FREEMASONRY
AND AMERICAN CULTURE

Officers of Live Oak Lodge

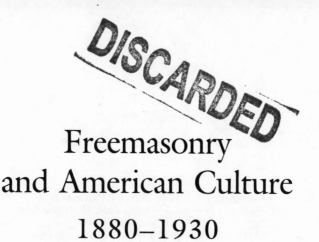

Freemasonry
and American Culture
1880–1930

LYNN DUMENIL

PRINCETON UNIVERSITY PRESS
PRINCETON, NEW JERSEY

Copyright © 1984 by Princeton University Press
Published by Princeton University Press, 41 William Street,
Princeton, New Jersey 08540
In the United Kingdom: Princeton University Press,
Guildford, Surrey

All Rights Reserved
Library of Congress Cataloging in Publication Data will be
found on the last printed page of this book

ISBN 0-691-04716-2

Publication of this book has been aided by a grant from
The Andrew W. Mellon Foundation

This book has been composed in Linotron Galliard

Clothbound editions of Princeton University Press books
are printed on acid-free paper, and binding materials are
chosen for strength and durability

Printed in the United States of America by
Princeton University Press
Princeton, New Jersey

For my mother,
Margaret Dumenil

Contents

Illustrations

Frontispiece. Officers of Live Oak Lodge, Oakland, California, 1894 (reprinted from *Souvenir: Fortieth Anniversary Celebration*, p. 64)

(Illustrations appear between pages 112 and 113)

Preface

In the late nineteenth and early twentieth centuries, organizational activity engulfed America. Charles and Mary Beard called the proliferation of women's clubs, professional societies, civic groups, reform associations, and other organizations a "general mania."[1] A striking and ubiquitous form of organization was the secret fraternal society. Largely neglected by historians, these orders were immensely popular. Over 460 originated between 1880 and 1900, and in 1901, one observer estimated that more than five million Americans were in 600 orders.[2] Similar in structure and function, fraternal orders served highly diverse groups. There were orders for natives and immigrants, Catholics and Protestants, blacks and whites, men and women, adults and children. The archetypical secret fraternal order, as well as the most popular and prestigious, was the Ancient and Accepted Order of Freemasons.

This study examines Masonry between 1880 and 1930. A white, male, primarily native, Protestant society, Masonry had long existed in America, but saw its greatest growth after the Civil War. Fully recovered from an antebellum crusade against Masonry, the fraternity in 1879 claimed 550,000 members and had dozens of imitators. By 1925, it was over three million strong. Although Masonry by the end of the 1920s was beginning to lose some of its popularity, the history of the organization during the period of its greatest appeal illuminates the significant cultural role of voluntary associations in modern America.[3]

Fraternal orders, like churches, are "expressive" organizations—they are directed primarily toward meeting the social and personal needs of their members. In contrast, "instrumental" organizations, such as trade unions or professional associations, have specific goals to accomplish. They mediate between members and the outside world. Both types flourished in the late nineteenth and early twentieth centuries. The major impetus for instrumental organizations' rapid expansion may be readily grasped. In an increasingly complex and economically rationalized society, individuals sought political and economic power in organizational activity. Expressive organizations, however, generally did not pursue such tangible ends, and the reason for their proliferation is less clear. Examining the sources of Masonry's popularity and analyzing the functions it served provides insight into the more elusive aspects of such voluntary associations, particularly the way in which they created a sense of community based on the shared values and interests of their members.[4]

A desire to understand the appeal and function of fraternal orders furnished the initial impetus for this study. But as the research unfolded and the richness of the material became evident, my focus shifted to a much broader set of problems, centering on the way in which Masonry mirrored middle-class culture. In the late nineteenth century, the order was a quasi-religious secret society dedicated to the ideals of fraternity, charity, and moral behavior. It offered sociability, relief in times of distress, as well as possible financial and political advantages, but the most important aspect of Masonry was its commitment to moral uplift and self-improvement. Inculcating the traditional virtues of sobriety, thrift, temperance, piety, industry, self-restraint, and moral obligation, Masonry offered its members identification with the values honored in the middle-class world of late nineteenth-century America.

Another crucial aspect of late nineteenth-century Masonry was its religious character. One of the order's major activities was the performance of various esoteric rituals. Heavily infused with religious symbolism and allegories, the rituals emphasized man's relationship to God, the inevitability of death, and the hope for immortality. Masonic literature, in which authors debated the nature of Masonry's religious content, further underlines the sacred quality of the order and also illuminates the controversies over faith that characterized late nineteenth-century America.

Although Masonry mirrored the religious and moralistic content of American society's concerns and values, Masons took pains to distinguish between the internal sacred world of Masonry and the external world of the "profanes." In particular, they contrasted the stability and harmony of their fraternity with the disharmony and disorder of American society. Masonry, they argued, had separate standards and concerns from the immoral, competitive, and commercial world beyond the temple and provided a sacred asylum in which men could ignore the social, political, economic, and religious conflicts of their time while cultivating love of God, bonds of fellowship, and improvement of the individual.

Although the characteristics of Masonry described above existed in the twentieth century, by the 1920s, the order had undergone significant changes. Exceptional growth altered the character of the membership, swelled the size of lodges, and created serious problems for leaders faced with assimilating the mass of new Masons. In particular, Masonic officials felt that the rapid influx of members and the tendency to larger lodges undermined the order's ability to offer its members the fraternity and sense of community its ideals promised. Even more significant than the expansion of Masonry was the widespread movement to de-emphasize the ritualistic, religious, and moralistic aspects of the order to create a more secular organization. This nationwide trend, evident in the actions of leaders as well as the rank-and-file membership, resulted in changes in Masonic ideology, structure, and activities.

Attempts to adapt the fraternity to changing conditions in the external world, these changes illuminate the secularizing and modernizing trends in American society. For example, in the 1920s, Masonic social activities took precedence over ritualism, revealing a preoccupation with the consumption and leisure-time pursuits made possible by advanced industrialization and general middle-class prosperity. Similarly, the movement to modify the goals and ideology of Masonry reflects an encroaching secular spirit. Feeling that newer and younger members were dissatisfied with Masonry because it was too old-fashioned, many leaders made conscious efforts to update Masonry. Minimizing the order's religion and ritualism, they sought to provide it with "modern" goals, such as community service and the practical application of Masonic ideals.

The changes in Masonry also illuminate American ethnic and cultural conflicts in the 1920s. The desire to promote 100 percent Americanism, an outgrowth of the postwar Red Scare, led Masons to a militant expression of their own cultural identity, as well as to a demand that Masonry as an institution take a stand in the efforts to meet the problems posed by radicalism, unassimilated immigrants, and "political" Catholicism. Taken together, the demands for a modern Masonry and the concern to reinforce native, old-stock American ideals prompted Masons to depart from the traditional emphasis on individual morality pursued in a sacred environment in favor of becoming more involved in the profane and secular world.

The attempt to modernize Masonry was widespread, but it was not prosecuted consistently enough to insure the order's vitality. The weight of Masonic tradition and conflict within the organization over de-emphasizing ritual and religion hindered the process of secularization. This inability to jettison its religious component left the order unacceptably out of step in an increasingly secular world and led to a decline in popularity and prestige from which it never completely recovered. Limited in their success, the significance of the attempts to modify Masonry lies in the way in which they illuminate the transformations of middle-class values concerning work, leisure, success, morality, and religion, and facilitate analysis of the social and cultural changes accompanying America's industrialization, urbanization, and modernization.

Although Masonry is a secret society, a wealth of material about the organization is available. I have used dozens of magazines and local lodge bulletins from all over the country. In addition, *Journals of Proceedings* from the various state Grand

Lodges proved immensely helpful. These yearly journals contain administrative business, speeches, accounts of charity and of Masonic trials, summaries of lodge conditions, occasional eulogies and biographies, and reports on activities of other Grand Lodges in the United States. In addition, *Proceedings* include statistical records for local lodges and, in many instances, complete membership rosters. An extensive reading of this literature provides a general picture of the opinions, activities, structure, and function of American Masonry in the late nineteenth and early twentieth centuries.

Statistical material from Live Oak Lodge No. 61 of Oakland, California has been used to probe the composition and character of Masonry. Although minutes of the lodge's meetings were secret, and thus not available, I had access to membership records for the entire period studied. Data on age, occupation, length of membership, officeholding, attendance, and participation in auxiliary Masonic organizations are provided throughout the text and in detailed appendixes to exemplify the nature and composition of what I suspect was a typical urban lodge. I offer the caveat, however, that with thousands of lodges in the country, there was room for variety, especially in composition, and I urge other scholars to continue research on Masonry that will provide more definitive statistical data.

I have divided this work in two parts. Part 1 covers late nineteenth-century Masonry. Chapter 1 describes the composition, structure, and appeal of the fraternity. The following two chapters explore themes of religion, morality, and brotherhood and place Masonry in the context of late Victorian American culture. Part 2 examines Masonry in the 1920s. These chapters investigate a variety of topics—religion, nativism, public education, leisure-time activities—and address the broad theme of the transformation of America into a heterogeneous, "modern" society. By studying the fraternity's ideology, structure, activities, and composition, I have striven to comprehend a complex and important organization that touched the lives of millions of American men. Above all, I have sought to illuminate some of the key facets of American cultural change.

Acknowledgments

I have been particularly fortunate in the people I have encountered in the process of completing this book. I owe a special thanks to the many Masons who gave me access to a wealth of material and patiently answered my questions. Clarence A. Severin of Live Oak Lodge in Oakland, California, and William F. Klesow of the California Grand Lodge Library were an immense help. I also benefited from the aid of Joseph Friedman, Robert C. Hollow, Max King, Robert A. Klinger, Raymond A. Leavitt, Francis Lewis, Irban Makins, T. L. Roberts, Al Sontag, Frank B. Stimson, and Clare W. Wilson, Jr. I would like to thank the libraries of the Supreme Council of the Southern Jurisdiction of Scottish Rite Masons (Washington, D.C.) and the California Grand Lodge of Free and Accepted Masons for the use of their materials. Mrs. Inge Baum, of the Scottish Rite Library, was most gracious and helpful.

This book began as a dissertation at the University of California, Berkeley. I appreciate the help of the History Department, which was generous with its fellowships, research, and computing funds. I also benefited from the assistance of Ann Hernandéz of the Humanities Computing Service, who provided access to computer facilities and gave helpful advice in text editing. A number of people contributed to the preparation of the manuscript for publication. Gail Ullman and Alice Calaprice were my very helpful editors at Princeton University Press; Alison Seidel did a fine job on the index; and Robert A. Skotheim provided Whitman College funds that aided in the completion of the manuscript.

I was fortunate to have Lawrence W. Levine as dissertation

director. A superb teacher and good friend, his criticism and encouragement were invaluable. My other readers, Paula S. Fass and Claude S. Fischer, offered many excellent suggestions. In addition, James H. Kettner generously gave much time to the manuscript. His careful reading of various drafts was immensely helpful. My intellectual debt to all my teachers at Berkeley extends well beyond their specific contributions to this book. I am also indebted to Paul Boyer of the University of Wisconsin, whose insightful suggestions at a critical juncture facilitated the final revision of the manuscript. Many graduate student colleagues read portions of the manuscript. The efforts of Susan Glenn, E. Wayne Carp, James Gregory, Paul Spickard, Deena J. Gonzalez, and Lucy Kerman not only improved the product considerably, but helped to make the process far more rewarding. Other friends and family—Marlene Keller, Barbara Loomis, Anne E. Sayre, Dorothy A. Shannon, Paul T. Roberts, and my mother, Margaret Dumenil—have been warmly supportive and enthusiastic. Finally, John May has been a constant source of good criticism and good humor.

Part 1

Masonry in the
Nineteenth Century

1

Masonry Revealed: An Introduction to Nineteenth-Century Masonry

> When a citizen of these United States kneels at the altar of masonry, when he swears allegiance to her laws, he snaps asunder the ties that bind him to his country; he cannot at the same time be the citizen of a free republic, and the subject of a despotic empire. . . .
>
> Free-masonry, by mingling prayers with bloody and profane oaths, by uniting the mummery of masonry with passages from holy writ, by its impious titles, such as "Most Worshipful," and "King of Heaven," by insinuations in the lower degrees, and direct declarations in the higher, stands forth as the apostle of Deism, if not of Atheism.
>
> —Speech by Samuel W. Dexter of Michigan, 1830[1]

In 1830, anti-Masonic sentiment permeated much of American society, and comments like Dexter's were common. Critics accused Masons of being irreligious libertines and potential subversives of American democracy. Once a popular organization, the ranks of Masonry were decimated in the 1820s and 1830s. However, by 1880, the starting point for this study, Masonry had largely recovered from the inroads of anti-Masonic hysteria. Its membership had grown and its lodges had multiplied. Moreover, Masonry had achieved a position of respectability as an important and prestigious organization. This chapter explores the reasons for the order's reestablishment by examining its history, composition, structure, and activities. Many factors contributed, but crucial to its success was its multifaceted nature, which gave it broad-based appeal to America's middle-class men.

ANTECEDENTS

Although Masons have been fond of claiming that their order originated in antiquity, it is probably descended from a medieval English guild of stonemasons. Its recorded history begins in early eighteenth-century London, where the order included not only "operative" Masons, but also "speculative" Masons, men who were honorary members rather than craftsmen. Eventually, the speculative Masons predominated, and the brotherhood devoted itself to building "spiritual instead of material temples." Speculative Masons, led by noted scientists and clergymen, drew upon the Bible, stonemasons' legends, and geometry and physics (the builders' sciences) to fashion an elaborate Masonic system. The tone of the order reflected Enlightenment thought, with its emphasis on deism, rationalism, science, and man's relationship to nature. Masonry was pictured as a "progressive science." As the candidate advanced through the first three degrees—Entered Apprentice, Fellow Craft, and Master Mason—he advanced in his knowledge of Masonry and its moral lessons. Each degree entailed an esoteric quasi-religious initiation ritual. These secret rituals were the central component of Masonry. Through lectures, allegories, and symbols, they imparted Masonry's commitment to equality, charity, fraternity, morality, and faith in God. This form of Masonry spread to America during the colonial period, and by 1800, the order claimed 18,000 Masons and was growing rapidly. In 1825, in New York state alone, there were 20,000 Masons.[2]

One study of early American Masonry suggests that the order offered its members many advantages. In *Freemasonry in Federalist Connecticut, 1789–1835*, Dorothy Lipson indicates that as a social club, Masonry provided conviviality. As a charitable organization, it offered relief in times of distress. And as a far-flung network of "brothers," it was useful to geographically mobile men and those engaged in trade. One of the most significant aspects of the fraternity, however, was the way in which Masonry served as a vehicle for dissent from

Connecticut's standing order, particularly its established Congregationalist church. For many men, Lipson argues, Masonry could have been a surrogate for the church. Its rituals included not only initiation ceremonies, but also elaborate funeral services. Moreover, like the church, Masonry propounded a code of ethics. Apparent parallels notwithstanding, Masonry's religious ideas conflicted sharply with Connecticut orthodoxy. Beyond a faith in God, the order made no doctrinal demands on its members. Rather, as Lipson notes, "Masons could unite on universal principles whatever their 'private speculative opinion.' " Masonry could thus be interpreted as condoning a wide range of religious belief from dissenting churches to deism. This latitudinarianism, embracing individual choice in spiritual matters, presented a striking contrast to the more demanding, rigid Calvinist orthodoxy. In offering men an alternative religious framework, Masonry engendered church disapproval, which occasionally erupted in open conflict between lodges and local clergy. In general, however, the tension was kept in abeyance, in part because ministers were unwilling to create controversy over an organization endorsed by many prominent laymen.[3]

An incident in Batavia, New York in 1826 shattered this quiescence. William Morgan, a Mason, threatened to publish Masonic secrets. Before he could do so, he was abducted, never to be heard from again. A number of Masons were tried for conspiracy, but all but four were acquitted. The incident, exacerbated by the acquittals and the fact that many jurors and court officials were Masons, touched off a violent wave of anti-Masonic hysteria that was felt throughout the Northeastern, Northwestern, and mid-Atlantic states. Anti-Masonic sentiment invaded politics as anti-Masonic parties emerged in many states.

The sources of the anti-Masonic crusade were complex, and they varied from region to region. David Brion Davis has analyzed the movement in the context of American susceptibility to conspiracy theories. Davis views the eagerness to uncover conspiracies as an irrational response to the social disorder accompanying antebellum egalitarianism, laissez-faire individualism, and economic expansion. The movements against Masonry, Catholicism, and Mormonism shared a rhetoric of defending both democracy and Protestantism against organizations viewed as antithetical to cherished American values. Davis suggests that these movements helped to unite "Americans of diverse political, religious, and economic interests," thereby forging a sense of national unity and stability. Davis's comparison of anti-Masonic with anti-Catholic and anti-Mormon rhetoric is helpful in understanding how a minor event like the Morgan affair could explode into an emotionally charged crusade against a seemingly innocuous organization.

More recently, however, other scholars have suggested that anti-Masonry was not so irrational after all. By examining Masonry itself, it is possible to understand more precisely the sources of anti-Masonic rhetoric. Ronald P. Formisano and Kathleen Smith Kutolowski, for example, have demonstrated that there was some foundation for the criticism that Masonry challenged democratic values. In the aftermath of the Batavia incident, New York Masons, many in official capacity, blocked effective investigation of the matter. Moreover, Masons were well represented among judges and jurors sitting for conspiracy trials involving Masons. Those not acquitted received light sentences. The whole thing smacked of a cover-up, and the power of Masons to subvert the law for their own benefit seemed ominous. Masons were not only suspect for their cavalier attitude toward the law, however; the order also seemed antithetical to egalitarianism. Although Masonry appears to have cut across class lines, members of the elite may have been especially plentiful in the order. In addition, with its rituals, its secrecy, and its internal hierarchy of officers with ostentatious titles, Masonry set itself up as a group apart from the rest of society. Thus Masonry, an organization that seemed to flirt with aristocratic notions and to view itself as above the law, became a prime candidate for suspicion in an age whose watchword was "the common man."

Masonry could also be viewed as a serious threat to Christianity. Lipson and Formisano see religion as the central component in anti-Masonry, both in its political and social manifestations. Masonry's tension with the established order was compounded by the highly charged religious atmosphere produced by the second Great Awakening. Evangelical Christians saw Masonry as an agency of the devil. They mistrusted its oaths and considered its religious rituals blasphemous. It is not coincidental that anti-Masonry saw its strongest outpouring in New York's "burned over" district, the area visited by repeated religious revivals in the late eighteenth and early nineteenth centuries. In politics as well as religion, there was a rational basis for hostility to Masonry. Yet, the hysteria, the extremism, and the hyperbolic rhetoric that pitted good against evil seem to have sources well beyond the specific circumstances of Masonry and the Morgan incident, and to be, as Davis suggests, symptoms of deep societal strain.[4]

Anti-Masonry as a political movement was of short duration; it was dead by 1832. Anti-Masonic sentiment persisted longer, effectively blocking the fraternity's growth for many years. Many Masons renounced the order, few new men joined, and many lodges suspended operation altogether. Lodges that did function found it necessary to meet secretly, and while many men remained loyal to the order, they did so discreetly. The 1830s were troubled times for the fraternity, but by the 1850s, it had begun to recoup its losses. Between 1850 and 1860, its membership almost tripled, from 66,142 to 193,763, and the following decade saw much expansion. By 1870, there were 446,000 Masons in over 7,000 lodges. After 1870, the growth was slower, but steady, as the institution consolidated its position (see Appendix A). Accompanying Masonry's revival were the founding and expansion of many other fraternal orders.[5]

Masonry's enhanced popularity and restored reputation were evident in the public quality of the order in the late nineteenth century. It was still a secret society, but most men proudly wore the Masonic symbol (a square and compass) on their watch chains. Prominent men—businessmen, politicians, and clergymen—joined the order and lent their respectability to the organization. In addition, Masons made many public appearances. The tradition of Masonic funerals accompanying traditional church services was revived, and in some areas lodges periodically attended church as a group. Another important public appearance was the cornerstone-laying ceremony, which Masons performed for both public and Masonic buildings. These ceremonies, such as the one for the Statue of Liberty in 1885, began with colorful parades and ended with a Masonic ceremony and speeches by public and Masonic officials. In a day when parades and oratory were forms of popular entertainment, Masons were important and highly visible participants in major events. Newspapers gave ample coverage to these ceremonies. In Chicago, for example, the laying of the cornerstone of the Masonic Temple in 1890 was front-page news. The press also covered major Masonic meetings and offered fraternal columns. Whether favorable or neutral in their coverage, newspapers gave clear indication that Masonry had returned and was a significant and prestigious organization.[6]

The renewed popularity and prestige of Masonry in late nineteenth-century America may be attributed to several factors. Certainly, part of the explanation lies in the abatement of anti-Masonic sentiment. In the 1850s, ethnic, religious, and sectional conflict displaced concern over the threats posed by Masonry. For those predisposed to see conspiracies against American democracy, the menace of Irish Catholics or a conspiracy of slaveholders posed a much more serious threat than a convivial fraternity of respectable men. After the Civil War, with the Union preserved, it was even less likely that much popular credence could be given to the fear that Masons menaced the Republic. Moreover, the liberalized religious climate of the late nineteenth century made Masonry more innocuous in the eyes of the churches. Hostility to secret societies still existed. The Catholic Church and some Protestant denominations condemned them on religious grounds, but these dissenting opinions had relatively little impact on the prestige and the growth of Masonry and other secret societies. But while the waning of anti-Masonry cleared the way for the fraternity's revival, the key to understanding the sources of Masonry's popularity is the nature of the order itself, in particular its composition, structure, activities, and ideology.

COMPOSITION

Late nineteenth-century Masonry's structure and principles had changed very little from earlier Masonry. Ritualistic content and format were similar, and the lessons they taught were the same: equality, charity, fraternity, morality, and faith in God. The candidate continued to advance through three initiatory degrees in the Blue Lodge, the basic unity of Masonry. Blue Lodges in each state were under the authority of a Grand Lodge, which collected dues from its subordinates and sought to maintain conformity to Masonic rules and rituals. Grand Lodges were jealous of their sovereignty and successfully resisted the occasional attempts to create a national organizing body. However, they kept in close contact with one another and exchanged information about interpretation of laws and procedures. As a result of this cooperation, the differences in ritual and law among the Grand Lodges in the various states were generally slight. Thus, hundreds of thousands of American men scattered throughout the country shared very similar Masonic experiences.

Who were these men who shared in the experience of Masonry? Masons insisted that their order was committed to the principle of *universality*, which they defined as the association of good men without regard to religion, nationality, or class. The prospective candidate must be a physically sound, freeborn male who believed in God and lived a moral life. Beyond these requirements, Masonry theoretically imposed no policy restricting membership.[7] Although Masonic principles technically allowed for heterogeneity, the fraternity was, in fact, predominantly a white, native, Protestant, middle-class organization.

Despite its insistence on the equality of men, for example,

in practice the order excluded nonwhites. Not only did Masonry not admit blacks, but Grand Lodges also denied that Prince Hall Masonry, a black Masonic order that had existed since 1774, was an authentic part of Masonry. Although the refusal to grant legitimacy to Prince Hall Masonry was undoubtedly rooted in racism, there were few racial overtones in white Masons' explanation for their denial that the black fraternity was "real" Masonry. Instead, white Masons justified their position on the basis of Masonic law, claiming that Prince Hall Masonry had not been legally established. This recourse to legalism may be attributed in part to the Masonic obsession with rules and laws that permeated Grand Lodge proceedings. More significantly, however, the legalism reveals Masons' unwillingness to address the order's de facto racial exclusion. Masons were proud of their order's ideals and were unwilling to acknowledge that its commitment to equality was imperfectly realized. The avoidance of overt racist arguments was typical of Masons' desire to be consistent with the order's commitment to universality and the brotherhood of man.[8]

In contrast to its racial exclusivity, Masonry was somewhat more receptive to immigrants. Available data on Oakland's Live Oak Lodge members' nativity are scanty, but suggest that the order had a small number of immigrants from northern Europe. Immigrants in Masonry probably gathered in distinct ethnic lodges in major urban areas. California had three such lodges, all in San Francisco—Italiana Speranza, Parfaite Union, and Hermann. New York City, not surprisingly, had many ethnic lodges, and German Masons in New York state were plentiful enough to establish their own Masonic home for elderly and ill German Masons. While ethnic lodges answered to the authority of Grand Lodges of their states, they do not appear to have had extensive intercourse with regular lodges. Conducting ritual and business in their own language, these lodges self-consciously retained their native culture, a factor that served to separate them from mainstream Masonry. Although immigrants were represented in Masonry, the literary material used for this study—magazines and Grand Lodge proceedings—indicates little recognition that a substantial foreign-born Masonic population existed.[9]

Masons were primarily of Protestant stock. There was little or no overt anti-Semitic sentiment in Masonic literature, but the order was self-consciously Christian, and one Masonic organization—the Knights Templar—permitted only Christians. Membership lists for Oakland indicate Jews' minority status in the fraternity in that city. For example, in 1900, Jewish names accounted for no more than 1.5 percent of all the Masons in Oakland's four lodges.[10] In other cities, the percentages may have been higher, with Jews congregating in heavily Jewish or ethnic lodges. A Grand Master of New York, complaining about disreputable saloonkeepers who had been "smuggled" into the order, for example, suggested the existence of primarily Jewish lodges in New York when he noted that most of the trouble had come from "lodges composed of Hebrews." While he claimed that he had no objection to Jews, his comment indicates that even in cosmopolitan New York, Jews were not considered part of Masonry proper.[11]

Similarly, while Masonry had no policy barring Catholics, it is doubtful that many Catholics sought or received admission. Although it was not universal, many Masons shared the anti-Catholic sentiment characteristic of the 1880s and 1890s. In some cases, Masons objected to Catholicism on religious grounds, but in most cases the objection was based on their fear that the Catholic Church planned to Romanize America. Priests were pictured as diabolical, their parishioners as sheep. Authors pointed to armies of Catholics within America kept ready to "substitute, at some time, the Pope for President and make the Catholic the religion of the State." Most frequently, Masons condemned the Catholic Church for its perceived attack on the public school system and its attempt to shackle the minds of children through its own schools. The Church, it was argued, would first control the schools and schoolchildren, and then the state.[12]

In addition to sharing the pervasive American suspicion of Catholicism, Masons had another special grievance against the

Church: its historic animosity to secret societies. As early as 1738, Pope Clement XII had forbidden Catholics to join Masonry under penalty of excommunication. Throughout the nineteenth century, the Catholic hierarchy continued to warn Catholics about the dangers of secret societies. A new encyclical from Leo XIII in 1884, which condemned European Masonry as politically subversive, enraged American Masons. Ignoring the differences between Continental and American Masonry, they railed against the bigotry and ignorance that could view the fraternity as a threat to religion or society.

The Church's opposition helped to make Masonry self-consciously Protestant. It also led Masons to argue that despite Masonry's religious universality, Catholics should be expressly prohibited. One author in the *Masonic Advocate*, for example, suggested that since Catholics were likely to renounce Masonry and reveal secrets to priests, application forms should ask whether a man was Protestant or Catholic. Even without formal strictures, however, it is unlikely that many lodges admitted Catholics. As one man wrote in a letter to the editor of the *American Tyler*, his Port Huron, Michigan lodge would not knowingly accept a Catholic: "It's against his religion, and thus they would worry that he had some sinister motive in applying." And in any case, few Catholics would be willing to risk excommunication for the sake of Masonry.[13]

That reality did not completely mesh with Masonic rhetoric about universal brotherhood is also apparent in the occupational composition of the membership. Although Masons claimed that their order was composed of all classes, observers and historians have generally reported that it was predominantly middle class.[14] A study of the membership of Live Oak Lodge helps to confirm their observations. Between 1880 and 1900, men in white-collar occupations of all levels constituted between 75 and 80 percent of the total. Skilled workers ranged from 15 to 20 percent, while semiskilled workers never comprised more than 5 percent. The bulk of the membership was drawn from the low-level white-collar group (clerks, salesmen, accountants, etc.) and proprietors (mostly small businessmen such as restaurateurs, contractors, and retail merchants). Live Oak, then, did include a number of workingmen, but it was primarily a white-collar, middle-class lodge (see Appendix B-1).[15]

The high percentage of white-collar workers does not necessarily indicate that working-class men had difficulty obtaining admission. While some lodges may have discriminated against workers, it is also possible that few working-class men sought Masonry out. Many blue-collar workers would have found the cost of Masonry prohibitive. The Live Oak initiation fee in this period varied from $50 to $100, with dues ranging from $6 to $12 annually—a typical sum for California's urban lodges. Small-town lodge fees were generally lower, averaging about $30. Since the census figures for Oakland in 1880 reveal that the average annual wage of people employed by Oakland manufacturing concerns was $570, it would be an unusual skilled or semiskilled man who could readily afford Live Oak's $50 or $100 fee.[16]

These Live Oak figures provide a good sense of the composition of an urban lodge, but generalizations about Masonry as a whole should be made carefully. In 1880, there were over 9,000 lodges in the United States, which permitted much variation. Lodges thrived in both rural and urban areas, and the composition of lodges probably reflected their immediate environments.[17] Moreover, lodges may have varied within a given city. In some cities, for example, ethnic lodges served the needs of immigrant groups. Urban lodges may have also been distinguished by their occupational character, with some lodges attracting a higher socioeconomic class than others.[18] Future research may well indicate other patterns for Masonic lodges; but the possibility of variety does not diminish the essential native, middle-class, Protestant nature of the order that was underlined by Masons' insistence on identifying the fraternity with the respectable virtues. The values Masonry inculcated—industry, sobriety, self-restraint, honesty, and fear of God—could be found in any sermon, schoolbook, success novel, or Horatio Alger tale. Masonry's native, middle-class nature was not expressed only in terms of social structure, then, but also in terms of social values.

APPEAL

If caution must be used in generalizing about the composition of Masonry, even more must be invoked in speculating about the reasons hundreds of thousands of men were attracted to the fraternity. Ultimately, each man who joined had a personal motive, but some sense of the order's appeal may be gained from an examination of Masonry's structure and activities, which reveal the fraternity's potential for offering prestige, financial aid, business and political connections, entertainment, and sociability.

As many observers of secret societies have noted, fraternal orders provide average men with avenues for achieving distinction.[19] One major vehicle for attaining prestige within Masonry was officeholding. Masonry had a complex system of government staffed by numerous officials. On the local level, the lodge elected the Most Worshipful Master, Secretary, Treasurer, Junior and Senior Wardens, and Tyler. The new Master appointed the Senior Deacon, Junior Deacon, two Stewards, and a Chaplain. Although not part of Masonic law, the general custom provided that an officer "pass through the chairs," or "go through the line." Thus, over a period of several years, a Mason would progress through the offices of Steward, Junior Deacon, Senior Deacon, Junior Warden, and Senior Warden to become Master. The lodge's election for Master, then, was usually automatic confirmation of a process begun years before with the initial appointment of a Steward to the "line."[20] As a result, the names on the roster of lodge officers changed only slightly each year. Over a twenty-year period at Live Oak, for example, only 84 men filled 258 offices. The oligarchic nature of this arrangement was compounded by the fact that Secretaries, Treasurers, and Tylers frequently held their positions for years. Consequently, access to office was not so open as the order's provisions for democratic elections might suggest. While there was limited access to offices, however, officeholding was not a function of high occupational standing. Blue-collar workers were underrepresented in the ranks of officers, but men in the high-level occupation group did not monopolize lodge offices. Rather, the greatest percentage was drawn from the low-level white-collar category.[21]

Few men succeeded in becoming Master, and those who did found it a lengthy process. Nonetheless, for the perseverant, the results may well have seemed worth the effort. The Master was the supreme authority in his lodge. In addition to presiding over proceedings, he regulated admission of visitors, settled disputes, presided at trials, and determined all questions of law. Once elected, only the Grand Lodge had authority over him. The Master's position of power was underlined by the trappings of his office. During meetings he wore a hat, usually a top hat, while others remained bareheaded. His seat in the "East" was usually on an elevated dais and frequently of thronelike design. Other officers shared in the trappings of official rank. Each wore around his neck a special insignia, called a "jewel," which distinguished him from his brethren. And like the Master, officers occupied special seats in the lodge room that further enhanced their exalted position (Figure 1).[22]

Another means of achieving distinction in Masonry was advancement through its organizational hierarchy. After becoming a Master Mason in the Blue Lodge, a man could then join auxiliary organizations commonly known as "higher bodies" or "higher degrees" (Figure 2). One major branch of Masonry was York Rite, which contained Royal Arch Masons, Royal and Select Masons, and Knights Templar. Parallel to York Rite was Scottish Rite, consisting of a Lodge of Perfection, Chapter Rose Croix, Council of Kadosh, and Consistory. There was also an honorary "thirty-third degree" for men of long standing or who had made an outstanding contribution to the Rite. In both Rites, members advanced to the higher grade by progressing through the lower ones. At the apex of Scot-

tish and York Rites was the Ancient Arabic Order of the Nobles of the Mystic Shrine, prerequisite for which was the thirty-
second degree of Scottish Rite or membership in Knights
Templar.[23]

York and Scottish Rites and the Shrine were perceived as
elite groups. They were characterized by elaborate rituals and
celebrations and were noted for their social activities and for
their colorful regalia. The York Rite's Knights Templar, os-
tensibly modeled after Christian knight Crusaders, was traditionally the most distinguished Masonic order. It held conclaves at major cities attended by thousands of Knights. The
conclaves included parades, with the Knights arrayed in full
regalia (Figure 3). A description of one such display, as well
as a sense of the impact it could have on sympathetic observers, is given in these effusions appearing in the *Chicago Tribune* on the occasion of the laying of the cornerstone of the
Masonic Temple in 1890:

> Then came the horses, prancing with military spirit, while
> the air was filled with the brilliant fanfare of martial mu-
> sic. Men bearing glittering swords came by, their snowy
> plumes shining against the black background of the
> Knights' dress. There were red crosses, black crosses, and
> double-barred crosses, and every uniform as neat as wax,
> each uniformed man wearing spotless gloves. Magnifi-
> cently embroidered banners with Knightly crests on them
> floated on the breeze.[24]

Higher degrees frequently drew fire from Blue Lodge
spokesmen, who criticized them for deflecting interest away
from Blue Lodge. It was a common complaint that men attracted to the "high sounding title and the glory of a gorgeous
and showy uniform" joined Blue Lodge as a "stepping stone"
to the other orders, and quickly lost interest in the plainer
lodges.[25] Blue Lodge leaders also complained that these groups
undermined the egalitarianism of Masonry. As John Arthur,
Grand Master of Washington, noted, Masonry has "allowed a
childish longing for feathers and titles to destroy the democ-

racy of our Fraternity and convert it into a system of castes more complex than those of [India]."[26]

The critics were right. Masonry did harbor exclusive groups. Part of the exclusivity stemmed from the fact that the higher degrees were expensive. York Rite total fees for all degrees were $75 in New York, $100 in Chicago, and $230 in San Francisco. Oakland Scottish Rite fees during the 1880s were $125 for all the degrees. Uniforms and jewelry brought the total up substantially.[27] Relatively few Masons made this expenditure. Between 1880 and 1900, only 149 (29.4 percent) of the 506 men in Live Oak Lodge belonged to York or Scottish Rite. Approximately one-third of this group were in the highest ranks of their respective Rites. While higher degrees did constitute an elite group, as was the case with officeholders, they did not necessarily segregate Masons on the basis of occupational standing. The sample is small, but for three of the five years studied, the occupational distribution among Live Oak Masons who belonged to the Rites was similar to that for the lodge as a whole. While higher bodies did contain many men of high occupational standing, they were not limited to this group. Both officeholding and higher bodies, then, could provide men of relatively little status in the outside world with a vehicle for achieving prestige within the Masonic network.[28]

In many ways, the higher-degree system paralleled the characteristics of officeholding. Both were hierarchical; both created an elite group, offering prestige to men on the basis of Masonic qualifications—advancement through the degrees and service through officeholding. But, in addition to conferring status on a small number, they also contributed to Masonry's image as an ordered and stable society by adding to the ceremonial and formalistic qualities of the order. In particular, the higher bodies, with their impressive parades and costumes, helped to impart a glamorous aura to the fraternity. As one Knight Templar put it, "The building of the temples and the rich display of the commandery, etc., inspires men and [breeds] in them the desire to join the Fraternity." Both helped the order to "grow strong and powerful."[29]

As the Knight observed, the Masonic Temple was another important factor that enhanced the prestige derived from Masonic membership. Increasingly in the late nineteenth century, lodges built their own temples rather than adapt existing structures. The trend in urban areas was for lodges and other Masonic bodies to combine their efforts into one large building. Most temples were designed on relatively secular lines, resembling such public buildings as courthouses and libraries of the period. Whatever the specific design of these new temples, the effect desired was monumental. Descriptions of the buildings emphasized their massive quality, equating size and bulk with evidence of the permanency and stability of Masonry itself. Thus in 1890, the *Voice of Masonry* described the seven-story Denver temple: "[It] is massive, and conveys at once an idea of permanence and safety."[30]

A description of Oakland's temple also emphasized its size and splendor (Figure 4). The entrance was a "gothic portico of polished granite, with . . . [a] massive arch over the door way." Outward display was matched by interior furnishings (Figure 5). Two huge marble columns, topped by orbs representing the earth, flanked the doorway. The main lodge room, a rectangle with seats along the walls, was richly appointed. In the center of the room stood the altar, on which lay an open Bible. The Master sat in the East; behind him was a lighted panel emblazoned with the initial *G*, representing God. This interior layout was similar to most other lodges, although not all were so sumptuous as Oakland's.[31]

The Oakland temple, obviously a source of pride to Masons, was also a community landmark. The *Oakland Tribune* publicized the 1881 dedication of the temple, and characterized it as "one of the most superb structures ever erected in Alameda County." Similarly, other publications put out by the *Tribune* and Oakland's Board of Trade, designed to extol the virtues of Oakland, frequently noted the Masonic Temple and included drawings of it. The temple was classed with such major public buildings as the courthouse, a bank building, and schools. Similarly, the Chicago Masonic Temple was considered an important community structure (Figure 6). Twenty-two stories tall, in 1894 it was the highest building in the world and, according to Masons, the most expensive. Temples, then, clearly served a larger purpose than merely housing Masonry. They stood as imposing symbols of the wealth and permanency of Masonry. Access to the Masonic Temple, along with the right to participate in Masonic ceremonies and acquisition of Masonic secrets, set a man apart from the outside world. As a member of such a worthy institution, a man need not be an officer or a "high-up" Mason to share in the distinction of Masonry.[32]

In addition to the potential for prestige, another major component essential to understanding Masonry and its popularity was the order's commitment to charity. At initiation, Masons gave their oath to aid their brethren and their brethren's dependents in time of need. While ideally Masons were expected to help one another personally, most Masonic charity was administered through the lodge. *Charity* covered many services, including visits to the sick and funerals and burials for out-of-town Masons who had died away from home. In addition, Masons and their families in need of temporary financial help, as well as those with more chronic problems, could look to the lodge for aid. Lodges tried to handle requests discreetly, and Masonic spokesmen regularly took pleasure in recounting how silent Masonry was about its good deeds, explaining that Masonic relief was not tendered as "charity" in the usual sense, but rather was considered aid to a deserving and worthy brother.

The procedure for aiding a needy brother or his dependents varied. Some lodges placed a hat on the altar for specific cases, others had a permanent charity fund. In addition, while continuing to take care of their own lodge members, many city lodges combined to form a relief board. These boards saw to the needs of "sojourners," those Masons who belonged to lodges in other cities, states, or countries.[33] Another form of Masonic charity addressed the chronically needy. When they could afford to, lodges took on the responsibility of indefinite assistance to their elderly or enfeebled. The usual practice was to grant a stipend to the needy Mason, but this frequently strained the resources of individual lodges.[34] Looking for a more efficient means of caring for permanent dependents, in the late nineteenth century, state Grand Lodges began building Masonic homes. By 1893, eleven jurisdictions had built homes; by 1914, thirty had done so. Homes varied in size, with few occupied to their full capacity. Affecting a relatively small number of people, these homes were expensive propositions, with yearly average operating costs of over $1,800 per resident. While few people were served by Masonic homes, accounts of the operations of homes suggest that they met well the needs of their orphans and elderly. Attractive buildings, generally in rural settings, with Masonic leaders anxious to make them homes rather than institutions, Masonic homes provided real alternatives to state aid or to a lonely, impoverished existence.[35]

Masonic homes served another function, however. Relieving distress was their primary purpose, but contemporaries also clearly viewed them as monuments to Masonry. With their impressive physical layouts, homes were much like Masonic Temples in that they served to symbolize Masonic stability and munificence. They were physical embodiments of Masonic charity. Moreover, home building and fund raising gave Masons interesting projects that had tangible results. The California home, for example, had a popular fund raising for money to be used in the reception hall. The room was to have a marble floor, staircase, and wainscoting. Above the wainscot would be ornamental tiles. Each person who made a $5 donation to the home would have his or her name embossed on the tile, which would serve "as perpetual evidence of the liberality of the contributor, and remain a befitting memorial of the brethren whose hearts have gone into the superstructure."[36]

As the dual purpose of home building indicates, Masonic

charity functioned on two levels. Proffering honorable aid to needy brethren and their families, it was an important self-help institution. It also gave more fortunate Masons an opportunity to demonstrate their altruism by their contributions to the charitable endeavors of the Craft. While some men may have been attracted to the order by the idea that it might provide for them in unemployment and old age, others could find in Masonry that sense of well-being which participation in charitable activity so often brings. Moreover, charity helped to give Masonry a raison d'être—it legitimated the order as a practical organization with an important moral purpose.

Masonry's commitment to aiding brothers must have been particularly attractive to geographically mobile men. The order gave men contacts—of both a personal and a business nature—in new communities. A letter in the Live Oak files suggests the practical uses of Masonry. Frederic H. Kent, Secretary of King David Lodge in Taunton, Massachusetts, wrote Live Oak in 1883 to find out something about Oakland. In particular, he wanted to know about the Judson Manufacturing Company, as he was a tack maker and had applied to the company for work. A more famous Mason also found the order helpful. Samuel Gompers, head of the American Federation of Labor, passed through a West Virginia town in 1897. A man stopped him on the street, and they exchanged Masonic signs of identification. Informing Gompers that he had been hired by the neighboring mining company to watch him, the man gave the labor leader pictures and negatives that had been taken of him previously. Gompers noted that he "frequently found that my affiliation to the Masonic order has been a protection to me."[37]

Masonry's practical advantages also extended to more geographically stable men, who found political and trade preferments in the Masonic connection. Live Oak Lodge had a large percentage of men engaged in occupations for which a Masonic network of contacts would have been useful. Of the 506 Masons in Live Oak Lodge between 1880 and 1900, a total of 245 were either proprietors, salesmen, or service professionals, such as attorneys and doctors, at the time of their initiation.[38] While these men may have joined the order with the hope of gaining useful connections, it is difficult to demonstrate the financial potential inherent in Masonry. Only occasionally did Masonic authors endorse the idea of Masons' patronizing one another. In "Masons Should Prefer Masons," for example, a *Trestleboard* author urged that Masons trade with one another, stressing that this would insure keeping business out of Catholic hands and in Protestant ones. Masonic spokesmen also occasionally encouraged Masons to hire one another. Employing a fellow Mason not only helped a brother, but also was supposed to assure the employer of an honest, upright employee. As C. M. Hammond put it: "Employers seeking help could secure the best in the land, men who could be depended upon in any emergency. Where could any man have better credentials than the square and compass?"[39]

These calls for Masonic patronage and preferment were unusual, however. As a rule, Masonic spokesmen were dismayed by the possibility that men joined Masonry for mercenary reasons, and they repeatedly emphasized that one of the Masonic pledges included the oath that the initiate had not been influenced by the desire for personal gain. To counter this tendency, many Grand Lodges passed laws against having Masonic emblems printed on business cards or stationery. Nonetheless, the laws and the remonstrances themselves suggest that Masons did have a reputation for "sticking together."[40]

It is similarly difficult to demonstrate the political advantages of Masonry. One of the order's basic rules was that politics, as one of the topics that produces discord among men, must not be discussed in lodge. The Masonic press was largely silent on political questions and elections. However, this does not mean that Masonic affiliation was not useful to politicians. Certainly many politicians joined the order. Live Oak Lodge members included mayors, councilmen, and state representatives. Oakland Lodge No. 188 had an even more illustrious list of government officials, which included two state governors. On a national level, Masons could claim senators and presidents. In the realm of both patronage and politics, then, Masonry may have been very useful to individuals, providing a network of personal connections that established a basis for accessibility and cooperation.[41]

Charity, prestige, and practical benefits were important components of Masonry. Another key to understanding the nature of the fraternity is the Masonic meeting. Much of the activity at a Masonic meeting was prescribed by the Grand Lodges, which laid down detailed rules for procedures and demanded conformity in ritual performance. Thus invariably, to prepare for a meeting the assembled Masons donned their costume, a white "lambskin" apron worn over their street clothes. In some city lodges, members might also wear white gloves and, less frequently, dress clothes. Masons entering the lodge room signed an attendance ledger and were admitted by the Tyler, an officer who remained outside the lodge to guarantee the secrecy of the proceedings.[42] Assured that no one was present without right, the Master "opened" the lodge. The agenda of the required monthly "stated" meeting included an opening prayer, an esoteric opening ritual, administrative business (including the consideration of charity cases and candidates for admission), the conferment of degrees, and a closing ritual and prayers. Other meetings, held for initiations, funerals, and installation of officers, were generally devoted primarily to ritualistic activity.[43]

In the late nineteenth century, rituals were the major Masonic activity. For funerals, cornerstone ceremonies, and initiations, Masters of lodges drew upon "monitorial" works, which contained printed speeches, prayers, and biblical passages, all of which they memorized and delivered at appropriate points in the ceremony. In addition to the monitorial sections, the rituals had an esoteric component, passed by word of mouth. This secret "work" included symbolic actions, spoken comments, administration of oaths, and revelations of passwords, grips, and other secret signs of recognition. To some extent, these rituals, which were essentially dramatic pageants with the officers and candidates the main actors, may be considered entertainment. Despite this potential for amusement, however, the rituals were meant to be taken seriously. Their central purpose was to give each new Mason the same initiatory experience, thereby forging a bond with the fraternity. Moreover, the rituals were highly religious and moralistic in content, inevitably giving Masonry and its meetings sacred overtones. Never-changing, highly sacred, rituals, like the hierarchical aspects of Masonry, infused the order with a sense of formality and stability.[44]

All lodges shared in the ritualism of Masonry; all Masons had similar ritualistic experiences. Lodge social activities, however, were far less uniform. Some lodges had regular social hours; others socialized less frequently. Some served alcoholic refreshments; others did not. Officers' enthusiasm, financial considerations, regional circumstances, and local customs determined the nature of the social activity that followed the "closing" of the lodge. In many places, especially in cities, Masons adjourned to nearby taverns or restaurants. Other lodges served refreshments and provided entertainment in the lodge building itself. Thus, a California Grand Lodge official described the social feature prevailing in some lodges in 1883 as consisting of "*bonafide* refreshments, no reason-destroying wines or liquors, but good substantial food, with tea or coffee for beverage," followed by "music, songs, recitations and speeches by the members and their visiting brethren."[45] While in some lodges such activities may have been a regular feature, organized by lodge officers, in others degree nights were the festive occasions when newly made Masons were expected to treat their new brethren. In 1886, for example, the *Freemason's Journal* reported that in an Indian Territory lodge, Brothers Cleland and Reigle "in accordance with a time-honored custom, furnished the lodge and all their friends they chose to invite, with a sumptuous supper . . . P.G.M. Doyle presided at the organ, and others did their level best to make it a truly social and profitable entertainment, refreshing both the outer and inner man."[46]

While lodges might have varied in the nature of their social activities, there was one area of universal conformity. With the exception of occasional banquets, women were excluded from lodge rooms. Indeed, one of the most striking aspects of the lodge meeting was its maleness. Dorothy Lipson, arguing that women resented Masonry's intrusion into their sphere as custodians of morality, and that they distrusted its latitudinarianism in religion, suggests that women may have constituted a major force behind anti-Masonic sentiment in the early nineteenth century. Early nineteenth-century Masons were sensitive to women's criticisms and frequently defended their male exclusivity. Late nineteenth-century Masons, however, gave little indication that they thought women were hostile to the order. Women's acceptance may have been promoted by the Masons' repeated insistence that the order did not threaten to supplant Christianity. Masons' sympathy to the temperance movement in some areas may have also helped to reconcile women to the fraternity. In addition, the development and spread of the Order of the Eastern Star, an organization composed of female relatives of Masons, mitigated women's resentment of the order, as it allowed them to duplicate their husbands' experience of secrecy, ritual, and sociability.[47]

There is some evidence to suggest that men sought in Masonry an escape from women, although Masons did not openly express this desire. The attraction of Masonry as a male social group fits well with what is known about Victorian relationships between the sexes. Men and women had separate spheres. Women's world was the home, men's the work place. Moreover, women's and men's leisure time was segregated. Contemporary observers in the late nineteenth century noted men's propensity for spending their free time outside the home. Depending on their class and temperament, men passed evenings at clubs, brothels, saloons, or lodges. The Masonic lodge was one of many places where men might gather for relaxed fraternal camaraderie.[48] Apparently, however, this segregation of leisure was not accomplished without some tension. Masonic authors occasionally noted that lodge night created friction between husband and wife because it kept men away from home. This theme was particularly evident in lodge humor:

> "Did your wife listen to your excuse for staying so late at the Lodge last night?"
> "Oh, yes, she listened to me, then—I listened to her."[49]

Frequently, lodge jokes hinged on the idea that men used the lodge as an excuse for a night out with the boys—or perhaps with the girls. One Masonic poem, "boisterously received" at a lodge in Aurora, Illinois, termed a Mason's life "free," for while he's "enjoying a spree," the wife sits at home, "Never dreaming it all a dodge, / But thinking the sad belating / Is caused by 'work' at the lodge."[50]

Masonic humor depicted women as domestic tyrants who must be tricked if their husbands are to have their freedom, and described Masonry as a justification for men's having secrets from their wives and nights away from home. The picture that emerges, then, is not the stereotyped vision of Victorian husbands ruling their wives with iron hands, but rather of women possessing a certain amount of domestic power to which men felt it necessary to cater. While we cannot be sure whether men really did use lodge meetings to deceive their wives, Masonry's male exclusivity and its humor illuminate the separate spheres of Victorian men and women and the tension that accompanied the segregation of their leisure.[51]

Whatever men may have found in lodge meetings—entertainment, religion, fraternal camaraderie, or an escape from women—it is important to note that many men were not interested in participating in lodge activities. Poor attendance was a source of concern to Masonic spokesmen who contrasted the lodges of their own time with lodges of the past, which they pictured as vital, active places, well attended and universally important in the lives of their members. Unfortunately, authors offered no statistics to document this perceived decline. Some statistics for the late nineteenth century are available, however, and they support the notion that many

Masons were not active participants in their lodges. At Live Oak Lodge, attendance figures are available for 1880, 1885, 1890, 1895, and 1900, and reveal a decline in attendance: in 1880, 26 percent of the 105 members attended monthly meetings; 9 percent of 379 members attended in 1900 (see Appendix C).[52]

Masons themselves offered many explanations for lack of interest. Noting the patterns of individual decline in activity, for example, they suggested that men lost interest in the lodge after failing to gain office. Conversely, it was commonly thought that after serving as Master most men were unwilling to participate as ordinary members. Leaders also claimed that indifferent Masons were those men who had joined Masonry for the wrong reasons. Influenced by curiosity or the desire for trade or membership in higher bodies, these men had only a tenuous commitment to the order. Some Masons, however, found fault with the institution itself and suggested that lodges were not interesting enough. Although few men went so far as to say that the ritual was boring or monotonous, they did insist that men wanted a social time and urged that lodges institute regular social features.[53]

Occasionally, Masons suggested that poor attendance was an urban phenomenon, and romantically contrasted the warmth of the small-town lodge with the cold city lodge.[54] Few statistics are available to substantiate this claim. In 1892, a California Grand Lodge official conducted a systematic attendance survey of lodges in California and reported that country lodges, which averaged about 33 percent of their membership at meetings, were better attended than city lodges. If Masons were right about the urban-rural dichotomy, it is not difficult to explain the disparity. Rural communities had fewer attractions than urban areas, and thus lodges could have played a far more important social function. Moreover, city lodges tended to be much larger than rural ones. There are no data for nineteenth-century lodge attendance as a function of size, but twentieth-century data on lodges in Indiana and Minnesota reveal a clear connection between size and attendance.

Large lodges may have suffered because there was less opportunity to establish fraternal feeling in a larger group. In addition, the larger the lodge, the less opportunity there was for participation or officeholding.[55]

Lack of interest in lodge activity can be traced to many factors. Insincere motives on the part of Masons, boredom with the ritual, competition from other activities in urban areas, and the difficulties of large lodges all played a part. Masonic indifference may also be examined in the context of voluntary associations. Membership apathy is an almost universal complaint of voluntary association officials. Addressing this problem, the sociologist Robert Michels explored German political parties and theorized that with increased size and complexity, voluntary associations inevitably become oligarchic. This concentration of power leads to less active participation on the part of the rank and file. Certainly Masonry was oligarchic, and it also displayed another tendency of voluntary associations—goal displacement. Organizations are usually established to accomplish certain goals or provide specific services. Frequently, however, the association becomes sidetracked, either because the original goal was accomplished or because the problems changed. In addition, it appears that through time, a major concern of voluntary-association officials becomes the aggrandizement and perpetuation of the organization. Its survival becomes an end in itself. Goal displacement is expressed by increased bureaucratization, formalization, and conservatism. This process was evident in nineteenth-century Masonry. Temple- and home-building projects, for example, were undertaken as much to establish monuments to Masonry as to house lodges and provide charity. In this period, moreover, Grand Lodges were extending their power over local lodges, demanding uniformity in ritual, work, and adherence to laws and regulations. Lodges had to follow specific forms for balloting, voting, transaction of business, and trials; they were routinely inspected by Grand Lodge officials to insure their conformity. Individual lodge members frequently had little to say in the conduct of the lodge. Legalism, combined with the formality and routinization of the ritual, could well have hampered the conviviality of the lodge. The formality and ritual might have appealed to many, but it is easy to see how the regimentation could have affected attendance, particularly in lodges that did not offset the ritual and business work with social activities.[56]

As intriguing as the problem of why some men failed to participate in their lodge is the question of why Masons maintained their membership without retaining much interest in the social and ritualistic aspects of the order.[57] The desire to remain in good standing in case of hard times may have influenced some men to keep their ties with the charitable institution. Others may not have wished to sacrifice the commercial and political benefits accruing to members of the order. A letter to Live Oak Lodge from Joseph Cairn Simpson, a man who had been a Mason for thirty-eight years, but who attended infrequently, suggests another major source of inactive Masons' persistence in the order. Cairn sent some books to Live Oak's library and in his cover letter apologized for his lack of attendance. He explained that his job as editor of the *Daily Call* made it difficult for him to find time to attend lodge. He acknowledged that this explanation was "not sufficient to fully exonerate," but noted that he had been a zealous member in his youth, "enthusiastically devoted to Masonry the greater portions of time I worked a mill." He hoped that the "dereliction of later years may be pardoned by the Supreme Grand Master of all." He continued, "I have just as much reverence as of youth for the grand principles of Masonry. I hope . . . in the near future to be [able] to be present at the meetings of the [lodge] which has honored me with a place on its rolls."[58] Cairn's letter indicates how a Mason's participation might decline after his initial years in the order. Moreover, it reveals how a man's earlier participation in Masonry could establish a bond with the order and his brethren that remained when interest in Masonic activity had waned.

Cairn's example makes it clear that the appeal of Masonry transcended the specific advantages the order offered individuals. Masonry served many men in many ways—it offered charity, trade and political preferment, social activity, and the prestige of higher bodies and officeholding. These attractions were well suited to the male, middle-class world of the late nineteenth century. In a period of increased leisure time for middle-class men, the lodge was a respectable gathering place, filling the gap between the exclusive clubs of the wealthy and the saloons of the poor. Masonry's charitable feature could not fail to appeal to men in a society characterized by nationwide depressions and economic fluctuations. In addition, men in the expanding white-collar sector of employees could find in Masonry avenues for prestige denied them in the outside world. Moreover, for geographically and socially mobile men, Masonry provided extensive opportunities for connections— both in their communities and throughout the nation.

The appeal of the fraternity went far beyond these practical advantages, however. Masonry also had a more intangible appeal that was rooted in the order's ability to confer respectability. Far from being suspect as a cabal of deists, libertines, and subversives, late nineteenth-century Masonry was a prestigious and important organization. Joining Masonry was the accepted thing to do. To some extent, Masonry's public image of respectability was enhanced by the prominent men within its ranks, the fanfare of its higher bodies, and the impact of its impressive temples. But equally important in Masonry's bid for respectability was its ideology. As the following chapters will demonstrate, Masonic leaders, sensitive to popular attitudes, molded Masonry to reflect the religious and moralistic viewpoints of the Protestant middle class. Masonry did more than mirror late nineteenth-century cultural values, however. Through its rituals and emphasis on fraternity, Masonry created a bond among most of its members. In offering them identification with a religious and moralistic organization that upheld societal norms, Masonry provided men with a vehicle for expressing their commitment to the respectable virtues of industry, sobriety, self-restraint, honesty, and faith in God.

2

Sacred Masonry: Ritual and Religion

Look at its ancient landmarks—its sublime ceremonies—its profound symbols and allegories—all inculcating religious doctrine, commanding religious observance, and teaching religious truth; and who can deny that it is an eminently religious institution.

—Albert Mackey, 1889[1]

One of the most important characteristics of nineteenth-century Masonry was its religious component. Its parallels with organized religion were striking. The building was a temple; the Bible stood open at the altar; meetings were opened and closed with prayers; lodges had a chaplain; the ritualistic exchanges between Master and brethren resembled responsive readings; and the ritualistic ceremonies provided dramatic pageantry. In short, the aura of a Masonic Temple was a solemn one that underlined the sacred quality of the order. A Kansas Mason, also a minister, made the churchlike quality of Masonry quite clear:

Freemasonry is not only a brotherhood but a church. . . . It is an essential part of our ceremonial to joyfully recognize our relationship to God, our dependence upon Him, and to express our sense of need. A Masonic temple is a religious temple. The very word "temple" implies worship.[2]

There are two main avenues for exploring the religious character of Masonry. The first is the order's rituals. Rich in

31

religious themes, they suggest that Masonry provided individuals with opportunities for religious experience and expression and indicate the importance of Masonry's sacredness in creating loyalty among Masons to their order and their brethren. A second source of Masonic religious attitudes is periodicals and proceedings, which in the late nineteenth century and the prewar years included extensive treatment of the nature of Masonry's religion. While it would be an overstatement to suggest that most Masons were attracted to the order primarily because of its religious quality, religion was nonetheless so pervasive in Masonry that it must be taken into account in explaining the function of Masonry in the lives of its members.

The religious component of Masonry also provides an opportunity to explore the religious crisis prompted by scientific challenges to traditional faith in the late nineteenth century. Conflicts within Masonry over religion paralleled controversies in the churches. Both institutions grappled with such fundamental questions as the interpretation of the Bible and the nature of God. Masons' concern to delineate the fraternity's religious content indicates the vitality of religious issues in this period and illuminates both the variety and persistence of faith.

RITUAL

The importance of ritual to late nineteenth-century Masonry is indicated by the extensive attention officials and spokesmen gave it. Grand Lodges, for example, insisted upon "uniformity" of ritual work, and developed a system of inspectors to visit lodges and insure that their ritual conformed to Grand Lodge specification. This concern for exactness in ritual may be traced to several factors. Inevitably, there were those Masters and Grand Lodge officials who saw insistence upon obedience to laws as a means of aggrandizing their authority. Much more significant, however, was the conviction that the immutability of the ritual was evidence of the changelessness and importance of Masonry itself. In 1899, a California Grand

Lodge committee clearly articulated the connection between uniformity and Masonic prestige. Referring to the expenses of the Grand Lecturer who visited lodges to instruct or inspect ritual performance, the committee's report noted:

We are aware that the Grand Lodge has an unusual call upon its resources in carrying out its grand system of charity, and that every effort should be exercised to guard against the extravagant expenditure of its means. We do not think, however, *that its most important work—the preservation of its Ritual in its integrity*—should be neglected in any event, for upon that depends its honor and reputation.[3]

The insistence on uniformity was also related to perceptions of Masonry's antiquity. As Robert Macoy, the author of a widely used "monitor" (or ritual guide) explained, "it is the pride of our institution that its forms and ceremonies cannot be changed, and that all intelligent Masons endeavor to perfect themselves in the ancient work."[4] While thoughtful Masonic writers recognized that Masonry and its ritual were not of ancient origin, nonetheless Masonry's antiquity was continually stressed in the rituals and the literature. Some Masons traced the order to Adam and Eve; others emphasized its Christian origin. Most frequently, Masons dated it to the building of King Solomon's Temple.[5] Thus, emphasis on ritual uniformity underlined the important myth that the esoteric parts of Masonry's ritual had been handed down over many centuries and served to imbue the Craft with a serious and important purpose.

While lodges strove for uniformity, there was some variety in their rendition of the degrees. The initiations were essentially dramatic pageants. Enthusiastic lodges might employ elaborate costuming as well as dramatic lighting techniques to make the ritual more exciting. Although the degree of embellishment must have depended upon the financial resources of lodges and the energy and skill of officers, the tendency toward theatrical accouterments was becoming widespread toward the end of the century. The *Masonic Constellation*, for example, in 1894 called Masonry "the greatest of all plays, containing the highest sentiments, the most beautiful allegories, historical representations [with] dramatic force and settings," and urged that lodges be required to obtain "proper paraphernalia," because the acting out of the ritual in street clothes dimmed the force of the performance.[6]

The desire to make the ceremony more impressive was a crucial factor in the innovations, but frequent references to how much costumes and other elaborations revived interest and improved attendance suggests more mundane purposes operating in ritual modification. In 1896, a full-page ad by the M. C. Lilley Company in the *Masonic Chronicle* outlined the connection between costumes and lodge prosperity:

HAVE YOU EVER SEEN THE WORK OF THE LODGE DONE IN APPROPRIATE ROBES? If you have seen it you know how much the use of Robes beautifies the work. . . . Neat Robes add much to the beauty of the Lodge Work. New Robes cause members to talk and think about the Lodge. Talking about the Lodge induces new applications for membership. The purchase of a set of new Robes is thus made a profitable investment.[7]

The emphasis on the dramatic and entertainment quality of the ritual does not indicate that the content of the ceremonies was secondary. In fact, the great attention given to ritual indicated its central role in Masonry and served to direct attention to the ritual's message: commitment to morality, loyalty to Masonry, and obedience to God. A brief synopsis of the three degrees, drawn primarily from the printed monitors, will provide a sense of the religious and moral views expressed in Masonic ritual.

The three degrees of Masonry symbolized the stages of life. Entered Apprentice was youth; Fellow Craft was middle age; and Master Mason was old age. The rituals took the form of a journey; a checkered carpet, representing "human life, checkered with good and evil," served as the terrain for the journey. As the candidate proceeded in his travels, he stopped at certain points for a lecture, prayer, or dramatic presentation in which he participated. Throughout, the novice learned the history of the order and the meaning of Masonry's key symbols—the square, the plumb, the twenty-four-inch gauge, and so forth. The candidate was also instructed in moral virtue and on his responsibilities as a Mason. His duty to his brethren and their dependents was a key theme, as was the oath of secrecy.[8]

Religious motifs were pervasive. The central drama of the ritual—the building of Solomon's Temple and the death and resurrection of its master builder, Hiram—was just one of many biblically inspired parts of the ceremony. Short passages from both Old and New Testaments, including Genesis ("In the beginning . . .") and 1 Corinthians ("And now abideth faith, hope, charity, these three; but the greatest of these is charity . . ."), were read to the candidate. In addition, the Mason's required belief in God and the themes of death and immortality were reflected throughout.[9]

In keeping with the religious tone of the rituals, the Entered Apprentice degree, like all others, contained numerous prayers. This Prayer at Initiation was typical:

Vouchsafe thine aid, Almighty Father of the Universe, to this our present convention, and grant that this candidate for Masonry may dedicate and devote his life to thy service, and become a true and faithful brother among us. Endure him with a competency of thy Divine Wisdom, that, by the influence of the pure principles of our Order, he may the better be enabled to display the beauties of holiness to the honor of thy holy name. Amen.[10]

Within the degree, the candidate learned that the Bible was the "cornerstone" of Masonry and that he must be obedient to God, but the major thrust of the degree was to teach Masonic moral tenets and virtues. Brotherly love, charity, and truth were the mainstays of the order; its "cardinal virtues" were temperance, prudence, and justice. Their constant practice would allow the Mason to fulfill his Masonic obligations to God, his neighbor, and himself.[11]

The Fellow Craft ritual stressed the idea of continual upward progress as the Mason started on the "journey of life, with the great task before him of self-improvement." The symbolism of the winding stairs dramatically presented the message of this degree. With each step the Mason progressed in his Masonic enlightenment until he reached the top and found "the hieroglyphic bright, which none but Craftsmen ever saw, as the emblem of divine truth."[12] This degree also contained references to Masonry's connection with architecture and geometry, both of which were used to illustrate religious and moral lessons. The degree was notable for its deistic conception of a God known through reason and nature.

> By Geometry, we may curiously trace Nature, through her various windings, to her most concealed recesses. By it, we discover the power, wisdom, and goodness of the Great Artificer of the Universe, and view with delight the proportions which connect this vast machine. By it, we discover how the planets move in their respective orbits, and demonstrate their various revolutions. By it, we account for the return of seasons, and the variety of scenes which season displays to the discerning eye. Numberless worlds are around us, all framed by the Divine Artist, which roll through the vast expanse, and are all conducted by the same unerring law of nature.[13]

Masons considered the third degree, Master Mason, to be the sublime degree, for it taught the immortality of the soul. Here, the Mason learned the "last, the most important, and the most necessary of truths, that having been faithful to all his trusts, he is at last to die, and to receive the rewards of his fidelity."[14] The charge of the Master Mason was to follow the instructions of the first two degrees so "that in age, as Master Masons, we may enjoy the happy reflections consequent on a well-spent life, and die in the hope of a glorious immortality."[15] The significance of the themes of death and immortality was dramatically represented by having the candidate play the part of Hiram, King Solomon's builder, and experience a symbolic death and resurrection as a climax to the whole series of degrees.[16]

Although the second degree embodied a deistic conception of God, most of the ritual was clearly influenced by the Bible. Some passages came from the New Testament, and the major theme of the third degree was the assurance of immortality. There was, however, almost no direct reference to Christianity. One exception was that in the first degree, the Entered Apprentice was taught that all lodges were dedicated to the Christian saints John the Baptist and John the Evangelist.[17] Another exception was that some monitors invoked Christ's name in the discussion of death and immortality. Robert Macoy, for example, in his widely used *True Masonic Guide*, described the Christian belief in immortality, "which strengthens him, with confidence and composure, to look forward to blessed immortality" and urged Masons to "imitate the Christian" in conduct and faith.[18]

The rituals, then, contained a hodgepodge of religious elements—with some deistic influence and an extensive borrowing from the Judeo-Christian tradition and Bible. The result was to leave Masonry with an ambiguously defined religious content, open to several interpretations. Jews and Christians could find the God of their Bible in Masonry; deists and freethinking believers, a God revealed through nature and reason. Although there was ambiguity in Masonry's notion of God, there was no question that Masonry was religious and demanded religious expression from its devotees. Participation in Masonic ritual involved an acknowledgment of the individual's belief in God. Moreover, the ritual's emphasis on death and immortality was highly conducive to contemplation of profoundly religious topics.

In addition to revealing the sacred quality of the order, the ritual also demonstrates an important aspect of the mechanics of Masonry. Much like the emphasis on uniformity and antiquity, the confluence of ritual and religious belief invested Masonry with serious overtones and gave the oath of loyalty to the order and to one's brethren increased importance. This helps to explain how so many Masons could be inactive, yet still desire to maintain their Masonic "mystic tie." For many men, the order succeeded in creating a lasting, meaningful bond infused with religious overtones.

Crucial to the process of bonding was the sense of Masonry's sacredness. Masonry was sacred not merely because it had religious ideas, but also because it portrayed itself as an asylum from the secular or profane world outside the temple. The insistence that religion, politics, and business could not be considered within the lodge walls was one aspect of the sacred-profane dichotomy stressed in Masonry. The ritual's emphasis on secrecy was another means of establishing the barriers between Masonry and the outside world. In each degree, the candidate repeated a vow of secrecy that included a threat of violence. The Entered Apprentice, for example, agreed to the following:

> All this I most solemnly and sincerely promise and swear . . . binding myself under no less a penalty than that of having my throat cut across, my tongue torn out by its roots, and buried in the rough sands of the sea at low-water mark where the tide ebbs and flows once in twenty-four hours, should I ever knowingly violate this my entered apprentice obligation. So help me God and keep me steadfast in the due performance of the same.[19]

The importance of secrecy was further underlined in Masonic literature, where authors frequently alluded to the Mason's possession of ancient secrets. As a writer in the *Trestleboard* remarked, "Over and above all, it should be remembered that Freemasonry is in its very essence a mystery."[20] In fact, Masonic secrets were less concerned with ancient truths and more with the order's ritual, passwords, and .signs. As many social scientists have suggested, the content of secrets frequently is less important than their existence as secrets.[21] Masonry's secrecy served to emphasize the common bond between brethren by giving them shared knowledge unknown to the outside world.

Other aspects of Masonry's ritual forms also accented the sacred-profane demarcation between Masonry and the rest of the world. The complicated procedure necessary before outsiders could enter the lodge room, as well as the presence of the Tyler at the door, symbolized the sanctity of lodge proceedings. The major device for isolating Masons from the profane world was, of course, the ritual of initiation. Masons described the candidate for the first degree as standing "on the threshold of this new Masonic life, in darkness, helplessness, and ignorance. Having been wandering amid the errors and covered over with the pollutions of the outer and profane world, he comes inquiringly to our doors, seeking new birth, and asking a withdrawal of the veil which conceals divine truth from uninitiated sight."[22] In each degree, the candidate gained more "light" until with the third degree, he became a full Master Mason.

The three rituals, then, served as rites of passage. The initiate passed from being a profane outsider to occupying a position of equality with other Masons. Having successfully completed each stage, he earned the right to sign his name on the roster, to attend meetings, to speak and vote in lodge, and to have a Masonic funeral. He now knew the secrets of Masonry. He was entitled to wear the lambskin apron at meetings and the square and compass on his street clothes. The process of initiation integrated the individual into the community of brothers and set him apart and above the outside, profane world.[23]

While the initiation rituals integrated the novice, they also had meaning for the older members who witnessed it. The ceremonies reminded them that they were members of an important and mysterious organization. By participating in the rituals, as observers or actors, they could reaffirm their allegiance to Masonry and its teachings. For them, as well as for the candidate, the ceremonies could promote the sense of communal solidarity with Masonry and fellow Masons.

39

In all of the official ceremonies of the order, the possibility of renewing Masonic commitment is evident. At dedications and cornerstone-laying ceremonies, for example, Masons appeared before the public as a group set apart from the rest of the crowd by their distinctive garb and special Masonic knowledge. In 1881, when the Oakland Masons dedicated their temple, a huge procession formed according to specific guidelines set out by the order. The assembled Blue Lodge, Scottish Rite, Royal Arch, and Knights Templar Masons wore the regalia of their lodge or body. Representatives of the state Grand Lodge joined local Masons in a formal and solemn march that brought them to the temple. This appearance in public as a member of the group could not help but enhance one's identification with Masonry. Moreover, in witnessing the ceremony dedicating the temple, only Masons would know the significance of each act. When the Grand Steward circled the altar three times and then handed a jar of corn to the Grand Master, Masons shared in their understanding of his actions.[24]

Cornerstone and dedication ceremonies took place relatively infrequently, but another major Masonic ritual, the funeral, occurred all too regularly. While there were some complaints about insufficient attendance, funerals, which frequently included burial in Masonic cemeteries or Masonic sections of public cemeteries, occupied an important place in Masonry. According to Robert Macoy, the Masonic funeral was so desirable that many brethren who had lost interest in lodge activities retained membership for that reason alone. If he or his family requested it, a Mason was guaranteed burial with an impressive service, which he could hope would be attended by a large number of his brethren. Even if a Mason were buried away from his home lodge, he received this tribute, for local lodges would perform the burial and send delegates to the funeral.[25]

The funeral service, like other rituals, was carefully prescribed by Grand Lodges. Wearing their lambskin aprons, as well as a sprig of evergreen (symbolic of immortality) in their coat lapels, Masons formed a procession from the lodge to the funeral site. After a memorized exchange between Master and brethren that resembled a responsive reading, the Master offered a prayer in which he called upon the brethren to "advert to the nature of our solemn ties, and pursue with assiduity the sacred tenets of our Order," so that they might be prepared to travel "to that undiscovered country where no traveller returns." Following the prayer came another exchange. Then the dead man's apron was thrown into the grave. At the conclusion, the group passed around the grave three times, casting their evergreens into it, and saluting the dead man with arm stretched out straight.[26] Like initiations, the funeral ceremony reveals the importance of themes of life, death, and immortality, and indicates the bonding process inherent in the order's rituals. Masons performing funerals together shared in the most sacred secret of all: death.

Masonic rituals aptly demonstrate two of the classic functions of ritualistic activity. In "Magic, Science and Religion," Bronislaw Malinowski called attention to social as well as personal functions served by "primitive" societies' initiation rites. Such rites, he argued, are both an "efficient means of transmitting tribal lore, or insuring continuity in tradition and of maintaining tribal cohesion," and are a vehicle for providing the individual with a religious experience involving a "spiritual metamorphosis."[27] The same can be said of Masonry's rites. While Masonic rituals clearly served the function of cohesion for the group, the personal impact on the individual should not be underestimated. Ritual not only could give him a sense of belonging to a community, but also could provide an opportunity for religious expression and experience.

Mircea Eliade, in *Rites and Symbols of Initiation*, sketched a brief but provocative analysis of the significance of modern man's interest in the initiatory themes of symbolic ordeal, death, and rebirth. Noting their prevalence in books, poems, films, and dreams, he suggested that "nostalgia for an initiatory renewal which sporadically arises from the inmost depths of modern nonreligious man . . . would appear to represent the modern formulation of man's eternal longing to find a posi-

41

tive meaning in death, to accept death as a transition rite to a higher mode of being."[28] Applying Eliade's analysis to Masonry, it may be argued that Masonic ritual could be spiritually meaningful even to a man usually indifferent to religion by providing him with a dramatic experience that encouraged him not only to contemplate his relationship to God, but also to undergo a symbolic death and rebirth. Masonic ritual could create at least a temporary sense of spiritual renewal.

The possibility that Masonry provided religious experience to "nonreligious" men is an intriguing one. It is clear from the rituals that Masonry could function as an alternative to traditional religious worship. Attendance at a Masonic meeting necessarily involved participating in a religious activity. With relatively little precise theological content, ritual activity provided the opportunity to affirm one's religiosity in an unemotional, highly stylized manner. It should not be inferred, however, that all or most Masons were indifferent to organized religion. Figures on Masons' church membership do not exist. It would have been out of keeping with Masonry's "universality" to ask candidates for their denominational affiliation. Nevertheless, one can surmise that for many traditionally religious men, Masonry, containing the pageantry and ritual largely absent from Protestant churches, could serve as a dramatic addition to traditional religious expressions. Masonry's success in creating a candidate's bond with the fraternity or in promoting religious feelings obviously depended upon individual needs and proclivities. Yet whether men recognized it or even desired it, Masonry clearly functioned as a religion.

RELIGION

Religious concerns permeated Masonic literature and official transactions. Masonic spokesmen repeatedly reaffirmed the Mason's belief in God and his hope for immortality. In addition, the emphasis on tracing the ancient history of the order frequently led them to biblical times and the claim that Masonry had preserved religious truths and duties throughout the centuries.[29] As a prominent Masonic writer, Albert G. Mackey, explained in 1889:

> Look at its ancient landmarks—its sublime ceremonies— its profound symbols and allegories—all inculcating religious doctrine, commanding religious observance, and teaching religious truth; and who can deny that it is an eminently religious institution.[30]

Although it was evident that Masonry was a religious institution, the nature of its religious content was much debated. In the 1880s and 1890s especially, spokesmen grappled with the problem of whether Masonry merely contained religious elements or actually functioned as a religious system. Must a Mason believe in the inerrancy of the Bible? What was the nature of a Mason's God? What was Masonry's relationship to Christianity? And these questions frequently led to a larger one: What is the nature of religion? The rest of this chapter analyzes a wide range of conflicting opinions about Masonry and religion, showing that the variety of interpretations resulted from a malleability in religious matters that allowed individuals to mold Masonry to their own religious views and needs.

Masonic religious questions did not exist in a vacuum, however, and the intensity of Masonic interest in religious questions cannot be explained without preliminary reference to conditions in the churches in late nineteenth-century America. The social disruptions accompanying industrialization, urbanization, and massive immigration had a major impact on Protestant churches. Beginning in the 1870s, churchmen began worrying about their lack of influence over the urban masses (particularly Catholic, Jewish, and non-English-speaking Protestant immigrants) who constituted a large sector outside the pale of American Protestantism. The concern over the "unchurched" became especially acute in the face of widespread labor unrest in the last quarter of the nineteenth century. Fearful of class conflict and unassimilated immigrants, urban churches sought to reestablish social order by reaching out to workers, immigrants, and the poor via missions, revivals, and Sunday schools. But while social conditions produced fear, they also induced guilt. In the face of glaring social inequalities and widespread poverty, many churchmen abandoned the traditional notions about poverty being the fault of the poor and departed from their earlier support of the economic status quo. Proponents of the Social Gospel criticized the churches for their smugness and for their indifference to pressing practical problems of society. Insisting that churches must save men before they could save souls, they demanded that the churches take an active role in effecting social reform. Whether stemming from a desire for social order or for social justice, urban Protestantism in the late nineteenth century changed dramatically as it developed a heightened social consciousness, and took an active role in secular affairs.[31]

A second major preoccupation of the Protestant churches was the challenge offered by science to traditional faith.[32] Darwinian evolutionary theory created the greatest shock, since it could be seen as not only contradicting the account of creation in Genesis, but also as supporting a scientific determinism that denied the existence of God. Geology provided the evidence against the literal interpretation of the Bible by revealing the extreme age of the planet and uncovering fossil remains substantiating evolutionary claims. And, to cap the assault on the Bible as divine revelation, historical scholarship produced evidence for the Bible's mundane origins, viewing it as ancient literature, not divine revelation. Further challenges to Christian tradition came from the emerging academic discipline of comparative religions. The sophisticated nature of Eastern religions in particular presented the rather shocking possibility that Christianity was only one of the world's great religions.[33]

The responses of leading churchmen and theologians have been amply documented. Orthodox, or conservative, Christians denied the accuracy of Darwin's and other scientists' work and persisted in the literal interpretation of the Bible.[34] Yet there were many theologians and ministers, generally termed "liberal" Protestants, who felt persuaded by science and were anxious to salvage the relevance of Christianity.

Liberal Protestants denied that evolutionary science undermined religion. They accommodated scientific challenges to the accuracy of the Bible by denying that a literal interpretation was necessary to faith, and arguing instead that men could depend upon religious experience or reason or both for their knowledge of God. The Bible was an important guide to religion and morals, but not the sole foundation of faith. Relinquishing Biblicism, they de-emphasized doctrine and creed while emphasizing morality based on the life of a historical Jesus. Liberal solutions gained wide acceptance in seminaries and seem to have been especially popular in the North and West among the urban middle class. For the most part, the predominantly rural South continued to be a stronghold of religious orthodoxy.[35] A complex movement, which frequently overlapped with the emerging Social Gospel, liberal Protestantism was above all a positive, optimistic faith, reassuring concerned Christians that the essence of faith need not be sacrificed on a scientific altar.[36]

Liberals were attacked from two sides. Conservatives vilified them and denied their claim to be Christians. Rationalists criticized them for having made untenable compromises that misrepresented science and failed to salvage religion. Scientists and those persuaded by science were an important component of the body of freethinkers who opposed religion, but not all opponents of religion were moved primarily by scientific arguments. The bête noir of late nineteenth-century religious leaders, the "infidel" Robert G. Ingersoll, was schooled in the Enlightenment tradition of rationalism and anticlericism. A militant agnostic and a highly skilled orator, Ingersoll was well known, and his books and lectures were popular.[37]

In addition to the outspoken atheists and agnostics who challenged nineteenth-century Protestantism were those freethinkers outside of Christianity who persisted in their belief in God. Representative of this viewpoint were the members of the Free Religious Association who sought a religion of humanity based on "pure religion." Founded in 1867, the organization was hostile to traditional creeds that hampered man's search for religion. As one Free Religionist explained in 1885, the association sought a "rational religion without a priesthood; a moral code without a theology; a God without a dogmatic system."[38] Challenging the validity of organized religion, the Free Religionists, despite their small numbers, evoked as much hostility as the agnostics and atheists.

Most historians, noting the persistence of orthodoxy and the success of liberal Protestant adaptations, have minimized the extent of freethinking. The impressive success of urban revivalists Dwight L. Moody and Ira D. Sankey, the popularity of religious themes in novels, the prestige of ministers, the growth of churches, and the spread of the Sunday-school and missionary movements seem clear indications of a vital Christianity.[39] Paul Carter, in *The Spiritual Crisis of the Gilded Age*, however, has suggested that freethinking might have been more widespread than historians have recognized, and he has emphasized the spiritual crisis that many Americans must have faced in the late nineteenth century. Against evidence of the success of Moody and Sankey, he places the popularity of Ingersoll. Against swelling church membership, he offers churchmen's belief that skepticism was widespread.[40]

It is difficult to document Carter's thesis. The task of tracking private spiritual crises is a hard one, made more difficult by the role Protestant churches played in defining American culture. With no established church, Protestantism was nonetheless the dominant religion, with its version of observance pervading the public schools and the popular culture.[41] Protestant morality was inseparable from the morality of middle-class, native Americans. As Sidney Mead argued in *The Lively Experiment*,

> it is a commonplace that toward the end of the nineteenth century Protestantism largely dominated the American culture, setting the prevailing mores and the moral standards by which personal and public, individual

and group, conduct was judged. If a culture is the tangible form of a religion, in the United States that religion was Protestantism.[42]

It is also a commonplace that the late nineteenth century brought a major challenge to the dominance of Protestantism in the form of massive immigration, consisting heavily of Catholics and Jews, which was met by increased identification of Protestantism with respectability and Americanism.[43] The Protestant churches' role in identifying cultural norms contributed to their ability to overcome the challenges of science. Thus, while organized freethinkers comprised a very small number of people, it is legitimate to ask how many others shared their doubts, but did so quietly, because of their support for Christianity as a moral force or because of their unwillingness to provoke the opprobrium of respectable churchgoing America.

Unfortunately, popular religious ideas escape historical quantification. The responses to the challenges to religion were varied and were undoubtedly influenced by region and economic class. Although it is difficult to know how individuals ultimately resolved the problems of faith that whirled around them, one thing is clear: the last quarter of the nineteenth century was a period of religious ferment. The challenges to traditional faith were well publicized. Magazines, books, sermons, and chautauquas dealt with the matter, making it difficult for a religious person to avoid addressing the issues.[44] Whatever secularizing tendencies were at work in American society, religion continued to be of vital concern. Its content may have been undergoing significant changes, but the question of faith was a pertinent one to large segments of society.

Masonry proves to be most helpful in exploring the persistence and contours of faith in the late nineteenth century. While very little of the Social Gospel appears in Masonry, the order reflected many of the concerns that occupied the churches. It, too, was anxious to counter the spread of atheism; it, too, grappled with such questions as the literalness of the Bible,

47

the primacy of Christianity, and the essential nature of religion. Within Masonry both conservative and liberal religious viewpoints were well represented, with the majority of Masonic writers eager to assert Masonry's harmony with organized religion, particularly Protestantism. In addition, a significant minority believed in a divine force, but were unwilling to embrace a more specific conception or subscribe to organized religion. Differences not withstanding, Masons shared an insistence that faith was valid. Masonry could accommodate freethinking, but it drew the line at skepticism. Conflicting Masonic opinions about religion are significant, then, for what they demonstrate about the tension in late nineteenth-century American religious life and about the individual's struggle to resolve important spiritual questions.

The most prevalent version of Masonry's religious character in the late nineteenth century described Masonry as being religious, but not a religion, meaning that while not claiming to serve the function of a church, Masonry was interested in directing the attention and concerns of its members toward spiritual considerations. Men of this school of thought held that the fraternity ought to nurture belief in God and immortality as well as the morality designed to serve God. As one author explained, in setting out "A Mason's Responsibility," the Mason promised at his initiation to "live a pure, blameless and holy life before God and man." Standing before his brothers, he "pledged himself literally to a faith in God, a hope in immortality and a charity for all mankind."[45] The majority of Masonic writers were unwilling to push Masonry's commitment beyond this simple statement of belief. They emphasized the fraternity's "ancient landmark," which held that Masonry was "universal," requiring only that faith in which all men could agree. Beyond that fundamental belief a man was left to shape his own doctrines. Furthermore, in the sanctuary of the lodge, religious questions must be eschewed; no sectarian creeds could be discussed or promulgated. This 1900 statement in the Los Angeles *Freemason* aptly summarized the Masonic principle of universality:

Masonry has no creed but the fatherhood of God and the brotherhood of Man. It would bridge over and heal differences existing between various beliefs in order to unite the family of Man in the service of one God. Masonry is not religion, but it is religious. It bows in humble recognition of the homage due from the creature to the Creator, but forbids narrow and sectarian bigotry that would condemn to outer darkness all who differ from a certain belief. Masonry is the world's religion, in that it contains the foundation of all faith and practice; for Jew and Christian, Mohammedan and Parsee, Roman and Protestant may enjoy the privileges it affords. One thing all must believe—there is a God. After that the manner of serving God, the form of doctrine is left to each individual. He reads the message from his Father and obeys it according to his understanding and agreeably to the dictates of his conscience.[46]

As the passage indicates, one of the major advantages of universality was that it could unite mankind and promote brotherhood. Repeatedly, Masonic "universalists" used the imagery of a worldwide Masonry, which allowed men of every religion to be linked by the commonality of the Masonic altar.

Universalists were proud of the order's broad tolerance and respect for individual conscience, "It is the proudest boast of Masonry that it has always been a jealous conservator of this right of individual thought."[47] On occasion, they linked Masonry's toleration to the American provision for religious freedom and boasted of Masonry's role in influencing the Founding Fathers in their concern for religious and political freedom. "Through Washington, Lafayette and other master minds and heroic brethren," one claimed, "Freemasonry gave to this country the principles of civil and religious liberty, and has preserved those very 'fundamental laws and principles' which guarantee to all freedom and equality."[48]

At the same time, universalists stressed that Masonry did not offer itself as a religious system, and they remonstrated with Masons who claimed that "Masonry is religion enough for me."[49] As the *Masonic Record* explained in 1877, Masonry "does not claim to be a church or system of religion, and to this end is content with a seat on the foot stool of religion."[50] More often, the term employed was *handmaiden to religion*, but the point was the same—Masonry fell short of religion. Unlike the churches, it was not concerned with theology; in particular, it offered no plan of salvation. An author in the *Pacific Mason* explained that Masonry "has nothing to do with the theological plans of salvation"; rather, it is concerned only with making men better "in this world."[51]

Universalists claimed that Masonry was not a religion, but they viewed it as a great aid to religion. Many noted that the fraternity served the churches through its inculcation of moral virtues and brotherly love. Others argued that by encouraging faith in God, the fraternity's teachings made it a bulwark against atheism and agnosticism. In 1896, an author in the *American Tyler* proclaimed that

> with a trust well-founded in God, a faith in the immortality of the soul, and the highest expression of the sentiments of universal brotherhood, Atheism may spread far and wide, but our Fraternity will continue a power on earth, and faith will ever find a sanctuary in its temples.[52]

Similarly, in 1906, the Reverend Henry W. Rugg, calling the belief in God "one of the fundamental, unrepealable laws of our Fraternity," claimed that Masonry served as a stabilizing force in the community.

> It counts for something of wholesome power, of good in the community, that Freemasonry takes issue with unbelief and agnosticism, that it opposes materialism and lawlessness, inculcating that essential faith which lays hold of eternal verities and gives promise of the life that now is and the life that is to come.[53]

In the universalist view, then, far from competing with churches, Masonry served them and society by promoting religiosity and taking a firm stand against immorality and atheism.

In arguing that Masonry did not threaten the churches, but rather promoted religious belief, authors frequently insisted that Masonry had a special relationship with Christianity. In 1890, for example, a New York Grand Lodge official insisted that Masonry is not, "in any sense, a substitute for Christianity, but rather, in its precepts and code, a handmaid thereto."[54] A Grand Master of South Carolina, Stiles P. Dendy, also stressed Masonry's close connection to Christianity when he claimed that Masonry allowed "absolute freedom in religious thought and modes of worship, exacting only as fundamental to its portals—belief in God," but then added that "Masonry has ever been the handmaiden of Civilization and Christianity."[55]

A concern to demonstrate Masonry's rapport with Christianity was also evident in the growing practice of lodges' attending church services in a body. A number of Grand Lodges officially endorsed the idea, and Masonic magazines frequently reprinted the minister's sermons on these occasions.[56] Significantly, there were no references to Masons attending a synagogue or a Catholic church. In a related vein, many Grand Lodges prohibited Masons from holding meetings on Sundays, out of deference to the Christian Sabbath. For example, in 1884, the Grand Lodge of Florida ruled that Masons must not confer degrees on Sunday: "It is contrary to the spirit and teachings of Freemasonry to transact business or work on the Lord's day, except on funeral occasions, or for some charitable work which cannot be postponed."[57] The *Repository*, when asked about the propriety of "work" on Sunday, replied that it was technically legal to confer degrees, but disapproved of the practice because it would bring criticism to Masonry. "It is no part of the functions or purposes of the Masonic organization to provide spiritual ministrations in the way of public worship, and thus usurp the place of the Christian Church."[58]

Thus, both church attendance and Sabbath observance under-lined the assumption that the religion for which Masonry was a handmaiden was Christianity.

Masons' attitude toward Christianity, particularly in its Sab-bath observance, is strikingly analogous to the relationship between church and state in America. Despite legal separation between the two institutions, until recently the state generally has acknowledged Christianity, particularly Protestantism.[59] Sabbath laws and the King James Bible and prayers in schools were just the official indications of the close connection be-tween the two.[60] Thus, as much as many Masons prided themselves on Masonry's universality, like the state, they ac-knowledged a special harmony between Masonry and Chris-tianity. And, like the state, because of the general absence of Catholics from the order, Masons implicitly equated Christi-anity with Protestantism. Masons trumpeted religious free-dom, but paid obeisance to the prevailing religious culture.

The reasons for the universalists' interest in demonstrating the order's support of Protestantism are not hard to find. Part of the concern, especially on the part of Masonic ministers, may be linked to the belief that whereas Masonry could not, Christianity could provide salvation. But a far more significant impetus was Masonic leaders' desire to maintain a harmonious relationship with the Protestant churches. Remembering the anti-Masonic furor of antebellum days and the hostility of the churches to the order, leaders were anxious to make it clear that Masonry was not that organization of irreligious deists and libertines which its detractors had portrayed. On the con-trary, they urged, it honored individual religious conscience, promoted love of God and morality, and contained nothing that need compromise a Christian's beliefs. Far from posing a threat to organized religion, Masonry shared many of its pur-poses and valued church and churchgoers' approval for the respectability it conferred.

To a large extent, Masonic leaders were successful in achiev-ing harmony with the Protestant churches; very few denomi-nations officially disapproved of the order after the Civil War.

The Disciples of Christ, for example, which had vehemently opposed secret societies in the antebellum period, generally adopted a much more lenient stance in the postwar years. A recent historian of the Disciples, David Edwin Harrell, Jr., relates that there was one "self-appointed Disciples champion of antimasonry" in the years immediately after the Civil War, but that "by the mid-1870s antimasonry was almost a dead issue." Church officials left the matter to the conscience of the individual. In 1895, when a Disciples newspaper featured a debate on secret societies, "a majority of the paper's readers approved of lodge membership." Harrell suggests that officials were probably not enthusiastic about secret societies, but that "there were many Masons in the church and few leaders were willing to offend them openly."[61]

Another sign of Masonry's respectability was the tendency of ministers to join the order. In 1900, the *American Tyler* noted with "pardonable satisfaction" and probable exaggeration, that "among the best, most earnest and most loyal Masons are the consecrated ministers of God. In every community it will be found that the preachers constitute a good percentage of the membership of the lodges."[62] Few records exist on the numbers of ministers in Masonry or their denominations. In 1889, Alabama reported 483 ministers in a total Masonic population of 7,950.[63] And in 1890, as evidence of Masonry's "goodness," the New York Grand Lodge reported that in that state there were 703 Masons who were clergymen, the majority of whom were Methodists, Episcopalians, and Baptists, and asked, "would these Clergymen, now in active Church service, labor with, or give countenance to, an institution that was not blessed by God and honored by man?"[64]

While Masonic efforts to tone down the order's deism and assume a subordinate status vis-à-vis organized religion contributed to its respectability, changes in the religious climate must be given equal weight. However much Masons might reiterate that the fraternity did not threaten to supplant Christianity, Masonic universalism could be viewed as quite challenging to traditional religion. A doctrine that ignored religious creeds and asked only that a man believe in God bordered on suggesting that belief in God was all that was essential in religion. However, the spread of liberal Protestant ideas had deprived Masonry of much of its potential radicalism. Masonry's dedication to universality, toleration, and morality was in keeping with the tendencies of liberal Protestantism, which placed less emphasis on creed and denominations, and which tended to stress ethics and morality as crucial elements in religion. Liberal Protestants, eager to stem the tide of skepticism and atheism, could well tolerate Masonry and welcome its efforts at encouraging morality and religiosity.

With church and Masonry moving toward one another, the breach was healed. The universalists' insistence that the order was in harmony with the prevailing Protestant culture undoubtedly contributed to its success. Masonry was no longer suspect as a society of atheists and libertines, and could thus have a broad-based appeal to the Protestant or nominally Protestant male population. By the late nineteenth century, aided by a liberalization of the religious climate, Masonry had largely disassociated itself from dissent and had established its respectability.

Masonry appealed to more than liberal Protestant sensibilities, however. In striking contrast to the universalists were those Masons who sought to invest the order with far more specific religious content by injecting Christianity into it or by insisting upon acknowledgment of the Bible's divine authenticity. These men, whose viewpoint was similar to that of conservative, orthodox Christians, were aided in their efforts by the fact that Masonic ritual clearly drew upon Christianity and the Bible. Although eighteenth-century deists had purged the rituals of most references to Christianity, a few remained: Masonry's reverence for John the Baptist and John the Evangelist, passages from the New Testament, the Bible on the altar, and the emphasis on immortality. In addition, the Knights Templar, the highest order in York Rite, was open only to Christians, a further basis for claiming a close connection between Masonry and Christianity. Drawing upon these elements in Masonry, a vocal minority of "sectarians" minimized the universality of Masonry and claimed that the fraternity was inherently Christian.

Perhaps the most common means of injecting Christianity into Masonry was the way in which both ministers and devout laymen referred to Christ in prayers and addresses. In this form, authors made no specific claim for Masonry's link to Christianity, but assumed that their audience was Christian, thus gainsaying Masonry's universality. Typical were the words of John H. Whipple, the Grand Master of Vermont, in an address to the Grand Lodge: "We may be truly one with Christ, a portion of that celestial mind. He is truly our brother, one of our family. Let us make Him our constant model."[65] More emphatically Christian was an Indiana Grand Lodge official's pronouncement that "there is but one true divine religion and its name is Christianity."[66]

Although few printed prayers referred to Christ, the tendency may have been pronounced in lodge meetings—especially if the lodge chaplain was a minister. In 1889, an Oregon Grand Lodge official complained of the habit, claiming that "nine-tenths of the prayers made in Masonic assemblies, according to our experience, close in the name of Jesus Christ."[67] A similar criticism was offered by the *Trestleboard*, a magazine emphatically hostile to Christianizing tendencies in Masonry. It claimed that Masonry as practiced in America had so many Christian influences that devout Jews were uncomfortable in the lodge:

> You initiate Jews into Masonry; you promise them on the word and honor of a gentleman and Mason, that they should enjoy all Masonic privileges without violating their conscience. But after their initiation, they find that they are obliged to join in Christian prayers to venerate Christian saints, to talk about the "Lion of the Tribe of Judah," and to listen to other allusions offensive to their religious beliefs.[68]

Years later, in 1911, Morris A. Sach, a Jew, made the same point when he complained in a letter to the editor of the *Masonic Home Journal* about the invocation to Christ in lodge prayers introduced by overzealous Christian ministers. The editor's response acknowledged that "sometimes a minister in offering prayers at a Masonic Meeting inadvertently uses the name of Jesus, but in all cases in our opinion it is the force of habit and never done intentionally."[69]

References to Christ in prayers and speeches may have been the most common form of linking Masonry with Christianity, but there were far more specific statements of the connection. In 1895, the Reverend J. C. Quinn argued that Masonry taught "the innocence of character which all men should possess, the resurrection of the dead, the immortality of the soul, and by inference safety in Christ." Masonry's main purpose, he noted, was to help men develop that holy character which "we attain through faith in Jesus Christ. Let us seek this!"[70] Similarly, in 1910, a Mason wrote a letter to the editor of the *Masonic Advocate* in which he claimed, "As I understand Masonry, it is second only to the church in the spread of Christianity. Its aim is to spread the Gospel and peace and good will and brotherly love. Is that not Christianity?"[71]

Perhaps the most militant of the Masonic Christianizers were the Brownell brothers, the editors of the *American Tyler* (Grand Rapids, Michigan), who vehemently insisted that Masonry was Christian. Their argument rested on the denial that Masonry had existed in pre-Christian times and on the claim that Masonry had been founded in the seventeenth century as a distinctively Christian organization. In tracing the Christian origins of Masonry, they acknowledged that much of Christianity had been purged from Masonry, and called for a return to Masonry's clear Christian purpose. Claiming that the "hour is fast approaching when the edict will go forth to humanity in all lands, saying 'Choose ye this day whom ye will serve,' " the Brownells predicted that as the millennium approached, Masonry would necessarily be divided. "The Christian branch of Freemasonry will lovingly agree to disagree with its brethren, even as did Abraham and Lot, and taking the purposes and principles of Masonic philosophy with it, will return to the 'old paths' of 1717, when Masonry was Christianity and Christianity was Masonry."[72]

In addition to citing historical evidence for Masonry's Christianity, the Brownells also argued that Masonry *must* be Christian because Masonry was *universal*. By their definition, this meant that "there is, and can be, in the very nature of things as they exist but one religion that is universal, and that is the religion of the Lord Jesus Christ."[73] Clearly, the Brownells' militant insistence on Masonry's Christianity was fueled by their own faith that Christianity represented the only true religion. This attitude was perfectly illustrated in the support in the *American Tyler*'s columns for the Morse Bill, which provided for recognizing God and Jesus Christ in the United States Constitution. Denying that the amendment would undermine either the American or the Masonic principle of religious freedom, the Brownells maintained that the amendment was imperative. The future of the nation's collective soul was at stake:

> It is of vital importance to this people as a nation that God hath the first place in their Constitution. He is still supreme, and He has declared that if we forget Him we shall be turned into hell with all the other nations that have denied his authority.[74]

The parallels between the Brownells' support of this amendment and the demand that Masonry be acknowledged as Christian are striking. Both stemmed from a Christian militancy that demanded the legitimacy of its position be recognized by the rest of the world. At issue was the belief that if America or Masonry did not specifically profess Christianity, they were tacitly accepting the viability of other religions. Although militants like the Brownells acknowledged that under Masonry and under the Constitution, men were free to worship as they pleased, they wanted it made clear that such worship was ineffective.

Other attempts to specify Masonry's religion by linking it to traditional faith focused on the order's relationship to the

Bible. Universalists usually argued that while Masonry demanded that Masons respect the Bible, it left "the interpretation of the Bible to the intelligence of the individual."[75] An Ohio Grand Lodge official's 1890 pronouncement was typical. He emphasized that Masonry required that Masons regard the Bible as the "Great Light" in Masonry—"nothing more, nothing less. The nature and definition of this belief are matters of his own, with which the Craft has no concern."[76]

Masonic sectarians disagreed. With striking similarity to orthodox Christian arguments about the Bible's relationship to Christianity, they insisted that a traditional interpretation was essential to Masonry. In 1897, for example, T. J. Larger of San Antonio, Texas wrote the *Texas Freemason* that "if the Holy Bible is not a divine inspiration, as it is claimed to be, it is a book of lies, and being the chief corner stone of our institution, makes Masonry a farce and a myth."[77] A Kentucky Grand Lodge official similarly linked the well-being of Masonry to an orthodox view of the Bible when he proclaimed in 1883, "We believe that the stability of Masonry has always been and is now due to the unshaken belief in God, and the authenticity of his word as taught in the Bible."[78] As this comment indicates, in addition to insisting that Masons must believe that the Bible was divinely inspired, sectarians also called for an acknowledgment of the Bible's "authenticity," by which they meant both its divinity and its accuracy.

While Texas and the South in general seemed particularly prone to Masonic Biblicism, this was not just a Southern position. In 1905, the *Masonic Advocate* (Indianapolis) printed an article criticizing Lyman Beecher for accepting the doctrine of evolution. "If he is right, then our whole Masonic system is erroneous; the Bible is discredited and is of no more value than any other book, and we are left without anything to inspire a hope for life hereafter."[79] Similarly, in 1885, J. R. Clymen addressed an audience of Scottish Rite Masons in Ohio and was vehement in his denunciation of Masons who denied the orthodox view of the Bible:

That man who proclaims himself a Mason and denies the authenticity or divine inspiration of the Holy Scriptures, is a perjurer before God and man, and when he presumes to minister at her altar, is an accessory to villainous fraud and delusion.

Arguing further that Masonry was responsible, along with Judaism, for preserving the Bible in historical times, Clymen exclaimed, "Let Atheism rage, and infidelity seek to destroy the Bible of our Fathers, but they will gnash their teeth in vain, for the sons of Freemasonry will be among its first, foremost and strongest defenders."[80]

The question was not just debated in the literature; in several instances Grand Lodges had to arbitrate expulsion proceedings stemming from a Mason's refusal to accept the Bible as traditionally interpreted. In 1888, the Texas Grand Lodge upheld the expulsion of two men who could not accept the divine authenticity of the Bible. Although the Grand Lodge felt that it should not debate questions "that belong to the church or church councils," it nonetheless felt that Masonry must insist that its members "respect and revere the Bible." It based its decision on a Grand Lodge resolution passed in 1877, which held that "a belief in the divine authenticity of the Holy Scriptures is an indispensable prerequisite to Masonic admission." The Grand Lodge concluded that if men who did not believe in the Bible did not have enough "respect for themselves" to withdraw from the order, the Grand Lodge must compel them to leave "so that they may no longer bring reproach upon the Order."[81]

In 1888, the Missouri Grand Lodge in two cases sustained "expulsion for denying the existence of God and the truth of the Bible." The vote in these trials was unanimous and enthusiastic, "the members all rising." In the case of A. G. Lobaugh, the defendant admitted that he did not believe in the Bible as revelation or in the Bible's God. Instead, Lobaugh claimed, "I believe God is a Supreme Being, and created all things, and made unchangeable laws to govern the same," and that he obtained his idea of God "from the works of Nature and what I can see around me." The Grand Lodge expressed regret over the incident: "We do not put him away as a monster, but rather as a friend, whose opinions, honestly formed, have placed him out of harmony with the symmetry of our edifice." Nonetheless, it was emphatic that Masons must believe in more than a God of nature and must accept the Bible as revelation from God.[82]

In Illinois the year before, the Grand Lodge took a radically different stance. John S. Crum, who had written a pamphlet expressing disbelief in the Bible and calling its first sentence a lie, was brought to trial for casting ridicule on the Bible and for atheism. Although the lodge found him guilty of the former, it failed to punish him. Crum, on his part, had preferred charges against the Master of the lodge for injecting sectarian matters into lodge proceedings. The Grand Master disallowed Crum's action, and because of the recalcitrance of the lodge in punishing Crum, arrested the lodge's charter. The whole matter was brought to the Grand Lodge, which essentially upheld Crum's position. The committee report on the matter invoked Masonry's universality and stressed that Masonry did not inquire into the specifics of a man's beliefs.

> The moment a brother assumes that the Supreme can be approached only through some one name—be that name Brahma, Jesus, Buddha or Allah—that moment he enters upon theological definition and interpretation, the very root of sectarianism, which, with its twin evil, political partisanship, Masonry seeks above all others to exclude.[83]

Lodges rarely acted on the matter of belief in the Bible, however, suggesting either that they took the universality of Masonry literally, or that most Masons who were doubtful about the Bible kept their skepticism to themselves.

It is evident from these cases that in demanding an orthodox interpretation of the Bible, sectarians were also insisting that Masonry required a belief in a specific God. In 1889, an Idaho Grand Lodge official responded to South Dakota's

F. C. Thompson, who had become notorious for his attacks on the Bible as divine inspiration.

> Do we, as Masons, believe in the Holy Bible? If we do, we must believe in the Bible's God. There is too much "free-thinking" among the Masons of to-day, and the questions that muddle Bro. Thompson should be left to profanes. Every Mason should believe in the teachings of Masonry, and the less we discuss these infidel and atheist notions the better we will be off as Masons and as men.[84]

Another author, writing in the *Masonic Review* in 1895, went further and specified that the Bible's God, and thus Masonry's God, was a personal God; "no pantheist, therefore, or one who believes in an *impersonal* God," or in "the sum total of all the forces which act and re-act in nature, can consistently worship at the shrine of Freemasonry. The trust, then, of every Mason, is not, *strictly speaking*, in God, but in a *personal* God."[85] Thus Masons who argued for the traditional view of the Bible also embraced an orthodox notion of the God of the Bible. They made it clear that belief in any other God was atheism. For Masons, there should be no midway position.

Both universalists and sectarians were generally sympathetic to the idea of a basic harmony between Masonry and Protestantism, but the differences between the two are important. Widely tolerant of religious variation short of atheism and agnosticism, the universalists' interest in construing Masonry as a handmaiden to religion seems heavily influenced by the desire to infuse Masonry with respectability. In contrast, Masonic sectarians who insisted upon the order's Christianity or the divine authenticity of the Bible were concerned not with the defense of Masonry, but with the defense of traditional religion. In demanding that Masonry adopt Christianity or a specific interpretation of the Bible, they were denying the validity of other religions, evolutionary science, and the accommodations of liberal Protestantism. Thus, despite Masonry's tradition as an asylum remote from the conflicts of the outside world, Masonry became one of the many battlegrounds over the content of Christianity.

Just as Masonry could accommodate Christians, it could also meet the needs of freethinking men. Almost as prevalent in the literature as a militant Christian orientation were the views of Masons who combined religious belief with criticism of traditional organized religion. Like the universalists, these men stressed Masonry's universality and insisted that it remain nonsectarian. They differed from universalists, however, in their critical stance toward churches and in their tendency to think of Masonry as a religion, not as a mere handmaiden to institutional worship.

A major theme in their criticism of churches was that Masonry was far more effective in teaching such moral virtues as brotherly love than the churches. Echoing the Social Gospel's criticism of the church's indifference to worldly matters, Masonic enthusiasts argued that churches had trouble filling their pews while Masonry flourished, because Masonry provided practical religion in the form of aid to needy brethren, widows, and orphans, while the church was slack in its duty to its parishioners. As this statement by F. A. Dixon in the *Kansas Freemason* makes clear, the assessment was highly colored by Masonic resentment over church criticism of Masonry:

> The church never has treated the fraternal orders of the day with anything but contempt, yet the Master commands us to visit the sick and dying and administer to their wants. Who to-day spends the most money to relieve the wants of the poor? Who is more ready to go deep into their pockets and assist the needy? Is it the church member or the lodge member?[86]

Along the same lines, the *Masonic Advocate* printed the purportedly true story of a dying man, Brother A, who was a Mason and a church member. While on his deathbed, he was asked by his pastor, a man hostile to Masonry, if he had not found Masonry an "empty profession." Brother A's response was a paean to Masonry. He claimed that the church people, "with whom I have labored and prayed," neglected him. "I have been left uncared for; my labors among them seem to have been forgotten, and my devotion to their interests entirely overlooked." The Masons, however, "daily visited me" and "every want was anticipated, quietly, and without a chance to return my heartfelt thanks."[87] Or, as the *Trestleboard* pointed out, while both Christianity and Masonry taught morality, "to the theory of Christianity, Masonry adds the practice; with the precept, she furnishes the example; for the picture, she gives the subject; for the word, the deed."[88]

A second major criticism of the churches focused on the sectarian squabbles and doctrinal issues that seemed to dominate organized religion and militate against the churches' ability to teach love of God and man. As C.E.J. White argued, "the religion of this world is but a field of sectarianism, where men and women wrangle and dispute about matters of opinion, and forget the weightier points of the law—'justice, mercy and truth.'" In contrast, "what the mass of religionists profess, Masonry carried out in those details, whereby the idea of brotherhood is exemplified in deeds of sympathy and extended charity."[89]

Masonic spokesmen frequently specified that it was impatience with the hypocrisy and the creeds of the churches that led men to Masonry. H. H. Ingersoll, the Past Grand Master of Tennessee, argued in 1891 that if the church

> had striven with half the energy to keep hell out of men, that it has to keep men out of hell, perhaps Freemasonry would not have had its present place and power. If the sects had fought each other less and fought the devil more, men might have felt less need of Lodges, Chapters, etc. Less of creeds and more of deeds would have won more of the hearts of men.[90]

Similarly, a *Masonic Review* article, entitled "Masonry Practices What Christianity Teaches," compared the "crimination and recrimination" found in churches with the harmony of the lodge room: "While churches are thus shut up in sectarianism, and can see no good and nothing but evil in those who are not of their particular faith, so long will even those of their own church seek an asylum where they are free from this fulsome laudation of themselves and wholesale condemnation of others."[91]

In 1897, the editor of the *Trestleboard* declared his preference for the universality of Masonry over the sectarianism of the churches. In response to a minister who had claimed that Masonry was the servant of the church, he denied Masonry's subordinate position and provided an account of his personal religious search, which, because such descriptions are rare, deserves quoting at length.

> Now, we protest against the placing of Masonry in this position. From our earliest years of childhood ... we were taught the fatherhood of God and the brotherhood of man, and to do right and deal justly with all men because it was right. It is not for us to profess that we have always performed these last duties, but these things we were taught before and since we became a Mason, both in the church and in Masonry; and while we listened to much more in the exhortations of the one which were conducive to division and dissension among men because of differences of opinion upon articles of faith, and conflicting ideas of polity and creed, we have never, in Masonry, heard but one universal faith and code of practice enforced upon the attention of its votaries. With half a century of close investigation of the one which claims superiority, and over three decades equal attention to the more modest retiring system of morality veiled in allegory and taught by degrees, we are prepared to protest against the placing of Masonry in the position of a handmaid to any system of religion, creed or opinion.[92]

The editor hinted at what many more traditionally religious Masons suspected and feared: Masonry could be and was interpreted as an alternative religion. In 1896, the *Trestleboard* offered an amusing—and revealing—anecdote.

In a discussion among some little girls in a Texas city on family, religious and social matters, says the *Texas Freemason*, one declared that her father was a Methodist, another that her papa was a Baptist, etc., until one bright little girl spoke up. "My papa does not belong to any church, but he's a Mason," which fact seemed to be in her mind amply sufficient for her father's high religious and social standing.[93]

The notion that Masonry occupied a position of equality with the churches was particularly evident in the attempts to promote Masonic Sunday services. A number of authors criticized as sectarian Masonic laws that prohibited Masons from meeting on Sundays and argued that Sunday Masonic services would fill a need. As the editor of the *Trestleboard* noted, "There are many Masons who are not sectarians or attendants on any regular church service. Many such would like to hear a good lecture from some intelligent Brother upon some subject proper for a respectful observance of the day, and a service which would be divested of all sectarian bias."[94] In a somewhat flippant vein, W. W. Lee of Connecticut also urged that Masons be allowed to have Sunday meetings. Terming himself a "backslider" who "never had enough religion to brag about," he expressed impatience with "our Masonic lawgivers and lawmakers, jurists and judges, poets and preachers" who

> reiterated and reverberated in long-winded orations that Masonry was not religion—Oh, no! but the handmaid and co-worker with religion. This being so (and who shall dispute them), and as Sunday is devoted to teaching religion, it occurred to me as a sinner, that it would be a handy thing to have that handmaid around on Sunday and give the sinners an extra means of grace.[95]

Formal means of establishing Masonry's status as an alternative to traditional religious worship were unsuccessful, but there was ample expression in the literature of Masonry's equality or superiority to traditional religion. Statements that

Masonry was a religion or on a par with the churches were particularly evident in, though by no means limited to, the Western states. The most prevalent argument was based on the Masonic concept of universality, taken one step further, to praise Masonry as "pure religion." The advantage of Masonry's religion was its simplicity. As the California Grand Orator, Niles Searles, explained, "Masonry discards as non-essentials much of the formula in which religious truth is enveloped and establishes as its tenets only the great central truths to which we all subscribe."[96] In effect, freethinking Masons argued that belief in God and immortality was not only all that Masonry required, but all that was essential to religion. Stressing that Masonry taught men to discover God through nature, Grand Master Edward Myers Preston of California claimed:

> By such methods Masonry teaches a conception of the Creator which is more comprehensive than that of those religions which are limited by creed and dogma. It inculcates a more reverent devotion than mere compulsory obedience to law, inspires a faith in God which cannot be impugned by heresy, and proclaims a recognition of the birthright of man, which is the foundation of religious and political liberty.[97]

In this light, Masonry's professed tolerance of widely different world religions within its temples takes on new significance. Although the Masonic praise of "pure religion" had much in common with a concurrent movement in Christianity to return to a purer form of the faith, rather than referring to Christianity, freethinking Masons viewed all religions as equal. They argued that Masonry's strength lay in its possession of the common denominator of all religions: belief in God and immortality. All else was irrelevant. Albert Pike, a prominent Scottish Rite Mason, whose book, *Morals and Dogma*, was often quoted, drew upon his study of world religions to praise Masonry as a religion. In a speech at the laying of the cornerstone of the Washington, D.C. Masonic Cathedral in 1888, he explained:

> It has been said that Masonry is not a religion. If it be said that it is not Christianity, or Hebraism, or Moham- medanism, or Parseeism, this is true; but there was reli- gion in the world before any of these were; and if the faith of the enlightened thinkers of Greece, Rome, of Egypt and India, who believed that there was one Divine Cre- ator and Preserver of the Universe, its Lord or Ruler, loving and adoring him as beneficent and wise, and that the intelligent soul of man did not cease to be, at the death of the body; if this was religion, surely Freema- sonry, having the same belief and trustful reverence, is likewise a religion.[98]

Similar to Pike in an appreciation of world religions was Richard Saxe Jones, who in 1896 wrote an article that in- cluded a critical examination of Christianity. He explained that biblical scholarship had made it evident that the Bible could not be literally interpreted, and argued further that "if the Bible itself is open to historical criticisms, can it be said that the higher truths of Christianity as explained to us by Bible authority, cannot be criticized." Having set up a challenge to the exclusive truths of Christianity, Jones proceeded to discuss the nature of true religion, which he defined as love of God and love of man.

> The Christian too often assumes that all which is good in Christianity is the sole property of Christianity and too often fails to learn that the golden rule of the Christian is at least the gilden precept of Brahminism, Confucian- ism, Zorasterism and Mohammedanism. No religion has ever prospered without genuine Creator worship, genu- ine brotherly love.

After placing Christianity in the context of other religions, Jones retreated somewhat and suggested, citing the works of James Freeman Clark, that "because Christianity has turned to account in human relations these basic ideas of all religion, that therefore Christianity is better fitted for a world's religion than any other present system." He stressed, however, that to succeed in becoming the world's religion, Christianity must include only the "essentials"—love of God and of man. Jones concluded, "This latter . . . was our general definition of religion, and is the true basis of all religion, and here Masonry takes its place, teaching love of God and love of neighbor, perhaps no better than other religions or semi-religious organizations."[99]

Masons sympathetic to the idea of Masonry as pure, undefiled religion also stressed that the fraternity did not attempt to define a man's God. Acknowledging the validity of different conceptions of God, the *Masonic Tidings* praised the order for recognizing that Masons did not have to agree about the nature of God: "Every man's conception of Deity is drawn from his own innate conception of the Infinite, and they must be and are as varied, as is the intelligence and observation of the individual."[100] Albert Pike echoed these sentiments when he answered a man who wondered if his agnosticism would bar him from Masonry. The man had questioned Pike in 1882 "as an authority in such matters, whether the insistence in the belief in a personal God . . . would be an insurmountable objection to his reception in the Order." Pike's response gave his correspondent a great deal of leeway.

> Dear Sir: You would have to place your trust in God, and kneel and unite in prayer to God. Whether this is a belief in a personal God you can judge for yourself.

Yet later in the letter, he was more specific.

> We do not require belief in a God having form or shape, but in one Supreme Intelligence, having unity of will, the source and origin of all that is . . . I should rather consider God as an all pervading Spirit,—Soul of the Universe—of whose intellect, that of every man is a ray, or spark that lives its distinct life.

The Los Angeles *Freemason*, which had reprinted the letter, obviously approved, "Such an epitomé of the religion of a Mason it would be hard to improve on."[101]

In fact, such a vague conception of God was probably not the "epitomé" of most Masons' religion. Yet both Jones and Pike explored in depth what most of those Masons hostile to creeds of churches and enamored of "pure religion" hinted at. Science, by challenging the literal interpretation of the Bible, had undermined the certainty of Christian truths, while comparative religious studies had led many men to recognize, as Albert Pike put it, that "men create Gods to suit their own particular spiritual needs."[102] Having much in common with the Free Religionists, this wing of Masonry persisted in an optimistic belief in God, while implicitly or explicitly rejecting traditional religion and its institutions.

Thus, despite Masonic universalists' attempts to deny that Masonry was an alternative to the churches, one group of Masons clearly contradicted them. This group is significant for an understanding of popular religious belief, for in arguing that it was legitimate to have religious faith consisting only of a belief in God, love of man, and hope for immortality, these men were indicating that Masonry could serve as a vehicle for religious expression outside the churches.

If Masonic authors and officials could interpret Masonry's religion so variously, there was little to stop rank-and-file Masons from doing so as well. They could make of Masonry what they wanted, short of agnosticism and atheism, although obviously in states like Texas and Missouri, unorthodox religious beliefs were best kept private. Thus the devout Christian could join without feeling he was violating his religious principles. Even without invoking the name of Christ, it could be clearly demonstrated that Masonry was influenced by Christian principles and morals. Moreover, Masonry could provide what most Protestant churches did not—dramatic pageantry that could reinforce religious expression. Jews (when they were admitted to the order), assuming they could ignore the occasional slip in prayer reference, could also find in Masonry a religious spirit congenial with their traditions and could have the satisfaction of knowing that much of Masonry was drawn from the Old Testament.

It seems, however, that Masonry's religion was particularly appropriate for those men with rather vaguely defined beliefs. For men unsettled by controversies surrounding the Bible and the validity of Christianity, Masonry provided a religious experience that was comfortable, not disturbing. "To the Lodge room the soul perplexed by religious differences may flee and be at rest."[103] With the important exception of the sectarians, Masonry offered the assurance that the questions science and history had brought into play were largely irrelevant, because they had challenged only creeds, not God. As one author put it, "While the warfare of science drives wedge after wedge into the rigid ecclesiastical dogmatism of creeds, it has no power over the subjective religion of the heart, in which alone man can be made to agree, and which, therefore, is the religion of Freemasonry."[104] Masonry could thus have special appeal to men who persisted in believing, but who were uncertain about what they believed.

The religion of Masonry is vital to understanding the attraction of the organization in late nineteenth-century America. With its conflicting traditions of Biblicism and deism, along with its emphasis on individual conscience, Masonry was highly malleable, and could have a broad-based appeal. While sectarians and freethinkers reveal the range of Masonic opinion and the flexibility of the order, perhaps the most helpful in explaining Masonry's appeal were the universalists. Given the history of anti-Masonry, the order could not have reestablished itself without first achieving respectability. The universalists' willingness to pay obeisance to the churches by stressing Masonry's handmaiden status helped to place the fraternity on the right side of America's Protestant culture. Moreover, Masonic universalism, which shared so much with liberal Protestantism, indicates how crucial a general liberalization of the religious climate was to the respectability and hence the growth of Masonry.

Thus Masonry's religious content provides insight into the broader religious currents outside the temple. Historians who have argued that most Americans were able to meet the challenges of science either by adaptation of their beliefs or reaffirmation of traditional religion are most probably correct, although Masonry suggests that freethinking believers may have been more prevalent than the meager size of organizations like the Free Religionists suggests. While Masonic beliefs varied, it is significant that all Masons agreed that their organization was religious. Although some Masons may not have taken the religious component of the order seriously, Masonry insisted upon a formal declaration of a belief in God. Moreover, no man could be made a Mason without undergoing three religiously oriented ceremonies. The spiritual crisis of the late nineteenth century—at least for the men of Masonry—was not one of belief versus disbelief, but rather a struggle within the confines of faith. Masonry represents a group of men widely divergent in their religious professions, yet insistent that God exists.

3

Brotherhood and Respectability

One marked characteristic of this good man which has made
itself felt with all who have known him, was his absolute sincerity in life, and character. . . . Mentally and morally he was
cast in a large and strong mould, a man of sterling integrity.
—Eulogy for William Paggett Allen, Grand Master
of Iowa, 1886[1]

This hall becomes a moral battle-ground where the contest is
waged between truth and error, virtue and vice, and only the
best material is selected for our spiritual building. Here the
outward turmoil reaches not; here the din of worldly conflict
is not heard; here the oppositions and clamors of worldly strife
prevail not. This spot is sacred to peace, charity, good will, and
to all those graces that exist and redeem man.
—Abraham H. Howland, Jr., Grand Lodge
of Massachusetts, 1884[2]

Just as Masonry mirrored dominant religious ideas, it also reflected the middle-class conception of moral behavior typical
of Victorian culture. Masonry, like pulpit and popular fiction,
promulgated a creed of self-improvement whose emphasis on
industry, piety, honesty, temperance, and sobriety stressed the
importance of self-restraint to a well-ordered personality and
a well-ordered world. And while affirming these values, Masonry's repeated contrast of the virtues of the Craft with the
competitive, commercial world outside the temple also reflected contemporary fears that the old morality was being lost
in a rapidly changing world. Masons, like so many other
Americans, viewed personal regeneration as an antidote to the
disharmony that characterized their society.

An analysis of the rhetoric of Masonic morality provides
more than a litmus-paper reading of popular ideology. Much

of the fraternity's appeal may be traced to Masons' insistence that theirs was an organization composed of moral men, whose actions were governed by honesty, restraint, and brotherly love. Masonic rhetoric promised men both a sense of brotherhood and a badge of respectability. Whatever the tendencies of the outside world, Masons could take satisfaction in the knowledge that they belonged to a community of upright, moral men.

RESPECTABILITY

Just as Masonic rituals were well suited to late nineteenth-century religious ideas, the moral lessons they inculcated were appropriate to the prevailing Protestant middle-class culture. In addition to religious lessons, the initiate received brief lectures on the Masonic tenets of brotherly love, charity, truth, fortitude, prudence, temperance, and justice, all of which emphasized the golden rule and the constant striving for moral perfection. Similar moral lessons were also imparted through an explanation of the elaborate systems of symbols and "working tools" of an operative Mason. The neophyte learned, for example, that the lambskin apron was to be a constant reminder of that "purity of life and conduct" so essential to gaining admission to the "Celestial lodge above." Similarly, he discovered in the Entered Apprentice degree that

> the common gavel is an instrument made use of by operative masons to break off the corners of rough stones, the better to fit them for the builder's use; but we, as free and accepted masons, are taught to make use of it for the more noble and glorious purpose of divesting our hearts and consciences of all the vices and superfluities of life; thereby fitting our minds as living stones for that spiritual building, that house not made with hands, eternal in the heavens.[3]

The theme of self-improvement was repeatedly invoked in Masonic literature. T. J. Wilson, the orator for an 1887 Saints

Johns' Day Feast in San Bernardino, California, aptly summed up the ideal Mason's attributes:

> Masonry teaches him [the neophyte] to be just, faithful, true and vigilant, to watch his own conduct, to circumscribe his desires and keep his passions within due bounds, to square his actions by the square of virtue, to do unto others as he would have others do unto him, to seize the golden moments as they pass and employ them in the pursuit of some useful calling, giving a due proportion of time to the service of God and the assistance of his fellow-man; to divest his mind and conscience of all the vices and superfluities and walk uprightly before God and man.[4]

Appeal to one or all of these duties constantly surfaced. In particular, authors stressed one of the cardinal virtues of the order—temperance. While the idea of temperance frequently included the specific injunction to avoid alcoholic excess, it generally encompassed the much broader notion of restraint and self-government. As one *Trestleboard* author noted, temperance "embraces subjection of all the appetites and passions, and the restriction of the Craftsman, in every respect of person, thought, word and act, within due bounds."[5] Restraint of one's passions facilitated brotherly love. It allowed one to banish selfishness and greed so that the Mason could treat others fairly, honestly, and charitably.

The Masonic view of morality, with its emphasis on self-improvement, honesty, industry, temperance, and sobriety mirrored Victorian American culture. This reflection was not altogether an unconscious one. Masonic spokesmen were quite aware of the values respectable society honored and sought to insure Masonry's reputation by identifying the order as an institution dedicated to inculcating moral behavior. This sensitivity to public opinion appeared constantly, as spokesmen urged lodges to guard against harboring immoral men. For example, in 1877, the *Chicago Tribune* reprinted Michigan's Grand Master's call for expulsion of the "notoriously profligate" and "profane." He insisted that Masters "purge your lodges of such. They are a source of weakness and a cause of shame and disgrace. A society making the professions that we do ought to be heard upon questions of public morality."[6] Masonic leaders wanted to maintain Masonry's respectability by guaranteeing that none but worthy men could claim Masonic membership. As one author summed it up, "The world has a right to expect that he [the Mason] will be a better citizen, a more considerate, truer friend, a man of probity, to follow whose example will be safe. . . . The fact that a man was connected with the Institution ought to be a passport into any respectable society. Membership in a lodge ought to give a man an undoubted reputation for honesty and fair dealing."[7]

Masonic leaders' sensitivity to public opinion and their determination to maintain the order's reputation were particularly well demonstrated by the widespread movement to prohibit saloonkeepers from joining Masonry. By 1897, twenty-four Grand Lodges had passed laws forbidding lodges from accepting petitions from men engaged in the saloon business; by 1912, all but seventeen jurisdictions had enacted similar legislation. Other fraternal organizations, as well as the Knights of Labor, followed the same policy. A movement started in the South and West, where temperance support was strongest, the condemnation of the saloonkeeper was quite in keeping with popular attitudes.[8]

In the late nineteenth century, temperance sentiment, long a part of Protestant middle-class culture, split over the issue of prohibition. Earlier reformers had concentrated on securing individual regeneration, but as the cities filled with immigrants and laboring people, and the widespread existence of poverty and municipal corruption became clear, the liquor problem assumed ominous proportions that individual reform seemed powerless to stem. Many reformers fastened on the saloon as the key to understanding poverty, vice, labor unrest, and graft, depicting saloonkeepers as immoral men who not only dispensed poison, but also fostered prostitution and gambling and who joined with ward politicians to keep a tight rein on the politics of the city. This popular image promoted a growing sentiment for prohibition laws that would supplement persuasion with the coercive power of the law.[9]

This view of the saloon and saloonkeeper was spread by churches, literature, the Woman's Christian Temperance Union, the Prohibition Party, the Anti-Saloon League, and by many other agencies. While the eventual support for prohibition laws stemmed in part from a conviction of the evils and immorality of drinking as such, it was also based on the belief that closing the saloons would help to establish control over the vicious and unpredictable people who inhabited the country's slums. Elimination of the saloon and the liquor traffic became a panacea for many—drunkenness was a convenient explanation for poverty and misery that would not challenge Americans' faith in their democratic republic.[10]

Masons shared the prevailing view of the saloon and reflected the complex attitudes about drinking that surrounded the prohibition movement. The Masonic drive to bar saloonkeepers from the order was influenced in part by a small sector within Masonry anxious to have the order officially endorse prohibition legislation. There were frequent complaints in the literature about temperance "cranks" who were trying to turn Masonry into a prohibition society.[11] But while some Masons were clearly motivated by a desire to use Masonry to stop the "crying curse of the age," the most important impulse behind the ban on saloonkeepers was to use the temperance issue to make Masonry's stand on the side of public morality clear to the world at large. For example, A. H. Barkley of Mississippi lauded the new spirit in Masonry and revealed the importance of Masonry's public reputation. He exclaimed that the banning of saloonkeepers "has placed Masonry on a high moral plane, and the good, noble and true men of our land are knocking at our doors, and earnestly, and of their own accord, asking for admission to the mysteries of Freemasonry." He continued:

We have lifted up the standard on high, planted it in the midst of the camp so that both those within and without may see it, read and know for themselves, that a Masonic Lodge is no place for the immoral, licentious, intemperate, and that our doors are forever closed against those who in anywise deal out ardent or intoxicating liquors, and God helping us, we intend to keep this standard lifted up as a warning to all such that they need not apply for admission among us.[12]

Similarly, an Arizona Mason, urging that his Grand Lodge exclude saloonkeepers, argued that it was imperative that Arizona Masons show "that we are unalterably on the side of law and order, and proclaim to the world that temperance is the chief cornerstone of our government."[13] Legislation barring saloonkeepers, then, was a symbolic device for underlining Masonry's commitment to the moral order.

That the measures were in large part symbolic is suggested by the fact that saloonkeepers do not appear to have been numerous in Masonry. Opponents of the laws frequently claimed that they were unnecessary. An Arizona Mason, explaining why his Grand Lodge had not banned saloonkeepers, reported that since it had long been an unwritten rule to reject them, there were very few liquor dealers in Arizona.[14] Another Mason, hostile to the "temperance cranks" trying to inject their views into Masonry, also indicated the operation of unwritten laws when he complained in a letter to the editor of the *American Tyler*, that his lodge "has got to the point where if a liquor dealer asks admission he can't find anybody to recommend him, and we don't have any [liquor] racket either."[15]

Legislation aimed at saloonkeepers, then, was "safe." Affecting relatively few men, it gave Masonry the opportunity to proclaim that the order—and its membership—supported public morality. The laws were designed primarily to demonstrate that Masons, like all respectable men, felt that saloons were anathema—the curse of the poor, the scourge of the cities—and that they condemned and excluded the men who ran them and who profited from the sins and weaknesses of others.

In a more general sense the laws established Masonry's commitment to the ideal of temperance, although Masons disagreed over what temperance entailed. As in the case of religious views, Masons varied in their perception of acceptable moral behavior. Some Masons insisted that the order should require total abstinence. The Reverend Gilbert Small, for example, criticized Masonry for closing its doors to the dram seller while still permitting the dram drinker, and claimed that intoxicating liquors' "use as a beverage, or even its manufacture or sale to be used as such, is a Masonic offense."[16]

Far more frequent than the calls for abstention, however, were the reminders that while Masonry embraced temperance, it was not a prohibition society. The Grand Master of Missouri, in the midst of the saloonkeeper-law controversy, was quoted in the *New York Times* as saying that "Masonry advocates temperance, but it does not prohibit the taking of a drink. It does condemn drinking to excess."[17] Frederick Speed, a well-respected Masonic official from Mississippi, explained that the temperance that Masonry teaches "is not the sort which runs to the extreme of forbidding the use of intoxicating liquors as a beverage, but on the contrary, we freely admit that it permits a moderate and reasonable use of them, but it denounces immorality in every form in which it may appear."[18]

The presence of intoxicants at Masonic functions is further evidence that many Masons condoned moderate drinking. Scanty evidence makes it impossible to judge how widespread was the practice of serving liquor at lodges. On the one hand, there are accounts of drinking such as the one the *Pacific Mason* ran in 1904. Reiterating Masonry's distinction between temperance and prohibition, the editor disapproved of lodges that "have cut out beer at the fourth degree." As an example of how moderate indulgence made for a pleasant lodge meeting, he printed an extract from the Milwaukee *Masonic Tidings*, which obviously approved of the beer-drinking German Masons who enjoyed an informal social hour "pregnant of the spirit of good fellowship and fraternity."[19] On the other hand, in 1891, the California Grand Master noted that in his travels he had observed "a great and growing feeling against the evil of indulging in wine at the banquet table. This disposition has grown to such an extent it may almost be considered to have reached the proportion of prohibition."[20] In general, sentiment appears to have been growing against drinking in lodges. However, it is probably the case that lodge indulgence depended on local custom and sentiment.

The clearest indications that Masons had intoxicants at their functions emerge in the discussions surrounding attempts to ban them from lodge rooms and lodge functions. For example, Georgia failed to enact a ban on intoxicants, despite the insistence of its Grand Master, Josiah I. Wright. In 1883, Wright acknowledged that liquor was permissible at functions held in hotels and restaurants, but deprecated the practice of "carrying into ante-rooms kegs of beer, baskets of wine, ale, porter and the like" as "exceedingly offensive to many brethren." Wright concluded by insisting that Masons, "who profess to be moral men," must lead the way and set a good example: "We know where we stand, and the outside world ought to know." However, Georgia's committee on jurisprudence did not concur. It decided that once the lodge meeting had been formally closed and the brethren "resolved into their individual conditions as men and citizens," intoxicants could be served so long as lodge members did not "indulge beyond that moderation which becometh a man and a Mason."[21]

Although legislation prohibiting intoxicants in lodge rooms was enacted in various states, it lagged far behind the saloonkeeper restrictions. Eager to condemn saloonkeepers, Grand Lodges were less willing to condemn drinking per se. By 1900, only six jurisdictions had passed laws; by 1913, the total was only fourteen.[22] This discrepancy between enthusiasm for prohibiting saloonkeepers and reluctance for banning alcohol from lodges is interesting and may indicate how support for prohibition could develop even among moderate drinkers. While most Masons did not condemn drinking, they did condemn saloons and excessive drinking. Trusting their own ability to restrain their passions, their antipathy to saloons indicates their belief that not all men were capable of self-government. The Masonic ambivalence to saloonkeepers and drinking suggests how much sympathy for prohibition could have emanated not from a belief in the immorality of drinking, but from the conviction that saloons, as major contributors to poverty, vice, and social disorder, were affronts to respectability.

The slowness with which sentiment developed to outlaw intoxicants, as well as the repeated insistence that Masons did not demand abstinence, indicates a surprising amount of toleration of moderate drinking. This sentiment is particularly interesting in light of Masons' sensitivity to the order's public reputation, and may indicate something of the broader culture's (or at least its male component's) attitude toward drinking. Despite the growth of prohibition sentiment in the late nineteenth century, Masonic attitudes suggest that one need not necessarily be an abstainer to be respectable. Division within Masonry over the definition of temperance suggests the variety of middle-class notions of respectability and morality, which would become far more apparent when national Prohibition became law and defiance among "respectable" people became commonplace.[23]

While not completely in accord on the drinking question, Masons shared the belief that a good Mason must be honest, industrious, and temperate. The question remains, of course, to what extent Masons conformed to their society's norms. Many spokesmen insisted that the order admitted only moral men. A frequent refrain was that while Masonry encouraged self-improvement, it should not be viewed as a moral reformatory. As Oregon's Grand Master, George E. Chamberlain, explained, Masonry cannot "reform the wicked by receiving them into its fold"; rather, "our upright lives, fair dealing and honorable conduct . . . should be an example worthy of emulation."[24] Masons, then, should be good men to begin with, who would use the order as a guide to their progress.

In short, Masonry was a reward for proven virtue, an honor extended to a select few.

Spokesmen could point to several safeguards for insuring that Masonry be an organization composed of moral men. Its admission policy was designed to make acceptance into the order difficult. A petitioner needed several Masons to endorse his application. Then the lodge appointed a committee to investigate the candidate. Theoretically, the committee inquired into his home and family life, as well as into his business reputation, and then made its report to the lodge, which, in turn, voted by secret ballot. The vote had to be unanimous. Many Grand Lodges insisted upon detailed written reports from committees to guarantee a thorough investigation. New York, for example, adopted the policy of having the committee members answer a series of questions about the candidate "over their own signatures" to insure a sense of personal responsibility in the committee. The questions included: "Have you seen the candidate in person? . . . Is he addicted to the intemperate use of intoxicating liquors? . . . Does he gamble, or associate with bad characters? . . . Has he a good character among his neighbors?"[25]

The procedures for disciplining Masons guilty of Masonic, moral, or civil offenses also served to maintain Masonic morality. Masonic jurisprudence was well developed, with carefully outlined procedures governing evidence, trials, and appeals. Masons could be tried for a variety of "crimes"— drunkenness, sexual transgression, embezzlement and fraud, atheism, and disobedience to Masters. Leaders constantly reminded Masters to be diligent in using the force of Masonic law to keep the order pure and its reputation spotless.[26]

Admissions procedures and jurisprudence methods were only as effective as each lodge's diligence, and there is evidence that lodges varied in how seriously they took their responsibilities. There were, for example, complaints of laxity on the part of investigating committees. The California Grand Orator's lament in 1900 of "moral cowardice" in the failure to use the blackball against unfit men was a familiar refrain.[27] A Tennessee official also criticized lodge admissions procedures, blaming the problem on laziness. He reported that he had asked committees why they had passed objectionable candidates, and found that their examinations had been cursory and that "while they knew 'nothing bad' in regard to the candidate, neither did they know he possessed any *good* qualities, such as we should expect to find in persons whom we are willing to receive as associates and brothers."[28]

Another indication that the selection process was not so demanding as officials often claimed was the record of rejections. In California, between 1884 and 1891, the number of yearly rejections ranged from 15 to 20 percent of the total applications. Other states had somewhat higher percentages, but it is rare to find a rejection rate of over 30 percent. These figures suggest some degree of selectivity, but not enough to make the order truly exclusive. Moreover, these statistics are not necessarily indicative of a decision based on moral grounds, since there could have been many causes of rejection, including religious or ethnic prejudice, business conflict, and personal pique. The rejection rates suggest that Masonry, while selective, was not so rigorous in its admissions as its spokesmen claimed. Although a truly searching investigation of candidates does not appear to have been the rule, nonetheless the procedure itself undoubtedly served to preclude notoriously immoral candidates and to corroborate Masonry's self-image of selectivity.[29]

Disciplinary action against immoral Masons also depended upon local lodges' dedication to maintaining moral behavior. Trial records are difficult to obtain, as Grand Lodge transactions reported only those cases which were appealed to Grand Lodge. Moreover, many Grand Lodges took pains to omit details of the charges and trials on the grounds that such activity should be considered part of Masonic secrecy and not available to profanes. However, a survey of California, Texas, and Missouri cases provides a spectrum of the attempts to safeguard Masonry's reputation as a moral institution and to use the order as a mechanism for assuring obedience to the moral law.

Missouri's appealed cases for 1887 are quite typical. Several trials concerned sexual transgressions. John H. Sheriff was expelled from a Kansas City lodge for adultery. Similarly, an Ilia man, L. C. Laughlin, accused of desertion and bigamy, and S. H. Hagle, from Austin, charged with "adultery and general lascivious conduct," were expelled. In other cases, the Grand Lodge sustained verdicts for drunkenness and saloonkeeping, libel, slander, and fraud, each involving a fellow Mason.[30]

Many lodges obviously took to extremes the injunction to make the lodge an arbiter of moral behavior and brought men to trial on scanty evidence or imposed excessive penalties. Grand Lodges frequently overruled local lodge decisions in such cases. For example, in 1893, the Texas Grand Lodge considered the case of a Pecos Valley Mason brought to trial for alienating the affections of a Mason's wife. The Grand Lodge, finding the charges vague and the evidence unclear, dismissed the case. Centre City Lodge presented the unusual case of a Mason expelled for "carnal intercourse" with a Mason's daughter. The Grand Lodge found that the couple was now happily married, that there was little evidence for the accusation, and that both sets of parents had testified to their belief in their son's and daughter's innocence. The Grand Lodge chided Centre City Masons for their overzealousness and lack of charity and reversed the decision.[31]

Masonic trials served two main functions. In altering the sentence of a man convicted of slander against two Masons from expulsion to suspension, a Texas Grand Master touched on one. "The brethren," he noted, "are usually more after retaliation than the good of the Masonic Order."[32] Lodge trials clearly lent themselves to personal grudges—sexual jealousy, paternal outrage, business disagreements, and other private conflicts. On a much broader level, however, trials served to make lodges engines of social control, acting much in the way early New England churches did in using disciplinary measures of suspension and expulsion to punish those guilty of violating the moral law and the community's standards. This component of social control would be particularly evident in small communities where misdeeds could not easily slip by unnoticed and where an action on the part of a lodge would be more likely to become known among the citizenry. It is not surprising in this context that the majority of expulsions and disciplinary suspensions in California for the period from 1880 to 1900 occurred outside the state's major cities.[33]

If the lodge could deprive a member of his respectability, it could also restore it. For example, in 1879, Live Oak Lodge in Oakland had expelled Oregon C. Luelling for embezzling the funds of a fellow Mason. The committee investigating his request for reinstatement reported that he was now a farmer with a "worthy" family, and that "with one simple exception he has led an honest, industrious, temperate and sober life and this exception was, that twice in the year 1882, between January and July of that year, much to the surprise of his neighbors, he was intoxicated, but since that time he has not taken one drop of liquor of any kind or description." The majority of the committee felt that he had been punished enough and recommended reinstatement. Live Oak's response was typical of lodges considering reinstatement in that it required confession of one's failing and evidence of reformation. It demanded, in effect, a recognition of the lodge's right to define and demand the respectability of its members.[34]

While trials and reinstatements indicate Masonry's potential as a moral force, they should not be overemphasized. Suspensions and expulsions were not numerous. For the twenty-year period from 1880 to 1900, when the average total membership was 16,000, the lodges of California expelled or suspended for un-Masonic conduct a yearly average of 12.9 men. Missouri was far more rigorous, but here, too, the numbers were small. For the years 1880, 1885, 1890, 1895, and 1900, the annual average of expulsions and suspensions was 71 out of an average total membership of over 25,000.[35]

There are other indications that lodges were not always diligent about prosecuting and punishing immoral Masons. Grand Lodges occasionally found it necessary to revoke the charters of lodges that failed to punish immoral Masons.[36] And many officials worried about how many more instances of laxity never reached their attention, sharing the concern of the Georgia Grand Master who reported that in his state lodges tolerated all sorts of immorality, failing both to investigate the "moral worth of the applicant" and to reprimand Masons for "profanity, drunkenness, gambling."[37]

Complaints of laxity on the part of lodges, both in admissions and in discipline, indicate that Masonic claims for the exceptional character of the membership did not always mesh with reality. However, there were at least sporadic efforts to insure that only respectable men could claim to be Masons. Furthermore, complaints about the character of the membership should not always be taken at face value. Many criticisms about declining standards emphasized intemperance among Masons and thus may reflect diverging views about the acceptability of moderate drinking. More importantly, complaints about laxity on the part of lodges in maintaining the order's standards existed side by side with assertions that the quality of Masons was continually improving. In 1884, a Georgia official claimed that "new discipline was being established in its lodges with a strict enforcement of our laws against immoralities—the vicious and unworthy are being expelled, and the good and true who had dropped off or retired in disgust are returning to renew their worship around our altars."[38] John D. Vincil of Missouri was also optimistic and wrote in 1887:

> It is the belief of this Committee that true Freemasonry is advancing steadily, and, for the most part, satisfactorily, in this country. . . . There is a grand moral reform going on in the ranks of our Brotherhood. To one who stands on the watch-towers of our Masonic Zion, the outlook, as to the moral elevation of the Fraternity, is more cheering than at any former period.[39]

Two isolated attempts to make a systematic study of the moral quality of Masons also revealed encouraging results. In 1895, the Texas Grand Secretary sent out a questionnaire to lodge Secretaries. The results revealed that of the 26,481 Masons in Texas, 889 used profane language, 71 were gamblers, and 419 drank to intoxication. How careful the individual lodges were in compiling these statistics is a matter of conjecture. Moreover, the Grand Secretary offered no comment on the figures, so it is not clear whether he considered the possibility (assuming no cases of multiple offense) that 5 percent of Texas Masons were immoral as disgraceful or encouraging. However, if the figures are at all accurate, it does not seem that Texas was plagued by un-Masonic Masons.[40]

E. C. Blackmar, Iowa's Grand Master for 1888, undertook a less ambitious investigation. He felt that the task of determining the morality of Iowa Masons was so large that it would be best to begin by investigating a single major problem, "the habitual use of, and illegal traffic in, intoxicating liquors," for, as he explained, "the drunkard-maker and his unfortunate victim have no business in a Masonic Lodge, or to be in any way connected with the institution." Blackmar was delighted to discover that Iowa Masons were "comparatively free from the curse."[41]

Despite the complaints, then, most spokesmen were encouraged that Masonry was fulfilling its moral role. They frequently insisted that the outside world recognized the moral worth of the order. In 1900, the *American Tyler* proudly quoted a daily paper's account of a Michigan Grand Lodge meeting. The article was so laudatory it could easily have been written by a Mason:

> Bad men, or men of doubtful character are never wanted in Masonic Lodges, though they do get in sometimes, much to the regret of the great majority, and it is a pretty hard case that cannot be changed for the better after becoming a Mason and mingling with the brotherhood. Everything in the order is of an elevating nature, and an influence on all to do right.[42]

A California official, arguing that "the fact that a man is a Mason ought to be a guarantee, not alone to the fraternity, but to all the world, that he is a man of honesty, integrity, liberality, and moral character," conceded that unfortunately there were many exceptions, but that "it may be assumed that as a general rule such is the fact."[43] Similarly, North Carolina's Grand Master claimed in 1895, "I believe that Masonry is better understood and appreciated than ever before, and that it is fast being recognized as a great moral force in the land and consequently is receiving the encouragement and support of the best citizens."[44]

Public opinion may have been impressed by the morality of Masons, but undoubtedly the order's reputation was particularly enhanced by its ability to attract prominent men. Masons themselves frequently confused morality with prominence, not a surprising assumption given the American tradition of equating success with virtue. Thus when Maine's Grand Master, William R. G. Estes, pointed to the high "moral and social worth" of Masons as the source of the fraternity's good reputation, he claimed that "as proof of this, it is only necessary to examine her lists, where we shall find the names of men illustrious in the affairs of government, in educational institutions, and in all the benevolent enterprises and business relations of the world."[45]

Estes was not exaggerating Masonry's illustrious membership. The order laid claim to many important historical figures, including George Washington, Benjamin Franklin, and John Paul Jones. In the late nineteenth century, national, state, and local politicians were numerous in the order, as were prominent business and professional men. Masonry was proud of these men, and collections of biographical sketches of important Masons always included a large number of successful civil officials and businessmen. The California Grand Lodge's "Prominent Members of the Masonic Order of California" praised well-known Masons possessed of outstanding character. Thus, Dr. C. H. Allen "enjoys a large and lucrative practice, and aside from his profession, is a prominent man in his community. He is whole-souled, genial and philanthropic— in fact, a courteous and refined gentleman, a credit to society, the medical profession, and the Masonic Craft."[46] Similarly, *Gems from the Quarry* (1893) offered biographies of over a hundred important American Masonic officials, the majority of whom appear to have been both prominent and moral men. Costello Lippitt was typical. A well-known banker in Norwich, Connecticut, he held "the respect of his friends and associates for his thorough manhood, dignity of character, and allegiance to the highest principles of morality and virtue."[47]

Whether because of its ability to attract moral men or its ability to attract prominent ones—and the two could be easily confused—Masonry did secure a reputation as a respectable and prestigious society. Undoubtedly, just as many Masons may not have taken the order's religious orientation seriously, many may have been indifferent to the morality it preached. Yet, while men who joined Masonry may not have been exceptionally moral men, it is significant that they sought out an organization whose rhetoric was overwhelmingly religious and moralistic. They found this rhetoric appealing because Masonry enunciated a moral code of self-improvement through self-restraint that harmonized with the prevailing Protestant middle-class culture. Men shaped by this culture found in Masonry more than a mirror reflecting popular values. Joining Masonry permitted them to make a symbolic statement of commitment to this moral system. More significantly, it allowed them to claim Masonry's morality as their own. Thus, the square and compass dangling from a watch chain stood for temperance, sobriety, honesty, industry, and self-restraint—it was the Mason's badge of respectability.

BROTHERHOOD

The importance of Masonry's commitment to morality and its promise of respectability can best be understood in the context of late nineteenth-century Americans' struggle to maintain their traditional ideology in the face of an increasingly complex and disordered world. Most of American history can be characterized as punctuated by periods of rapid social change,

but it would be hard to overemphasize the profound transformations taking place in the decades after the Civil War.
Robert Wiebe has described America in the 1870s as composed of "island communities." These small towns, dependent
on the outside world in many ways, nonetheless managed to
maintain a sense of local autonomy. Members of the community tended to share the same Protestant common-sense
values of "modesty in women, rectitude in men, and thrift,
sobriety, and hard work in both." As Wiebe notes, "Usually
homogeneous, usually Protestant, they enjoyed an inner stability that the coming and going of members seldom shook."
Not a static society, it was nonetheless an ordered one. However, beginning in the 1870s, economic and technological
changes shattered this relative isolation and stability. Rail-
roads crisscrossed the nation, bringing people and places together, and facilitating the eventual modernization of the national economy. National corporations undermined local
business as they brought efficiency to production and distribution, and finance capitalism brought local communities into
the web of financial control. This decline in community power
was particularly evident in periods of economic instability when
inhabitants of island communities became acutely aware that
their lives were shaped by conditions beyond their control.[48]

Not just community autonomy was affected, however; industrial development and urbanization also had a tremendous
impact on the lives of workers. The late nineteenth century
was a period of transformation of the old middle class as the
world of proprietors and farmers began to give way to a new
white-collar world of urban office workers. At the same time,
industrialization encroached upon the domain of the skilled
artisan, creating in its stead a huge industrial work force. On
both middle-class and working-class levels, workers lost much
control over the conditions of their employment. Affecting
individuals profoundly, these changes also brought significant
challenges to traditional notions of success. Hard work, temperance, and self-restraint might be the attributes of valued
employees, but as a guide to the self-made man, a figure so

treasured in American ideology, they seemed increasingly less valid.[49]

In addition to the decline of community and personal autonomy, one of the major characteristics of post–Civil War American society was its striking heterogeneity. This was particularly evident in expanding urban areas. The freedom of cities promoted diverse life styles and exposed individuals to strangers about whom they knew little or nothing. For the native middle class the most startling stranger in the city was the immigrant. The massive influx of immigrants in the late nineteenth century was unprecedented and was particularly threatening because it was composed of "new" immigrants— southern and eastern Europeans whose culture and religion (primarily Catholic or Jewish) blended less readily with northern European culture. Clustered in cities, generally poor, and retaining much of their native culture, they were perceived as a major threat to the homogeneity of American society.[50]

Americans traditionally were committed to the ideal that theirs was a harmonious society, where conflicting interests were all subsumed under the umbrella of democracy, equality, and Protestant respectability. In the late nineteenth century, this sense of harmony was shattered. Unassimilated immigrants were just one disturbing symptom. Economic developments brought even more distressing signs of disunity and discord. Devastating nationwide depressions, agrarian discontent, and a growing awareness of the problems of the cities and of the existence of poverty both dismayed and alarmed the native middle class. Labor unrest in particular made the array of conflicting interests obvious. Henry May has fittingly characterized the intense labor discontent that surfaced in 1877, 1886, and 1892–1894 as "three earthquakes," to suggest the fear that these incidents evoked in "respectable" Americans.[51]

Eventually, the development of huge corporations, the dreadful state of urban politics, the persistence of crime, corruption, and poverty, and the condition of labor would result in the Progressive movement and the call to use government to redress the problems industrial growth and urbanization had engendered and to restore that harmony and equality of opportunity so essential to Americans' perception of their society. But while Progressive thought was in the offing, an earlier mode of thinking about social disorder persisted. Antebellum Americans had viewed personal morality, especially self-restraint, as the ideal antidote to the disorder fostered by economic expansion and the rise of the common man. Moreover, this ethic, based on the belief in the power of the individual will to perfect itself, strongly permeated social reform in that period: Create moral individuals and a moral society will naturally follow. Although gradually being challenged, this view continued in the postwar years as men saw poverty, crime, and corporate malfeasance as the results of individual moral failings and offered, as a solution to these, moral regeneration.[52]

Faced, then, with a newly heterogeneous and complex society, beset with evidence of social conflict and the decline of community and individual autonomy, many late nineteenth-century Americans sought to bring order and harmony into that world by reaffirming the centrality of individual morality for the well-being of society. It was this world view that lay behind Masons' insistence on moral behavior, particularly their emphasis on self-restraint. But Masons addressed the need for social order and commitment to time-honored values far more directly. A major motif in the literature presented Masonry's emphasis on morality and brotherly love as an antidote to modern social disruption. Although one theme stressed that the teachings of Masonry, if adopted by all individuals, could promote a more harmonious, just, and moral world, the most pervasive view pictured Masonry as an asylum. Free of economic, political, and religious discord, Masonry provided a retreat from the materialistic, competitive, immoral world of late nineteenth-century America.

It would be a mistake to characterize Masons or Americans as universally fearful of change. One need only read accounts of the World's Fair of 1893 to find a sense of excitement about scientific and technological developments and a general optimism about the progress of civilization. Masons evinced this enthusiasm frequently. At the turn of the century, for example, John M. Carter, past Grand Master of Maryland, wondered at the technological marvels of the nineteenth century—the steamboat, locomotive, telegraph, telephone, sewing machine, and reaper—and congratulated America for its abolition of slavery and of imprisonment for debt, as well as its universal common-school education. He concluded:

The century behind us has been rolled away as a scroll and added to the ages of the past. Parting the rift of heaven, we may, with the eye of the faith, see the grander achievements of the era upon which we have already entered. Standing today at the closed portals of the old and upon the open, threshold of the new, may we not, in the language of the first message over the magnetic telegraph, fervently exclaim: "What hath God wrought."[53]

Many Americans, however, were ambivalent about progress, particularly in light of economic depression and social unrest. Henry Highton, the California Grand Orator for 1883, perfectly expressed this ambivalence in his address, "The Function of Freemasonry in Modern Society." Beginning with praise for the progress that had brought the individual more knowledge, rights, and luxuries, he worried that "extraordinary and unprecedented activity" had left social disruption in its wake. In Highton's view, "new social plans, inconsistent with the individual nature and history of man, with his family relations, and with order, subordination, and prosperity, are insidiously appealing, *first*, to the imagination, *second*, to selfishness, and covetousness, and *third* to the destructive instincts and passions." He argued that what was needed to restore order was "Rest . . . found only in Balanced Activity." *Rest* meant many things—the pursuit of duty, the rejection of anything not in keeping with God's scheme of things. But above all, it encompassed individual self-control. It meant "the development of individuality through the rational use of opportunities, through simplicity, through directness, through self-denial, and through self-abnegation."

Highton argued that Masonry provided an obvious means of achieving rest and control.

> Ancient, severe, changeless, it is the very type of immutable law. Beginning and ending in God, it antagonizes agnosticism, and it is freed from all doubt and fluctuation on the fundamentals of true religion. . . . It insists upon order and subordination, because without them the world would be a Pandemonium. It demands definiteness and simplicity, because without them there would be little else than confusion and strife.

In short, Masonry, with its emphasis on morality and its inculcation of religiosity, taught men to live orderly, upright lives before God. In doing so, it provided a clear corrective to the confusion besetting modern society.[54]

This notion of Masonry's role of improving individuals as a means of achieving social stability was also evident in the frequent analyses of labor problems. The *Trestleboard* was notable for its hostility to big business. In 1894, for example, it criticized "Pullman's Fraud Town," and traced the labor strife in this "model" town to scandalously low wages and unfair practices. "Pullman has become, through the labor of his men, so rich that he cannot count his wealth."[55] Most Masonic authors, however, were less radical. Hostile primarily to the commercial spirit of the age, not big business as such, they avoided specific labor disputes and rarely took sides. Invariably, their solution to the conflict between labor and capital was morality and brotherly love. If men honored the guidelines Masonry taught them, harmony would prevail. As Oliver A. Roberts argued at a cornerstone ceremony at Amesbury, Massachusetts in 1906, "If everyone lived up to his Masonry, vice, crime, poverty and war would cease; concord would be established among all classes; friendship would cement the now divided humanity and peace would shelter all nations with its outstretched wings."[56]

A *Dispatch* author developed the same theme at greater length in 1886. He reported: "We are in troublous times. The sky of the commercial world is dark. Clouds have arisen. The breeze of discontented labor has grown to a fearful magnitude." Recognizing that the "working man has much to complain of," he also insisted that destruction of property was no solution, and asked, "What then, can Masonry do now?" His answer invoked Masonry's principles of "peace, moderation, submission to rightful rule," and asserted that Masonry could serve as a mediator between capital and labor. This mediation should not involve any covert action by Masonry as an organization. Rather, because Masonry contained both capitalists and laborers, the order had the potential to teach both groups the principles of harmony and justice that could solve the dilemma. "If the magnates will meet with their employees in the spirit of Masonry, yielding to what is right on both sides, the question of labor and capital will be settled on a basis of peace and unity."[57]

As social analysts, these Masons reveal profound limitations; as representatives of the middle-class view of the source of labor-capital conflict, they are exemplary. Demonstrating a faith in the justice of the American economic system, they brought to new circumstances traditional notions of the nature of social problems. Discord and injustice in the world could be reduced to individual morality or the lack of it, and the solution offered was individual effort, not social restructuring.

The emphasis on individual morality as a key to understanding social disorder was particularly evident in Masons' preoccupation with the greed and commercialism that they felt permeated contemporary society. Rarely was a speech or article complete without reference to the "growing greed for worldly goods . . . [that makes] money the God to be worshiped."[58] In 1892, the *Trestleboard* printed an article on the "Decline of Politeness," which offered a typical summary of the spirit of the age:

This is an age of transition, and an age out of proportion; and between its exigencies and our faculties there is a discrepancy that leaves us neither time nor strength for mere formalities of speech or deeds. Money rules everything, and no one can escape its yoke; and money scorns the quiet habits of the old world; it pulls the old social machine to pieces, puts what was below above, and the ancient surface of society, so skillfully levelled, is made to sink and swell at random.[59]

Focusing on personal selfishness as a major source of the difficulties plaguing modern society, Masonic spokesmen promoted individual reform as the obvious solution. Masons, they insisted, should personally counter the spirit of materialism by remembering their "solemn duty to protect the reputation and administer to the wants of the distressed brother, the destitute brother, the destitute widow, the innocent maiden, and the helpless orphan."[60] But in addition to avoiding selfishness by pursuing charitable impulses, Masons ought to resist the spirit of the age by being scrupulously honest in business affairs. Albert Pike described the "Duty of a Mason as an Honest Man" quite simply: "It requires of us honesty in contracts, sincerity in affirming, simplicity in bargaining, and faithfulness in performing. The Mason must give fair measure for what he receives."[61]

Hostility to commercialism, with its emphasis on business morality, was pervasive. It was particularly prominent in Masonic fiction, which continually encouraged Masons to lead a moral and honest life. In "A Perfect Master," for example, a Mason learned that personal morality must characterize business transactions. When a merchant sold poor-quality merchandise that he represented as a much better product, his wife challenged the ethics of his commercial dealings and pointed out that his activities were inconsistent with his Masonic pledges. Seeing his mistake, the shopkeeper rectified his questionable policies and learned that ill-gotten gains were not worth the sacrifice of virtue. Furthermore, he repledged himself to Masonry, vowing that it had "lifted me out of self and selfish purposes, and introduced me into a higher and better order of being."[62]

Although Masonic authors decried materialism, they honored success achieved by honorable men. A typical short story described a successful Mason who disowned his sister because she married a poor man. Years later, the sister's daughter tried to show him his wrongdoing. He professed regret over his actions, and to test his reformed character, she introduced him to her fiancé, a shoemaker. With much effort, the Mason acknowledged that the fiancé was a good man and that his lowly status should not impede the match. Happily for all, the shoemaker was, in reality, a highly successful shoe manufacturer. While the story made the point that moral character was more important than financial worth, the happy ending of the story depended upon the niece obtaining a husband both virtuous and successful.[63]

The insistence that morality was not inconsistent with success also appeared in Masonic biography. The California Grand Lodge's souvenir booklet commemorating the opening of the widows' and orphans' home contained accounts of prominent Masons that clearly attributed success to sterling character. W. Frank Pierce, the president of Blue Lakes Water Company, was described as possessing excellent character consistent with Masonry. He was known to be a "genial, whole-souled gentleman" of "personal probity, business integrity and enterprise." Dr. Henry Wyle Emerson was characterized as "among the younger generation of the professional men of Alameda county, who, by their own ability and personal qualities, have successfully established themselves in their chosen profession."[64] A Knight Templar souvenir booklet for 1900 also provided biographical sketches of prominent Masons and emphasized that their success was well deserved. Thomas Morton, a coal supplier and city supervisor, for example, had prospered as "the legitimate result of intelligent push, coupled with incorruptible character."[65]

Masonic stories and sketches make it evident that Masons valued business and financial success. The conjunction of virtue and success was typical of late nineteenth-century success books in the Horatio Alger mode. Both John Cawelti and Richard Weiss have noted that these books generally criticized the materialism of the age and did not, as has so often been thought, offer a guide to attaining wealth. As Cawelti has argued, the success genre was not really about going from rags to riches, but from rags to respectability. The hero achieved very moderate financial success when judged by the robber-baron standards of the day. Moreover, the stories made it clear that it was not success in itself that was to be striven for, but rather the satisfactions of a moral life. Masonic writers, like success-story writers, made it evident that success was meaningless without good character. And in doing so, they, like popular authors, emphasized the validity of moral attributes. In linking character to success, they also reaffirmed a belief that greed and materialism were not necessary prerequisites for success—a worthy individual had the opportunity for social mobility, or at the very least, for respectability.[66]

Clearly, Masonry held no monopoly on hostility to materialism or on belief in the necessity for moral behavior to the well-being of both society and individuals. Yet, as part of the sacred-profane motif, Masons claimed a uniqueness for the order by repeatedly describing Masonry as an asylum where the commercialism and discord of the external world were excluded and morality, equality, and brotherly love prevailed. The asylum theme was far more inward looking than the rhetoric that ingenuously proposed Masonic morality as a solution to social disorder. Less optimistic, it offered a critique of American society, but not a program for improvement. The idea of the asylum fused American political and social ideals of equality and religious toleration with Protestant morality and brotherly love to create the idea of a homogeneous, harmonious community. It offered Masonry as an isolated microcosm of what America should be but was not.

The Grand Master of Kentucky, James A. Black, praised Masonry as a sanctuary from external conflict in a typical manner:

It is a significant tribute to Freemasonry that, amid the busy scenes of this driving, practical age, Masons realize pleasure and profit in breaking away from absorbing avocations of life to meet in the common bonds of our Fraternity.

Out in the rushing, struggling world, the gleams of a thousand goals beckon on the scurrying multitudes. There, in the midst of activity and fierce contention, the greed for personal aggrandizement pursues its unsatisfied lust. Comingling there with the clamor of effort, the thought of self and selfishness are the most potent incentives of life. But here, around our sacred altar, where gather the glintings of a purer life, personal ambition is subordinated to the higher attraction of a common cause and a common glory. Here the human soul, quickened by a faith that lifts above turmoil and struggles, delights in contemplating a loftier destiny.[67]

It was not merely that Masonry provided a spiritual environment that gave its members temporary surcease from commercialism and competitiveness. One of the major characteristics invoked in describing Masonry as an asylum was the order's distinctive standards for judging men: "Masonry admonishes us to regard a man, not for the wealth that adheres to him, but for the wealth within him."[68] The fraternity not only taught that men should be regarded for their character and not their wealth, but it also claimed to act upon these principles. Masons insisted that their order's commitment to equality meant that it ignored financial or social standing as a prerequisite for membership. Moreover, they claimed that this absence of distinctions carried over into the lodge room itself. As a *Keystone* author explained, "Whatever might be the insolence of wealth and power outside, within the mystic fold all were Brethren tied to each other's defense and support."[69]

That Masonry honored the man, rather than his possessions or standing, was emphasized in a speech by a prominent Mason, Theodore Roosevelt. Brother Roosevelt distinguished

Masonry's standards from the external world when he argued that Masonry achieved that equality promised but imperfectly achieved in American society:

> One of the things that attracted me so greatly to Masonry that I hailed the chance of becoming a Mason, was that it really did act up to what we, as a government and a people are pledged to do—of treating each man on his merits as a man.

He claimed that he enjoyed going to some

> little lodge, *where I meet the plain, hard-working men—the men who work with their hands*—and meet them on a footing of genuine equality, *not false equality*, of genuine equality conditioned upon each being a decent man, a fair-dealing man.[70]

A less illustrious Mason also stressed the equality operating within the lodge. In a speech to Live Oak Lodge, J. R. Glascock, a former Master of the lodge, discussed deceased members.

> I knew them all. Good men they were in the lodge and out of it; and who shall say that they were not better men for being good Masons? It was not given to all of them to stand in the prominent walks of life, but each in his own way wrought out a life squared with the principles of his order, and the sum of their efforts has gone to build up and beautify humanity. Their lives have taught us that if there is any one principle that, more than another, typifies the true spirit of Masonry, that lifts human life out of the rut of commercial accommodation into a broader touch with humanity and a closer communion with the divine, it is human love.[71]

Masons' praise for the common man also appeared in biographical accounts. In 1888, for example, Andrew Jackson Stevens, an Oakland Mason who at the time of his death was a master mechanic, was honored in the *Trestleboard*: "Few have led so eventful and truly successful a life, not such, perhaps, as worldly ambition would term it, but eventful in changes of location, and successful in always securing and retaining the confidence and friendship of all with whom he was associated. . . . Brother Stevens died with the peace and happy reflections of a well ordered and useful life."[72] A sketch of William P. Innes, a Michigan railway engineer, conveyed a similar message. Innes, "by the honest, persistent labor of brain and brawn, secured a competency, which, represented in the labors performed should show dollars where dimes are seen." But, his biographer noted, "it is in matters purely Masonic that Brother Innes shines. Bringing to the responsibilities he assumed, on taking his Masonic obligations all the force and persistency characteristic of the man, he has made himself, from his first step into Masonry, one of its ablest advocates and loyal servants. He has invariably recognized the fact that Masonry honors the man, and not the man who honors Masonry."[73]

Masons claimed that the order's commitment to equality also extended to the selection of officers. Just as Masons were chosen for their virtue, a lodge was supposed to select its leaders for their exemplary character. Officers should be the most Masonic of Masons. No criteria beside character should be considered; class or social standing should be irrelevant. As we have seen, at Live Oak at least, there was some truth to this claim. Blue-collar workers were somewhat underrepresented in the ranks of officers, but men in high-level occupations did not monopolize lodge offices. Rather, the greatest percentage was drawn from the low-level white-collar category.[74]

In general, lodge officers earned the honor not so much on the basis of character as by virtue of their constant attendance and willingness to perform various duties. Undoubtedly, such other factors as personality entered into consideration, but officers did need to demonstrate their loyalty to the order. While morality may not have been the operating factor, to some extent Masonry conformed to its ideal of having special criteria for achieving recognition within the order. As one Live

Oak Mason explained, "There are men in various lodges, who, while they occupy lower positions in the world outside, yet are far above, in point of value to the lodge, those who are socially their superiors. There is a difference between the standards of Masonry and the standards of the world."[75]

The message behind the notion of Masonry as an asylum was a recognition that the outside world was not governed justly. Masonry reassured men that despite the inequalities and immorality of the profane world, moral behavior was still the best ideal, and Masonry honored them for it. Masonry was proud of its many successful men who combined success and virtue. But equally importantly, by honoring character and criticizing the unrestrained pursuit of wealth, Masonry offered prestige and status to those men whose economic standing brought them little recognition in the outside world. Despite the myth of the self-made man, they need not feel themselves failures if they led moral, respectable lives. This recognition could have strong appeal in a world of employees whose chances for advancement and sense of job security were uncertain in the economic fluctuations of the late nineteenth century.

In addition to a belief in the equality of moral men, the asylum aspect of Masonry was also evident in the order's insistence that the lodge be free of discord. In explaining how the mystic tie of brotherhood was sustained, authors emphasized the spirit of harmony made possible by the exclusion from the lodge of a wide range of tension-provoking topics—politics, religion, business, and personal disagreements. Masonry, the rhetoric went, caused men to forget their differences, at least temporarily, and approach each other as brethren.

One of the major examples of the way in which Masonry allowed men to put aside the disagreements that separated them in the outside world were the Civil War anecdotes that portrayed Masons who forgot their wartime passions in order to succor a fallen or imprisoned brother Mason. The *Trestleboard* printed many such accounts. For example, General Horatio Rogers of Vermont reported finding the body of a dead

Confederate colonel who had a certificate in his pocket testifying that he was a member of a Georgia lodge. "Thereupon it was determined that this deceased brother, an enemy in life that had been striken down far from home and loved ones, should be buried by fraternal hands." Rogers buried him "tenderly and reverently" and had the grave clearly marked. Years later, the body was removed to Georgia, and R. W. Hubert, the master of the colonel's lodge, wrote Rogers:

> I am glad to know that his body fell into such hands, and that the blessed principles of our ancient craft are not forgotten or eclipsed by the clang of arms, the din of war, or anything else and that the nerveless embrace of death is no barrier to a Mason's charity.[76]

Masons also claimed that the harmony and brotherly love of Masonry surmounted the heated political controversies of the day. The 1880s and 1890s were strongly partisan decades, where voting turnout was high and local political issues deeply felt. Silver, populism, and prohibition, as well as religion and ethnicity, divided men and communities.[77] In 1880, an author in the *Freemason's Repository* commented on this "partisan electricity" that permeated the country and exclaimed:

> Is it not a matter of rejoicing that Masonry knows neither sect nor party, and that the Lodge-room is the one place where men of all opinions can meet in a blessed communion? In these days when there is so much excitement in the political world, it surely counts for something of good that so restful an atmosphere pervades the place of Masonic meeting, and that brethren who oppose each other on party grounds can here enter into sweet fellowship, and strike hands together for the advancement of those interests and principles which attach to the Institution.[78]

According to Masonic rhetoric, then, economic, political, and religious differences became unimportant as men sought their "common interests." In sharp contrast to the outside world, harmony prevailed; men were equal and shared the same moral standards. The asylum rhetoric and the harmony it promised catered to nineteenth-century Americans' sense of disorder and conflict. The asylum offered more than equality and peace, however. Another crucial component of the asylum motif was that Masonry established a community that allowed brotherly love to flourish.

The centrality of the Masonic commitment to brotherly love was evident in the order's emphasis on charity. For the fraternity required not merely that Masons treat one another honestly and equally and strive for harmony, but also insisted that Masons' commitment to brotherly love gave them sacred obligations to help one another in distress and to aid brethren's widows and orphans. These obligations came under the general heading of *charity*. Charity provided an excellent means of contrasting the commercialism of the external world with Masonry's selflessness. However, as beautiful as the ideal of charity was, it presented some ideological difficulties for Masons who were part of an individualistic culture that viewed unemployment or poverty as the product of individual intemperance or profligacy. In discussing Masonry's responsibility to aid distressed brothers, this assumption surfaced frequently. Chauncey M. Depew's oration at the 1891 dedication of a New York Masonic home included a warning about the possibility of charity "pauperizing the recipients":

> But there is a help which harms. It is always proper to question whether the independence and self-reliance of the individual are to be weakened. Vigor, success and good citizenship exist only among those who, being capable and in health, rely not upon charity but upon themselves for their own maintenance and support and that of those who are dependent upon them.[79]

The fear that undeserving men were taking advantage of Masonic relief surfaced frequently, and officials undertook a plan of systematizing relief that would weed out imposters and make sure that aid went only to the needy. To this end, the General Masonic Relief Association of the United States and Canada was established in 1885, with its main purpose to issue lists of known imposters and "unworthy applicants." Most jurisdictions insisted that Masons receiving aid be affiliated, dues-paying members—lapsed Masons were generally not received sympathetically. In addition, drunkards and other men considered irresponsible were given only minimal help and were rarely aided more than once if they failed to reform. An indication of the reluctance to aid undeserving Masons may also be seen in a comment by the New York Relief Board. Explaining that almsgiving is "an encouragement to pauperism," it put much effort into assisting needy brethren to find work, thereby allowing them to help themselves.[80]

Yet side by side with this traditional approach to charity, and more in keeping with the asylum concept, was the recognition that hard times and misfortunes caused many deserving Masons to need help. Not all men were responsible for their own difficulties. In 1890, one author discussed Masonic homes and the charity found in them as "that genuine article, brotherly love," and analyzed the sources of misfortune:

> In these revolving years of financial stress and change; of devastations by fire and flood, and accidents by sea and land, who can assuredly say, my status is fixed, my fortune will never be swept away, my family will never cease to surround and care for me. O! the wrecks which disease and death and misfortune cast upon the shores of time! In such a season what a blessed haven is a Masonic home! How its strong arms, and gentle hands, and fraternal voice, and sufficient means, uphold and comfort and cheer the unfortunate, the bereaved, the forsaken, the sorely distressed Freemason![81]

While some Masons clearly challenged the idea that poverty was invariably the individual's fault, most frequently Masons resolved the tension between charity and traditional notions by glorifying that Masonic charity which went to aid the sick, aged, or women and children. An account of the Grand Rapids Knights Templar's charitable activity, for example, reveals extremely worthy recipients of Masonic aid. A young Mason moved to Grand Rapids with his wife and child and immediately became ill. Significantly, he was so valued an employee that his company continued his salary; nonetheless, the family needed help. The Knights took up a subscription and provided food, a nurse, and other personal services. Both husband and wife died, and the Knights buried them with a "beautiful ceremony." The orphaned daughter was immediately taken in by a Knight and his family and "has received constant love and affection with all the benefits of a refined and luxurious home."[82]

A typical fictional account of aid to a sick Mason also stressed that the recipient was a good and kind man, facing a problem beyond his control. The *Masonic Review* offered the story of two men who lived in a small town. One was a Mason, a genial and generous man; the other a closefisted individual who claimed that Masonry "doesn't pay." Both men prospered until hard times came to the community. They moved to the city to look for better opportunities and once again prospered until they contracted yellow fever. Neither man had any friends in the city. The non-Mason depended on hired nurses who provided inadequate care. But "to the bedside of one there came a crowd of Masonic brethren, ready to watch, aid, comfort and console. Nothing that the tenderest affection could devise was left undone; nothing that the most untiring energy could accomplish was left untouched." Needless to say, the Mason recovered, and in turn nursed his friend. At last he, too, recovered and decided to join the fraternity. "Now Freemasonry has not in all its ranks a more devoted brother."[83]

Masons delighted in recounting the tender sympathy offered deceased brethren's dependents. George M. Moulton told the true story of "The Orphaned Succored." A California Mason moved to Mississippi and almost immediately was stricken with yellow fever. The entire family, with the exception of a small boy, died. The father's assets had been consumed by the disease, and the boy was left destitute. However, the father's

Oakland lodge, hearing of the tragedy, sent for the boy. There was no one to travel with him, so some Mississippi neighbors put him on the train and fastened a note to his collar: "This is a Master Mason's child, his father and mother are both dead, and he has no relatives to assist him. He is endeavoring to make his way to his father's lodge in the State of California, and is commended to the care and attention of all Master Masons throughout the world." Moulton described this note as a talisman "more potent than Aladdin's lamp."

> He was no longer friendless, for he had with him a pass-port and a key to the hearts of all Masons, which insured him friends and protection wherever he went. Rough, strong men bent over him, and as they read those words their hearts opened to him and each one felt himself to be the little fellow's special companion, every care and attention was lavished upon him, and he was carried safely to the end of his journey.[84]

Similarly sentimental accounts of widows and orphans surfaced in Masonic fiction, where kindly Masons appear after a bereavement, providing wives with business advice, keeping sons out of trouble and daughters from disastrous marriages.[85]

The Masonic affinity for stories about widows and orphans is not surprising. This genre was a favorite with success-story authors as well. If a young man were poor, the story was more acceptable if he were orphaned or lived with a widowed mother, for it was difficult to reconcile a living, respectable father with the poverty-stricken state. Masons gave aid to a wide variety of recipients, many of whom were unemployed or down-on-their-luck brethren, but this group was de-emphasized in the literature in favor of accounts of more obviously worthy re-cipients—women, children, the aged, and the sick. Thus, Ma-sonic charity rhetoric reveals Masons' ambivalent meshing of traditional individualistic notions of success with the order's commitment to brotherly love. On the one hand, Masons were critical of the outside world and proud of their own standards that honored character not wealth and that rejected competitive individualism in favor of the belief that men should aid one another. In this mode, Masons recognized the unpredictability of economic life and catered to the desire for security for oneself and one's family. On the other hand, despite their recognition of hard times, Masons' desire to believe that anyone who worked hard and led a moral life could achieve some degree of security and respectability created a suspicion that the needy Mason might be "unworthy."

There was ambivalence among Masons about the financial aspects of charity, but there was none when it came to the underlying basis for charity. Ultimately, what was most important about charity was not the financial aid that one might hope to gain if suddenly unemployed or taken ill, but the foundation for the Masonic conception of charity: brotherly love. As the stories of charity reveal, the financial element of the aid offered Masons was not the crucial ingredient; rather, it was the sense of caring and kindness, of sacred obligations. Even a stranger in a city could expect Masonic kindness in times of trouble. Masonry promised a nonmaterialistic familial basis for relationships between men. As Oliver A. Roberts explained in 1906, "friendship binds, brotherly love cements, place unites and the blessedness of a calm retreat from the anxieties and confusions of life pervades the soul."[86] A *New York Dispatch* author similarly extolled brotherly love, tracing it to the shared experience of the Masonic altar, rituals, and secrets:

> An intimate relationship exists between Freemasons. A feeling of confidence. A chord of sympathy. A kind of family kinship that draws one near to the other, and establishes a bond of union strong and abiding. It comes from the fact that all have dwelt under the same canopy, and have tasted the sweet waters of the same fountain,

and have a language of their own. How beautiful is a relationship so tender, a kinship so extensive![87]

One man, D. W. Simmons of Cave Springs, Georgia, was so moved by witnessing the tie of obligation that Masonry fostered that he joined the order. He explained that in 1873 he was working for the Texas and Pacific Railroad at Marshall, Texas when an epidemic of yellow fever paralyzed the town. Although there were many deaths, there were no funerals because people refused to leave their homes. Yet one Sunday he saw several men burying Rosenbaum, a Mason:

> I watched them perform their sad duty, and wondered and admired their loyalty. . . . There was a city literally deserted, business was suspended, the pastors of the different churches had deserted their flocks; yet those Masons, forgetting self, forgetting the disease to which their companion had fallen a victim, forgetting everything except that a brother had fallen, with loving hands bore his remains to their last resting place and laid him away with the usual formalities. That is why I joined the Masons. Some may say my motives were mercenary; call it what you will, I have given you facts, and if it was wrong to want to be identified with such people, then I did wrong.[88]

Simmons's experience may have been somewhat exceptional, but it illustrates the importance of Masonry's rhetoric of fraternity. Brotherly love and the ideal of the asylum promised that the individual belonged to a community of men tied to one another by sacred obligations. Here was an organization whose members were a select group. Chosen as respectable men, they experienced a sense of brotherhood forged by the order's secrecy, rituals, and commitment to traditional religious and moral values. Masonry might not always have provided men with this sense of brotherhood and community; the square and compass may not always have served to make a man welcome in a strange town or to insure that his dependents received loving care after his death. Yet the reality was probably enough to justify the rhetoric. And it is not difficult to see how appealing this rhetoric would have been in late nineteenth-century America.

Masons themselves offered the reason for this appeal: a rapidly changing world apparently dominated by conflict, commercialism, greed, and financial insecurity. An increasingly heterogeneous society, it was a world characterized by political and social clashes. Those who lived in cities were constantly aware of the diversity and conflict in their environment. But even those who stayed behind experienced the erosion of island-community autonomy, and their access to newspapers, magazines, and chautauquas made them aware of the changes in their society and the conflict of interests that characterized it.

Masonry offered a spiritual oasis, a retreat from this world. Its rhetoric, emphasizing individual morality, reaffirmed traditional values. Moreover, the idea of the asylum promised harmony in a world sorely lacking it. Although Masonry included men in widely differing occupations, it proposed a basis for homogeneity. It brought together men, primarily native Protestants, who shared beliefs in American social, political, and religious ideals. It perfectly reflected that fusion of Protestantism and democracy which characterized American middle-class culture. Masonry was a community that insisted upon religiosity, but tolerated a wide range of beliefs. Committed to equality, it tempered rugged individualism with an insistence on brotherly love. Most importantly, it demanded adherence to the moral virtues that made for respectability—temperance, self-restraint, sobriety, and industry. In describing the fraternity as an asylum, Masonic rhetoric promised a community of spirit to supplement the eroding community of place brought about by urbanization and the waning influence of the island community. It offered the same harmony, homogeneity, and commitment to moral and religious standards that was supposed to exist in small-town Protestant America.

The way in which Masonry promoted a sense of community is useful in understanding the general organizational fever that

109

swept the country in the late nineteenth century. Unlike Masonry, many organizations had specific functions. Moreover, as Robert Wiebe has shown, groups need not be nostalgic attempts to re-create an idealized harmonious society. Occupationally oriented organizations of the "new" middle class, for example, were forward-looking attempts to establish new patterns of social organization that would achieve status and power for their members.[89] But people could also turn to groups as a means of finding others who shared their values and goals. Group members expected much from the leadership of their organizations. Leaders kept their societies together and attempted to carry out their specific goals. Equally important, the leadership also articulated the ideology of its membership. In the case of Masonry, the world view was that of middle-class Protestant America. Other organizations— women's clubs, the farmers' alliances, ethnic associations, and professional groups—provided similar expressions of members' values and interests.[90] The proliferation of voluntary associations testified to a sense of varied purposes and interests in an increasingly heterogeneous society. Men and women turned to groups for political and economic power, but these groups had broader significance. Confronted with a world apparently composed of many conflicting standards, the individual sought in group identification a means of finding others who shared his ideals.

It is important not to conclude from this that organizations offered inferior alternatives to the "real" sense of community that existed in antebellum small-town America. This view idealizes the past; moreover, it presents a distorted view of modern urban life. Historians of American culture were for many years unduly influenced by the sociological school of Louis Wirth. In his seminal article on urban anomie in the United States, Wirth viewed organizational activities in cities as substitutes for the family, somewhat pathetic attempts to find meaning in the vast disorder of the urban environment.[91] More recently, however, historians and sociologists have recognized that communities do exist in urban areas, and not just among ethnic groups isolated in physical enclaves. Family ties continue to be important. Individuals find friends and meaningful relationships with many people and use the diversity of urban life to find others who share their values and goals. The sense of community may not be a spatial one, but nonetheless it is real and serves important functions.[92]

Thus Masonry should not be viewed as an inferior substitute for family and close personal relationships, but rather as a positive attempt by individuals to create a community based not on space, but on common values. Not the only means men had of establishing order in their lives, Masonry was one vehicle for expressing their views about the changes in their society wrought by industrialization and urbanization. Masons were not in perfect accord on politics, religion, or even morality. Nonetheless, they shared dismay over social conflict and disorder and sought to reaffirm the traditional values of temperance, industry, sobriety, and morality. Despite the alarming trends in the outside world, within the Masonic community, respectability was honored and fraternity achieved.

1. Officers of
Rising Star Lodge

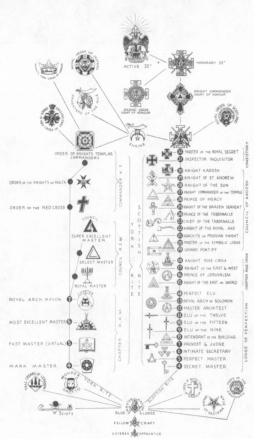

2. Orders of Masonry

3. Knights Templar Drill Corps

4. Oakland Masonic Temple, exterior

5. Oakland Masonic Temple, interior

6. Chicago Masonic Temple

Part 2

Masonry in the
1920s

4

The Defense of Americanism:
Masonry's Emergence into the
Secular World

It is now time for the Freemasons of the United States to lay aside . . . prejudice, to forget narrow traditions of the past, and to lay a foundation for a great organized effort which will make the fraternity a potent actor in the affairs of the world.
—Delmar D. Darrah[1]

The characteristics of nineteenth-century Masonry described in Part 1 persisted into the twentieth century. But in the second decade, there was an inkling of change, and by the 1920s, new ideas that challenged the older notions of the fraternity pervaded the order. In particular, the vision of Masonry as a sacred asylum receded before a widespread movement to create a more secular organization. This nationwide trend may be seen in the actions of leaders as well as of the rank-and-file membership, and resulted in changes in Masonic ideology, structure, and activities. Part 2 explores the changes that took place in Masonry in the years surrounding World War I and relates them to the broader cultural and social patterns of twentieth-century America. The changes in Masonry are significant because they reflect the attempt of leaders and members of an established organization to reshape their institution to meet the needs of a changed society.

WORLD WAR I AND MASONRY

The years of World War I marked a watershed of Masons' perception of the fraternity's relationship to the outside world.

115

In the Progressive period, some spokesmen occasionally insisted that Masonry as an institution take an active part in meeting the social problems of the day, but they were relatively few.[2] Prior to the outbreak of the war, the notion of Masonry as an asylum removed from the secular world continued to be the dominant motif. In the aftermath of World War I, however, a vocal segment of Masons demanded that Masonry ease its restrictions against involvement in the external world and lend its institutional power to combat the foes of Americanism. Masons still sought to have the fraternity embody respectable values, but the vocabulary had changed. Heightened ethnic consciousness made good citizenship on the part of white, native Protestants the keynote of respectability. Masonry as a moral and religious institution became less important than Masonry as a civic institution. Masons were still concerned with the conflict and discord that characterized American society, but in the 1920s, the preoccupation with Masonry as a harmonious asylum became supplanted by the impulse to use its power of influencing politics and public opinion to implement uniformity and harmony in the society as a whole.

The war itself was an important catalyst for promoting Masonry's emergence into the profane world. A national emergency of that proportion could hardly be ignored by the Masonic press or the lodges themselves. In discussions of the conflict, and of Masonry's relationship to it prior to America's entrance into the war, the major theme was pacifism. With the order's emphasis on brotherly love, it was natural that Masons should feel a responsibility to help relieve the suffering in Europe and to promote peace.[3]

Once America entered the war, however, nationalism flourished, and brotherly love, at least on an international scale, disappeared. Masons no longer pictured war as senseless, but rather as necessary for the preservation of democracy. With that noble goal, Masons launched themselves wholeheartedly into discussions of how Masonry could help to secure victory. On a symbolic level, Masons indicated their fraternity's commitment to the cause by universally introducing the American flag into the lodge room. Similarly, to promote 100 percent Americanism throughout the country, German-speaking lodges—either voluntarily or under orders from Grand Lodges—stopped using German in performing ritualistic work.[4] But symbolic gestures of loyalty were not enough; Masons, like so many other citizens, wanted to contribute something concrete to the war effort. Nationalism had eroded the walls of the asylum, and Masonic literature reverberated with calls for Masonry to serve the country in some practical way. Thus Masons were encouraged to enlist and told that they also had a role to perform in reminding citizens on the homefront that they, too, must make sacrifices. As a *Tyler-Keystone* author noted, Masonry's institutional power could be used to "arouse the spirit of the people to economize, to conserve, to eliminate waste, to eschew luxuries and useless, wasteful pleasures." He concluded exuberantly, "It is in our power to bring this country through to glorious triumph. We shall do it! We shall do it!"[5]

Despite their grandiose hopes for the institution's practical contributions to the war effort, Masonic activities appear to have been piecemeal and sporadic. Without a national coordinating body, there was no systematic effort. On the local level, one popular practical activity was fund raising. In 1918, for example, California lodges bought $300,000 worth of bonds and raised $66,000 for the care of returning soldiers.[6] The most prevalent form of war activity was providing services for soldiers. Occasionally, lodges offered aid to all soldiers, but generally the emphasis was on fellow Masons, the traditional recipients of the fraternity's charity. One author reported that in Michigan "many lodges have established funds to care for brethren and dependents distressed by the war, are eliminating banquets, looking after those who need assistance, helping in arrangements of their business interests and doing many other acts of kindness and helpfulness that speak well for the fraternity."[7] This sense of responsibility to brethren in the service was given particularly impressive expression in the actions of

Washington, D.C. Masons who declared the homes of all Masons in Washington open to Masonic servicemen. Breakfast, lodging, and a warm welcome were promised to all who made arrangements at the temple a day in advance.[8]

One of the most common wartime activities was the establishment of Masonic clubs for servicemen in the order. These provided a place near camps for entertainment, refreshments, and fraternal good will. Part of the motivation behind these clubs was to provide a wholesome place for recreation to counter the unsavory tendencies of army life. In addition to camps in the United States, a great number of clubs and lodges formed overseas. The Amex Masonic Club in Camp de Souge, France, for example, was very popular, averaging 350 members, and providing social activities as well as visitors to the camp hospital to cheer the wounded. "Each brother felt himself a committee of one, representing his lodge, and Masonry in general, charged with the duty of assisting the brethren, extending charity and relief to all his fellow men, and exemplifying Masonic principles and traditions in his daily relations with his fellow men."[9] Aid to Masonic servicemen—at home or abroad—was a logical outgrowth of the fraternity's principle of charity. It allowed Masonry to care for its own and to be patriotic at the same time.

Another indication of traditional Masonic values emerging in war activities was the emphasis Masons placed on inculcating morality among servicemen. For example, in keeping with both Masonry's religiosity and morality, a New York lodge composed exclusively of soldiers gave each of its new Masons a Bible with the following inscription:

> We undertake to maintain our part of the War free from hatred, brutality or graft, true to the American purpose and ideals.
>
> Aware of the temptations incidental to camp life and the moral and social wreckage involved, we covenant together to live the clean life and to seek to establish the

American uniform as a symbol and guarantee of real manhood.

We pledge our example and our influence to make these ideals dominant in the American Army and Navy.[10]

The moralistic tone of this pledge makes it evident that although the war caused Masons to become deeply involved in secular matters, participation in war work reflected traditional Masonic concerns. The major war activities involved acting upon the Masonic commitment to brotherly love and responsibility for fellow Masons. Furthermore, in describing the war in the idealistic terms of preserving democracy, Masonry's support of the war was pictured as bringing to pass the ideals of Masonry.

Given the consistency of wartime activities with traditional Masonic patterns, theoretically it should have been possible for Masons to withdraw from the secular world once the war was over and to reshape the Masonic asylum. In fact, the war seemed to focus attention on how ineffective Masonry was as a social institution. In particular, many men expressed resentment of those Masonic traditions and rules which hampered practical Masonic service. As the war came to a close, Masonic writers praised individual lodge contributions, but pointed to a lack of coordinated effort during the war. They contrasted Masonry's disorganized and sporadic showing with that of other organizations, such as the Red Cross, the YMCA, and the Knights of Columbus. There was a widespread regret that Masons, because of their tradition of keeping aloof from the external world, as well as their inability to coordinate the sovereignty-conscious Grand Lodges, had missed "the greatest opportunity for service to humanity the world has ever offered."[11]

The war had generated a spirit of patriotism and a desire for sacrifice. And when the war ended, Masons, like other Americans, were still primed for service. The struggle for the promotion of Americanism prompted by the Red Scare provided new avenues for Masonic participation in meeting the problems facing American democracy.

MASONRY AND THE FOES OF AMERICANISM

Although the most spectacular events of the Red Scare of 1919–1920 were the Palmer raids and the deportations of suspected alien radicals, perhaps the most significant ramification of the hysteria was the widespread insistence upon 100 percent Americanism. The militant demand for patriotic conformity originally concentrated on German-Americans during the war, but the campaign for Americanism was quickly widened to embrace radicals and immigrants in general. Even after the intense fervor of the Red Scare abated, nativistic sentiments and a general desire for conformity to American ideals persisted and contributed to making the 1920s one of the most intolerant decades in American history.[12]

Following the rest of the country, Masons reacted vehemently to the Bolshevik Revolution and the concurrent industrial strife in America. Condemnation of "IWW-ism, Bolshevism, and many other isms . . . preached by radicals and demagogues" pervaded Masonic speeches and articles. Masonic spokesmen seldom attempted to assess the causes of industrial conflict beyond assuming that it was fomented by radicals and immigrants. They rarely discussed or investigated the nature of such specific events as the steel strike of 1919 or the Palmer raids, but rather focused on the overall situation, which they perceived and discussed in generalities.[13]

This tendency toward generalities suggests that the Masons' harping on radicalism was symbolic more than practical. Its aim was less to expose disloyalty than to make Masonry's commitment to Americanism clear. Thus, Masonic accounts of radicalism were always accompanied by the call for Masons to take a stand on the side of law and order. As the New York Grand Master urged in 1920:

Preach to the brethren to be true to the Government, to be charitable to all, to spread the Doctrine of Universal

Brotherhood, to frown on and put down Bolshevism, Imperialism, Social Unrestism, I.W.W.ism, wherever found and always to stand on and to bank on Americanism.[14]

Similarly, a resolution against Bolshevism passed by the Grand Lodge of California in 1921 condemned the enemies of law and order and pledged "the entire membership to use all lawful means to check the growth of the destructive and treasonable doctrines that now threaten our free institutions."[15]

Masons' symbolic statements of loyalty to the government are analogous to saloonkeeper legislation. Always sensitive to public opinion, Masonic leaders were anxious to put the fraternity on the right side of prevailing ideas. Repeated Masonic expressions of Americanism also reflect a broad trend in the Americanism movement—a demand for expressions of unity on the part of respectable citizens. As the editor of the *Southern Masonic Journal* put it:

> No greater task presents itself to the American people at this time than that of securing unity of purpose and action. There are many differences to be reconciled, many factions to be brought into harmony. ... The great American public, representing the forces of social order, will soon be aroused to action: until now it has been a marvel of patience and long-suffering. The patriotic duty of the hour is the elimination of the radical elements from our political and industrial life and the achievement of national unity. To this end American Freemasonry is dedicated, and to this end all its influence and resources are solemnly pledged.[16]

Schooled by war to believe that victory required a clear conception of common purpose, 100 percenters brought to the domestic conflict a belief in the power of exhortations to patriotism. All patriotic groups harangued their own kind. The function of their rhetoric was to reassure themselves of the dominance of their values—to demonstrate that there existed a large number of loyal citizens committed wholeheartedly to the American system. While directed at the menace of radicals and immigrants, 100 percent Americanism needed to establish the undivided loyalty of respectable citizens before it could impose conformity on the enemies of law and order.[17]

The spectre of radicalism subsided a great deal after 1920, but the immigrant problem, inextricably tied to radicalism, persisted for many years. In striking contrast to the late nineteenth century, in the 1920s many Masons reflected popular anti-immigrant feelings. Part of Masonic hostility to immigrants may have been fueled by racism, and more specifically by anti-Semitism. Although Jews were admitted to the order and anti-Semitism was rarely expressed, there is some evidence that prejudice operated unofficially. The existence of primarily Jewish lodges in cities like San Francisco and Detroit may have stemmed partly from a desire on the part of Jews to meet separately, but there were also indications that Jews were not wanted in Gentile lodges. For example, one indignant letter to the editor written by a prominent Mason described the situation in his Detroit lodge. He claimed that in his thirty-nine years as a member, his lodge had never knowingly admitted a Jew. He further explained that the Detroit Jewish lodge recently organized was a result of this prejudice. Further evidence for Masonic anti-Semitism is provided by Norman Frederick de Clifford, a Mason who wrote *The Jew and Masonry* in 1918. Clifford explained that the purpose of his book was "to eradicate the hostile and Anti-semitic feelings now existing in some of our Christian Masonic lodges toward the Jewish Brethren and the race in general."[18]

Another indication that Masons were susceptible to the racism and anti-Semitism of the period was the popularity of the Ku Klux Klan with Masons. Although no reliable figures exist, the KKK appears to have been quite successful in recruiting Masons to its ranks. In Oregon, for example, the Klan had made significant inroads into Masonic membership: one former Klansman claimed that from 50 to 60 percent of the first 4,000 Klansmen in Oregon were Masons, and that once Masonic and other fraternal leaders could be claimed, "Klan-joining became contagious and ran epidemic through those organizations."[19] While its influence in local lodges probably varied widely, the infiltration of the Klan was noticeable enough that most Grand Masters, prompted by unfavorable public opinion and dismay over the dissension the Klan was promoting within Masonry, found it necessary to make a statement either condemning the Ku Klux Klan or denying Masonry's connection with it.[20]

Racism and anti-Semitism existed in Masonic circles, but they were manifested covertly. Little or no racism appeared in the Masonic press or official transactions. Masonic leaders' desire to be consistent with Masonic principles constituted the major impediment to overt racism. Central to Masonic ideology, of course, was the belief in the equality of man. Even when they tackled the problem of black Masonry in the 1890s, few Masons invoked racial inferiority. To argue publicly that "new" immigrants were racially inferior or that Jews were not wanted would be to undermine the idealism of Masonry, something that Masonic spokesmen were unwilling to do. In fact, Masonic magazines frequently ran articles calling for Masonic toleration, urging that Masons act to spread brotherhood and heal clashes in American society.[21]

Given popular conceptions, racist arguments were not really needed to criticize immigrants. The belief in immigrants' failure to adopt American norms was damning in a society committed to establishing ideological conformity among its people. Thus, the major thrust of Masonic rhetoric was to castigate immigrants' unwillingness to assimilate and to typify them as impediments to a unified America. Masonic authors resented immigrants for coming to the United States, seeking the benefits of the country without being willing to adopt American values. Keeping apart in isolated communities within cities, they persisted in their old-world customs and languages. These ethnic enclaves were pictured as breeding grounds for crime, disloyalty, and radicalism. In addition, immigrants were perceived as an organized force set in opposition to the broader goals of the society. As "compactly organized minorities controlled by gang and machine influences," they perpetuated corruption and challenged the political hegemony of "real" Americans.[22]

Closely linked to xenophobia was anti-Catholicism. Although not a prominent theme in the initial phases of Americanism, after the first wave of radical hysteria, anti-Catholicism experienced a strong resurgence. In Masonic literature, anti-Catholic rhetoric was far more pervasive than it had been in the late nineteenth century. Masons continued to describe Catholicism as the enemy of Freemasonry, but by far their most persistent theme was Catholicism as an enemy of democracy. Because many Catholics were immigrants, anti-Catholic sentiments followed the same pattern as anti-immigrant rhetoric. Masons criticized Catholicism because it promoted separatism via its parochial schools and its allegiance to a "foreign prince." The separateness of Catholics was even more troublesome than immigrant isolation because it was assumed that Catholics were well organized under the direction of American priests and, ultimately, the pope. Masons paid particular attention to Catholic political power, especially in urban areas: "The Protestant has been practically ousted from political life, the city is Catholic-governed, and schools as well as municipal departments reflect the influence of the Church of Rome."[23] But the influence was felt beyond the cities. Authors frequently expressed resentment of Catholic attempts to influence local, state, and national legislation. In particular, they cited Catholic opposition to immigration restriction and to public education legislation.[24]

This emphasis on Catholic organization and power was pervasive in the 1920s. John Higham has argued that the hostility to Catholicism in that decade was due in part to the resurgence of militant rural fundamentalism and that, after 1890, anti-Catholicism ceased to appeal to sophisticated, secularized urban populations and became the property of poorly educated rural dwellers. Yet Masonry had a strong urban middle-class component. As in the nineteenth century, Masonry in the 1920s kept pace with urbanization. In California, for example, 72 percent of all Masons were in urban lodges, while

69 percent of California residents were urban dwellers. And in the 1920s, white-collar men continued to be predominant in the order. With no indication that Masonic anti-Catholicism was concentrated in rural areas, Masonry suggests a much broader base for hostility than Higham recognized—an antipathy based on urban political and cultural conflict. Masons undoubtedly were influenced by the anti-Catholic tradition of rural Protestants, but they were also shaped by the conditions of urban America. Inhabitants of cities that housed large Catholic communities were exposed to the Catholics' numerical strength as well as to their ability to influence urban and national politics. Both urban and rural Protestant Americans could unite in dismay over the threat Catholic Americans posed to their own political and cultural dominance.[25]

While Masons identified their order with Protestantism, they were generally not invoking a religious system. Rather, the term *Protestant* had a much broader—and vaguer—meaning. As the *Masonic Review* put it,

> the Roman hierarchy hopes to destroy American institutions of liberty through the Knights of Columbus. The only way to defeat the purpose of the Roman hierarchy is for Protestants to as solidly unite to preserve the American school system, political liberty, and religious freedom as Rome is united to destroy them. Masons everywhere will unite with Protestants for this great and glorious purpose, for Masonry and Protestantism have made America and will unite to preserve it unimpaired to our children. The battle is on which will decide whether the Pope or American citizens will rule America.[26]

Protestantism was equated with Americanism—it was inseparable from the American political and cultural tradition. It became a shorthand term for native, old-stock, "respectable" Americans who were beleaguered by the influx into their society of a host of alien people who refused to adopt "American" ways. Masonry clearly reflected this heightened ethnic consciousness. Its emphasis on universality was supplanted by the tendency to define Masons as native Protestants. Ethnic qualifications and good citizenship, more than morality, became the primary standards for evaluating respectability.

ORGANIZED MASONRY: POLITICS AND PUBLIC OPINION

Although assessments of the threats posed by radicals, immigrants, and Catholics varied, they were all of a piece. These groups evoked hostility because they seemed to reveal a dire lack of unity in American society. More specifically, they challenged the hegemony of native, middle-class Americans. The assumption that the enemies of America were organized and powerful precipitated a desire on the part of "real" Americans to counter with their own organized activity. Responding to this need, many Masonic authors in the 1920s urged that Masonry take an active role in society and serve as a vehicle for promoting Americanism. Joseph Morecombe, an eminent Masonic editor and writer, continually harped on this theme, drawing attention to the lack of organization of the middle class. He claimed that because the "vast majority of the nation is at the mercy of noisy [alien] minorities and scheming groups, . . . the voice of real Americanism is not heard." Morecombe characterized "real" Americans as the middle class, which was "hugely helpless and inarticulate." Caught between the "upper and nether millstones of conflicting interest, it must find some agency or agencies fitted to represent its needs and put forth its demands." He offered Masonry as preeminent "among the institutions that can—that should—fearlessly and forcibly represent this inarticulate class."[27] Authors used many terms to categorize this endangered group—middle-class, native, Protestant, respectable, "real" Americans. Whatever the designation, Masons were perceived as its representatives. Consisting of the "best" men in the community, pledged to American ideals, Masons were the obvious force for the restoration of Americanism.

Masons had no doubt about their responsibility for stemming the widespread social unrest and loss of native middle-class power. But while they continually demanded "cohesive action," "coordinated activity," and "unity of purpose," there was disagreement over how to implement Masonry's potential influence. There were two major approaches, although the lines between them were frequently blurred. One approach was radical for Masonry—the notion that Masons should become involved in political activity. The second, more conservative, approach was to urge that Masons, while still eschewing partisan politics, abandon their traditional isolation and use the fraternity to mold public opinion on the problems of the day and on the duties of citizenship.

The different approaches may be explained in part by Masons' disagreement over the importance of adhering to the order's "ancient landmark," which required that Masonry take no part in politics or other profane activities. Many Masons who were willing to give up the notion of Masonry as an asylum in favor of emphasizing the order's role as a civic organization, were loath to extend Masonry's secularization to political activity. Others felt that the dangers of the Americanism crisis justified even more radical departures from Masonic traditions. In addition to reflecting differing sentiments about the inviolability of Masonic traditions and the extent to which Masonry should be secularized, however, the conflicting opinions about Masonic activities in behalf of Americanism also reveal varying sentiments about the nature and operation of power in America.

Private power had been an important preoccupation of the Progressive reformers. One of their central dilemmas was the problem of how to divest business interests and political machines of the authority they had established in both the economic and political sphere. Some Progressives, like Herbert Croly, embraced the idea of a federal government strong enough to protect the public interest against private power. But a pervasive distrust of power in the abstract, and federal power specifically, made this solution untenable for many Progressives, who assumed that reforming democratic machinery through initiative, referendum, and recall would return power to the people.[28]

Similarly conflicting and ambivalent approaches to the problem of private power seem to have operated unconsciously in the Masonic perception that "real" Americans had lost their power to the organized enemies of Americanism. Those Masons who wished to create a strong unified Masonry felt that the only way to fight power was with power. Significantly, Masons who advocated political involvement did not use the term *lobbying*, which would have a pejorative "special interests" connotation, but rather saw their proposed activities as righteous efforts in behalf of the general welfare. More prevalent within Masonry, however, were men unwilling to establish Masonry as an effective political force. Their solution, much like the major Progressive response, was to use Masonry's institutional mechanism to develop an informed and activist citizenry. Implicitly distrustful of institutional power in general, they were optimistic about the effectiveness of exhortations to civic duty. Even though most Masonic discussions of the methods Masonry might undertake in its Americanism movement were couched in terms of Masonic traditions, they were influenced by attitudes about the exercise of organizational power in a democratic society. Thus while Masonic response to Americanism is important for revealing the extent to which Masonry entered the profane world, it also indicates that Masons were grappling with a fundamental fact in modern American society: the increasing importance of organization for influencing public opinion and policy.[29]

Political Masonry saw its greatest expression in Masonic magazines. As the editor of the *Masonic Digest* argued in 1921, Masonry's strength must be "exerted as a unit when matters come for decision in the national legislature. There are questions of vital importance to the nation, presenting clearly issues of right and wrong, upon which the united Craft should take a stand openly and firmly."[30] In an effort to exercise Masonic collective power, authors occasionally suggested a Masonic office in Washington, D.C., designed for "combatting evil influences, and for supporting the hands of those who will tolerate no weakening of the world's greatest blessing—the American form of government."[31] Specific measures, however, such as education legislation and immigration restriction were the primary interests of politically oriented Masons. Authors who urged support of these measures argued that the issues were nonpartisan and so crucial to the well-being of the Republic that it was not inappropriate for Masonry to mobilize to support them.[32]

Some Masonic organizations, notably the Southern Jurisdiction of Scottish Rite Masons and the National League of Masonic Clubs, shared the press's enthusiasm for political involvement. However, except for a brief period during the especially intense years of the Red Scare, Grand Lodge officials tended to disapprove of official Masonic endorsement of legislation on the grounds that it would violate Masonic traditions and undermine the essential harmony of the lodge.[33]

But it was not just the press that clamored for a political Masonry; Grand Lodge officials also noted the desire of their members to have Masonry become involved in politics. In 1926, for example, the New York Grand Master felt compelled to issue a reprimand to twenty New York City Masonic clubs for petitioning the Senate to ask that the United States do something about the Italian government's persecution of Italian Freemasons. Similarly, the California Grand Master criticized a club in that state that had as its major purpose the investigation of political candidates and issues.[34]

Some of the impetus for political activity on the local level was revealed by the Texas Grand Master, who complained that he was constantly being asked when Masonry was going to get involved in politics. He further noted that lodges were "suffering from factionalism caused by political controversies, such as city, county and state questions and voting for some particular man for public office." Stressing that he did not wish to blame a particular organization for injecting politics into the lodge, he nonetheless singled out the Ku Klux Klan as a major source of discord.[35] Grand Masters throughout the country spoke out against the Klan-Masonry connection. Much of the official disapproval of the Klan stemmed from its unsavory reputation for lawlessness and violence, but part of the criticism resulted from the dissent that the Klan created among Masons. Conflict became so bitter in a Merced, California lodge, for example, that the Grand Master had to suspend the lodge's charter.[36] No details exist of the controversies that the Klan created in lodges, but judging from its usual political orientation, it is likely that Klansmen who were also Masons would be among those in the forefront of local attempts to embroil Masonry in politics.

Although there was apparently much interest in mobilizing Masonry for political purposes, Grand Lodge officials' hostility to political activity kept Masonry's political activity disorganized and sporadic. Only in one area—public education— was there ever much concerted effort, and even here the conflict over the propriety of political involvement prevented united activity.[37]

Disapproval of politics did not mean that Masonic officials were not interested in drawing upon Masonry's organizational strength to address the problems of Americanism. On the contrary, they firmly believed that Masonry had a duty to influence public opinion about the necessity for 100 percent Americanism. This vision of Masonry's role was a popular one— both with the press and with many officials—and led to widespread efforts to use Masonry to rally "respectable" citizens to the defense of Americanism.

One of the dominant themes in Masonic literature in the 1920s was that Masonry should be used to cultivate good citizenship. Good citizenship encompassed familiarity with American history and institutions, obedience to the laws, and respect for the flag, but more specifically it meant the duty of Masons to be informed and to exercise their vote. Reminding Masons that Americanism was needed among natives as well as immigrants, spokesmen urged that lodges encourage Masons to register and vote. Implicit in the emphasis on voting was the conviction that the problems facing America would not have become so severe if Masons and other "respectable" citizens had not abdicated responsibility. Citing voter apathy throughout the nation, Masons blamed the "better" elements who pursued business and pleasure, while "every element that is corrupt or vicious or un-American in idea or ideals has welcomed the opportunity to bring its full strength to the ballot-box."[38]

The emphasis on good citizenship in some ways suggests the traditional Masonic response to social problems: Urge Masons as individuals to apply Masonic principles to their lives in order to effect social change. Yet the increased attention to the Mason's role as citizen indicates a break with the former asylum emphasis in Masonry and also indicates the growing secularization of the order. Civic obligation had been noted in the past, but Masons traditionally were concerned with improving the private man, and thus concentrated on religion and personal morality. In the twentieth century, however, the emphasis shifted to the external world and to the Mason in his public role. As one author put it, "the Mason is primarily and essentially interested in the State."[39] The New Hampshire *Journal of Proceedings* in 1920 effectively illustrates the shift.

> Let us strive to prove to our less enlightened brethren that our spirit of brotherly love and affection is not solely confined to Lodge walls, but is part of our life, and that no matter who the individual may be or what creed he may profess, we are here to work hand in hand for the upbuilding of mankind, and the glorification of "True Americanism," thus demonstrating that our order is founded upon the principles of equality and justice.[40]

The replacement of the usual phrase "glorification of God" with the "glorification of 'True Americanism' " is a potent indicator of how important the civic side of Masonry had become. Certainly spokesmen still referred to the Mason's duty to God, but the notion of Masonry as a civic as well as a moral institution was becoming increasingly prevalent in the 1920s.

The call for Masonry to interest itself and its members in public issues came from all quarters; letters to the editor, local lodge bulletins, magazines, and official proceedings echoed the cry. Many Masons insisted that lodges should be able to address important contemporary topics. They called for the lodge to become a civic forum that would allow Masons to become better informed, and that would indicate Masonry's sense of public responsibility.[41] Chafing at Masonic traditions that prohibited non-Masonic subjects from being considered in lodge, these activists denied that discussing public issues would create dissension. They maintained that so long as partisan politics were eschewed, there would be no conflicts among the brethren; to suggest the opposite was to insult the capacity of Masons to hold dignified conversations. Implicit in the assumption that harmony would prevail was the notion that Masons were unlikely to have widely divergent ideas on general themes relating to the promotion of Americanism. As a *Masonic Review* author explained it,

> There is a right side and a wrong side to such questions as public education, the separation of church and state, immigration, war reparation, prison reform, religious bigotry and denominational influence, in politics and out. For Masons, as citizens, to permit these questions to pass without aligning themselves on the right side, is to let Masonry float like a cork in currents controlled by organizations more energetic but wholly devoid of the high ideals of our ancient and honorable fraternity.[42]

This assumption of harmony, founded on the sense that Masonry represented the interests of "respectable" citizens set in opposition to radicals, immigrants, and Catholics, was essential to the drive to turn Masonry into a civic organization. In contrast to late nineteenth-century Masons who prided Masonry on its asylum quality and who envisioned the lodge as a harmonious escape from the disorder of the external world, Masons in the 1920s argued that the institution must break through the barriers between Masonry and the profane world in order to promote cultural harmony in America as a whole. Aggressive action in the cause of Americanism could not disrupt the harmony that existed among Masons. Masons were of different religions, different political parties, and of varying occupational groups. When it came to Americanism, however, a group solidarity in need of expression was assumed.

The demands for Masonic civic awareness bore fruit. Magazine editors reported the new trend enthusiastically. Lodge bulletins from various cities revealed that lodges were offering speeches on such general themes as Americanization, Bolshevism, crime, law and order, and public education. In Los Angeles, a group of Masons formed a speakers' corps that addressed lodges throughout the city on the problems of the day. And the Grand Master of New York reported that a questionnaire sent out to all Masters revealed a widespread practice of providing speakers for the lodges, with the happy result of improved attendance and a better sense of the Mason's duties and responsibilities.[43]

Although it is evident that lodge meetings did change as it became acceptable for lodges to address non-Masonic topics, it is doubtful that all lodges developed into the vital civic forums that Masonic enthusiasts projected. Grand Lodges were divided on the issue. Several were vociferous in their disapproval. Other Grand Lodges, most notably California and New York, eagerly endorsed the new trend. Yet even in states where the principle of including speeches on current topics was widely accepted, the success of the program still depended on the initiative and interests of the Master and his officers. Difficulties in arranging for suitable speakers, especially in rural areas, must have affected the Master's ability to turn his lodge into a place of civic instruction.[44]

Recognizing the inherent difficulties individual lodges had in educating their members, a number of Grand Lodges went beyond merely sanctioning the civic activities of their subordinate lodges and actively promoted programs of addressing contemporary issues by setting up committees to coordinate programs and speakers and to disseminate information. The

Michigan Grand Lodge, for example, set up an education committee that was soon overwhelmed with requests for speakers. In an effort to develop new talent, it sponsored a Masonic speakers' contest. The response was enthusiastic, and the Grand Lodge was besieged with requests for research material. The speeches themselves reveal the tendency to view Masonry in a civic light. Of the 225 contestants, 36 chose to address strictly Masonic subjects, with the remainder concentrating on the relationship of Masonry to the outside world. More than 40 speakers chose "A Mason in His Community and Government," with the second most popular topic being "Masonry's Contribution to America."[45]

The majority of the states that pursued a systematic effort to promote Masonic civic consciousness operated through a state committee allied with the national Masonic Service Association (MSA). The association epitomizes the Masonic attempt to insist upon organization to promote the cause of Americanism and is a particularly good example of Masons' lack of agreement over the means of challenging the power of immigrants, Catholics, and radicals. The MSA grew out of the widespread dismay over Masonry's inability to send a mission to Europe to aid the troops by providing centers for soldiers' rest and relaxation. The United States government had refused permission on the grounds that Masonry was too disjointed to act effectively, and this decision embittered Masons. Because the Knights of Columbus had received permission, many Masons believed that their fraternity had been kept out of war service by a conspiracy backed by Catholics. To remedy the disunity that had hampered Masonry in war work, the Grand Master of Iowa sent out a call to other Grand Masters to attend a conference designed to find a means of coordinating the Craft into some sort of federation.[46]

By the time the organizational meeting had assembled in November 1918, the war was virtually over. Yet the enthusiasm for creating a central agency persisted, and the direction of the association was readily changed from meeting the problems of war to confronting those of reconstruction. The Masonic Service Association had as its goal the coordination of Masonic relief in time of national disaster, as well as the furtherance of Masonic knowledge. But the major interest of the MSA in its initial stages was to direct Masonry's energies to the problems presented by Bolshevism, socialism, IWW-ism, and other isms. No specific reference to Catholicism was made, but the veiled references to organizations opposed to American ideals, as well as the history of the Masonic war effort, suggest that offering an organized challenge to the power of Catholicism was part of the intent of the MSA.[47]

Although the thirty-two Grand Lodges that joined the MSA could agree on the importance of Masonry "doing something" in the cause of Americanism, there was a great deal of controversy over what should be done. Political Masons hoped to turn the MSA into an effective lobby that would agitate for Americanism legislation; others wanted to limit the association's activities to molding public opinion by disseminating information designed to promote good citizenship and Americanism. The latter group prevailed, but they, too, described the MSA in terms of power. They hoped the MSA would give the fraternity a "unified voice." By establishing a "foundation for a great organized effort," the MSA would "make the fraternity a potent factor in the affairs of the world." More specifically, the MSA would "help to outgeneral the strategy and propaganda of those enemies of America, who are working now from within."[48]

A majority of the Grand Lodges fell in with the scheme. By 1920, thirty-eight jurisdictions were members and were enthusiastic about the promise the MSA held. For a while, the MSA was able to sustain the initial enthusiasm. Many state educational committees drew upon the patriotic bulletins, movies, and slides it distributed. Despite its many activities, however, the organization quickly foundered. By 1928, only fourteen jurisdictions were still members. A large part of its decline may be traced to the fact that the original purpose of becoming a clearinghouse for investigating problems facing American society had lost its immediacy. It is not surprising that the MSA did not go very far beyond offering a few films and some accounts of public education and Americanism. The abatement of the Red Scare not only lessened enthusiasm for organizing Masonry to combat the enemies of Americanism, but also deprived the MSA of subjects that it could safely address. The issue of Americanism was one of the few questions upon which Masons could be united; without it, the MSA—and Masonry—were left with few avenues for concerted effort.[49]

Despite its brief tenure, the MSA is helpful for understanding the overall course of Masonry in the 1920s. It provides an excellent example of the way in which the emergency of the war and the Red Scare propelled Masonry into the secular world. Although the agitation over the MSA and the need for lodges to address contemporary problems such as Bolshevism or the immigrant threat was not of particularly long duration, it served as a vehicle for changing Masonry. Even after the Red Scare had abated, Masonry continued to have a civic orientation; Americanism had convinced Masons that as Masons they should address civic issues and other non-Masonic subjects; it had thus contributed to the permanent secularization of the order. The MSA further highlights the way in which Masonic commitment to Americanism was linked to nativism and anti-Catholic sentiment, and it demonstrates how the desire to promulgate Americanism and to reestablish the authority of native Protestants led Masons to call for cohesive institutional activity. Despite the desire for a unified national voice, however, the MSA reveals the limitations to that unity, for Masons were divided over what the institution could properly do.

While the association did not become the organized molder of opinion its founders envisioned, it nonetheless fulfilled an important Masonic need, one that much of the rhetoric of the period pointed to—it offered Masons an opportunity to formulate statements of Masonic purpose and identified the fraternity with 100 percent Americanism. Just as nineteenth-century Masons had sought to establish Masonry's respectability by passing saloonkeeper legislation, Masons in the 1920s seized upon the Americanism issue as a means of demonstrating the order's commitment to those values which its native, Protestant, middle-class constituency endorsed.

MASONRY AND EDUCATION

The secularization of Masonry, as well as the desire to bring organized Masonic influence to bear on behalf of Americanism, was particularly well demonstrated in the Masons' adoption of the cause of public education in the 1920s. Masonic interest in the schools paralleled a general popularization of the idea of an educational crisis in America. The results of the testing of soldiers during World War I received wide publicity in the 1920s, revealing a shocking amount of illiteracy and physical inadequacies among American youth. Subsequent federal investigations of education demonstrated that in addition to illiteracy, school systems were plagued with inadequate rural education, poorly trained teachers, and substandard physical plants.[50]

The exposure of educational deficiencies undoubtedly garnered popular attention for the issue, but what gave real weight to the question was the anxiety prompted by the war and the Red Scare. Public schools became a panacea for the problems facing American society. Better schools would help to insure that equality of opportunity so essential to the working of democracy. In addition to requiring improved educational standards, the future of democracy also depended upon special efforts on the part of public schools to Americanize immigrants and promote patriotism in all children. To this end, states throughout the country not only addressed educational problems, but also enacted a flurry of Americanism legislation, often under the prompting of such groups as the American Legion, the Daughters of the American Revolution, the Ku Klux Klan, and the Masons.[51]

These patriotic groups' support of public education was accompanied by criticism of private schools, especially Catholic schools. Patriots felt that such schools encouraged ethnic self-consciousness and contributed immeasurably to the ability of Catholics and immigrants to be organized opponents of Americanism. Thus, improving public education and keeping its direction firmly in native, Protestant hands became a major means by which patriots hoped to diminish the power of organized un-Americanism and achieve conformity to American ideals.

Although public education's strong link to Americanism made it inevitable that Masons would insist that their fraternity had a responsibility to support the public schools, the subject evoked the diverse responses that had characterized Masons' approach to the general cause of Americanism. While eager to "do something," Masons were again divided over the extent to which the order could legitimately involve itself in this worthy cause. On the one hand were those spokesmen who felt that Masonry should limit itself to publicizing the school crisis. On the other hand, political Masons argued for the use of Masonry's organizational strength to lobby for educational legislation aimed at counteracting the power of Americanism's enemies.

Masons who rejected the political role of Masonry nonetheless desired to have Masonry mold public opinion. The Masonic commitment to education permeated speeches, articles, and official transactions. In addition to making statements of the order's support, Masons also mounted publicity campaigns, frequently in conjunction with Masonic Service Association activities, to alert citizens to the needs of the public schools. California Masons' Public School Week was particularly ambitious. Started in 1920 and originally intended for Masons and their families, by 1925 it had become an important community activity throughout the state. California Masons reported tremendous success in attracting the public to its special meetings on schools and noted the cooperation of educators and other patriotic groups. Although few states duplicated California's extensive activities, Masonry throughout the country was an important force in alerting the public to educational conditions.[52]

Although many Masons felt that Masonry could not go beyond merely publicizing educational problems, there was a vocal contingent that insisted that the order exert itself in promoting education legislation. On the local and state levels, there were numerous instances of Masons lobbying for specific bills. Support of school funding was one of the most frequent forms of Masonic endeavor. In 1919, voters in Alabama, for example, were asked to adopt an amendment to their constitution to allow towns and cities to tax themselves for educational purposes. Alabama Masons heartily endorsed the measure and lobbied for its adoption.[53]

In addition to supporting legislation aimed at improving education, Masons also claimed credit for political victories over the "enemies" of public education. Masons in San Francisco on several occasions opposed attempts to make the school board elective. The *Junior Warden*, a publication of a large San Francisco lodge, frequently addressed the threat Catholicism posed to the public schools. In 1921, the editor, although vague about the means they had used, congratulated Masons on their role in passing a law to make the school board appointive, which he claimed would free the public schools from sectarian and political intrigue. "As elsewhere throughout the length and breadth of the land, Masonry has organized in San Francisco not alone to protect and perpetuate the public school system, but to place it beyond the reach of political organization and endeavor."[54]

Some of the most enthusiastic Masonic political agitation was directed toward promotion of legislation to create a federal Department of Education. The Smith-Towner Bill, introduced in 1919, provided for a cabinet position, the Secretary of Education, who through research and administration of appropriations would raise the standards of education throughout the country. Funds would be distributed to the states to combat illiteracy, to Americanize immigrants by providing instruction in English and civic duties, to supplement teachers' salaries (especially in rural areas), and to fund physical education and instruction in health and sanitation. To qualify for appropriations, states had to require children between the ages of seven and fourteen to attend some school for at least twenty-four weeks each year and had to have a law requiring that English be the primary language of instruction in private and public schools.[55]

Also called the Towner-Sterling Bill and the Sterling-Reed Bill, the measure was introduced unsuccessfully in Congress for several years. Even after its proponents dropped the appropriation component, calling merely for a Department of Education to carry out research and make recommendations about educational conditions in the various states, vigorous lobbying by dozens of organizations failed to get the bill through Congress.[56]

Masonic accounts of the education bill reveal how vital Americanism was to the enthusiasm generated for the measure. Masons repeatedly stressed the bill's potential for Americanizing immigrants. Particularly appealing was the requirement of English as the basis for instruction. However, the most prevalent theme developed in support of the bill was the Catholic issue. Masons claimed that the major opponents of the bill were Roman Catholics who sought to block the improvement of public schools. Indeed, frequently the major reason offered for putting the fraternity on record in support of the bill was Catholic opposition to it. The Grand Master of Utah, obviously concerned about the propriety of Masonic involvement in controversial issues, explained that Masons had no right to attempt to dominate public affairs. Nonetheless, he justified Masonic endorsement of the Smith-Towner Bill because it was a "proper function of Masonry to fight against other organizations" trying to dominate public affairs.[57]

Masons devised several methods of lobbying for the bill's passage. The Masonic press gave the bill thorough coverage. A number of magazines encouraged their readers to write their representatives in Congress, the president, and members of the committee investigating the bill. The *Trestleboard* offered a list of the religious and fraternal affiliations of the committee members and urged readers to write "each and every one of the Protestant members." It also printed petition forms in its pages for readers to tear out and circulate.[58] In addition, various Masonic groups, such as the Sciots and Southern Jurisdiction Scottish Rite Masons, undertook vigorous petition campaigns.[59]

Another means of promoting the bill was formal resolutions. Lodges petitioned Congress, and sixteen Grand Lodges overcame their hesitancy about political involvement and passed resolutions supporting the education bill. The most adamant Masonic support for the bill came from the Southern Jurisdiction of the Scottish Rite. The Rite, which was unhampered by restrictions against political activity, embarked on an exhaustive campaign to arouse public sympathy for the bill. Local Scottish Rite groups were instructed to promote public-school improvement and to publicize the Smith-Towner Bill. In addition, the Rite had a variety of publications, nativist and anti-Catholic in tone, which promoted both the education bill and immigration restriction.[60]

The Scottish Rite network of publications and local groups must have been tremendously influential in shaping Masonic and public opinion. Although it was not successful in its goal of securing passage of the education bill, nonetheless at the end of the decade, the Rite claimed credit for arousing the concern for public schools that had resulted in better buildings, better teachers, and general improvement. Although its influence may have indeed done this, it also helped to perpetuate traditions of xenophobia and anti-Catholicism, and it contributed to the intolerant drive for conformity that characterized the 1920s.

Historical accounts of the 1920s have given little attention to the education bill, which was well publicized and backed by a number of important organizations. The desire to improve educational conditions undoubtedly contributed to the support generated for the bill. However, as the endorsement of Masonry, the Ku Klux Klan, and other patriotic societies suggests, the education bill had much broader implications than merely educational reform. A Masonic editor offered an excellent statement of how the bill's educational features had become secondary to its larger purpose:

> Our Fraternity has no educational program whatsoever, so far as pedagogical methods, theories, or experiments are concerned; neither is it exercised over-much about the particular form into which the public school may at any time be cast. It is concerned, and concerned very much, to see that the whole educational institution is not quietly undermined by a swarm of separatist groups every one of which knows that it can never capture control of the nation so long as it leaves the schools free. The schools must never be permitted to fall under the control of the church, the politicians, the rich, the bolshevists, or any other divisive and sectarian party. . . .
>
> In the coming of a national Department of Education . . . the dream of the fathers will at last become true. Over and above all, the more visible and material advantages of that great political departure will stand its moral and symbolical values for all time to come, for the seating of a Secretary of Education in the Cabinet of the President will signify to all people the fact that in this land education is nationalized forever, and that private parties everywhere had best keep hands off.[61]

The education bill, then, became heavily imbued with symbolic significance. This was in part because the bill promised to promote 100 percent Americanism by Americanizing immigrants and insuring that throughout the nation all children would receive the education necessary to make them good citizens. In addition, the bill's passage symbolized a victory for the native, "respectable" citizens over the organized and pernicious influence of Catholics and immigrants. The fight for the school bill became yet another battleground of cultural conflict in which the native element attempted to assert its dominant position in American society.

Another highly symbolic battle over school legislation took place in 1922, when Oregon voters passed an initiative to make public school attendance mandatory for children between the ages of eight and sixteen. Scottish Rite Masons were instrumental in getting the initiative on the ballot by organizing petition drives. Once the campaign was under way, they organized meetings, provided speakers, and placed newspaper ads under Masonic auspices. The role of Masons in promoting the bill becomes somewhat unclear, however, for almost immediately the Ku Klux Klan jumped into the fray and claimed the measure as one of its special concerns. The Klan's participation gave the bill national prominence and helped to turn the school issue into what one observer called the most heated political controversy in Oregon since slavery. The school bill soon eclipsed the gubernatorial race in importance, as newspapers were filled with accounts, and public meetings were staged in every major community.[62]

Oregon voters turned out in record numbers to elect Klan-supported candidates and to pass the school bill by a vote of 155,506 to 103,685. Before it could be implemented, the state and Supreme courts ruled it unconstitutional. The bill's initial success is not surprising in light of Oregon's overwhelmingly Protestant and native-born population—in Oregon in 1920, there were 85 percent native-born and only 8 percent Catholic. Interestingly, much of the support for the bill came from cities, yet in contrast to other American states, hostility to Catholics in Oregon was not stimulated by contact with actual Catholic power. Catholics were too numerically insignificant to challenge native Protestant control. Rather, the strong anti-Catholicism reflected by the measure's success was based on a deeply rooted anti-Catholic tradition. In the past, Oregon had proved an exceptionally fertile field for Know-Nothingism and the American Protective Association. Fueled by the popular clamor for Americanism and enforced conformity, the Oregon tradition of nativism and anti-Catholicism easily resurfaced in the 1920s to make Oregon the ideal proving ground for anti-parochial-school legislation.[63]

The Masonic role in the campaign is difficult to assess. Although the Klan acknowledged Masonry's help in securing victory, it seems evident that the Klan was in the forefront. Nonetheless, Masonry was visible enough to create controversy among its members. Numerous prominent Masons spoke out against the measure, including the Grand Master, George C. Brown, who claimed that the bill did not have the sanction of the Grand Lodge. Brown criticized the Klan for its racial and religious prejudices. He admitted that the Scottish Rite had endorsed the measure, but claimed that the endorsement came from a "hand-picked" clique that had been won over by the Klan. Evidence of the conflict within Masonry is suggested by the disappearance of the names of Scottish Rite, Shrine, and Grand Lodge from ads late in the campaign.[64]

The dissension within Masonry over the school bill is not surprising. Many Masons had grave reservations about the advisability of Masonic political activity. More significantly, Masons may not have been divided over the school bill per se, but over Masonic association with the Klan. In addition to resenting Klan infiltration of their order, Masonic leaders were wary of Masonry being associated with an organization of such dubious reputation. The national press's condemnation of the Klan and the school bill may have contributed to the Masonic leaders' sense that the support of the Oregon bill was not quite respectable. The Klan's connection with the Oregon legislation, then, had as much to do with Masonic ambivalence toward the bill as the traditional fear of Masonic political involvement.[65]

It is unlikely that many Masons opposed the bill because of its unfair impact on parochial schools. Historians who have argued that Masonry was a dupe of the Ku Klux Klan on this issue have not recognized that Masonry's support of public schools and opposition to parochial ones was not at all unique to the Oregon situation. Although the Oregon legislation was exceptional, the sentiments behind the bill—an antipathy to Catholicism and a desire to fuse a homogeneous society by means of public education—were consistent with Masonic thought throughout the country. The Oregon example represents an extreme instance of the way in which Masons turned their organizational strength to political activity designed to promote cultural unity in America. For Masons, the Oregon bill, like the education bill, was a highly symbolic measure. Although it would have little practical impact on Catholic power—there were very few parochial-school students in Oregon—the bill's passage was a psychological victory. It formalized the relationship between Americanism and the public schools and signified the political and cultural preeminence of native Protestants.

Masonry's involvement in promoting Americanism, especially its commitment to public schools, is important for understanding Masonry's emergence into the secular world. The crisis of the Red Scare and the urgent need to insure conformity to American ideals led men to challenge the notion of Masonry as an asylum. They insisted that Masonry become a civic organization and use its influence to mold public opinion and reestablish control in the hands of "respectable" citizens. Although Masonic leaders concerned about the impropriety of political involvement kept their order from becoming the cohesive organizational power some enthusiasts envisioned, nonetheless Masonry in the 1920s presented a striking contrast with the sacred fraternity of the late nineteenth century.

Masonry's secularization reveals more than the dynamics of the institution's development, however. It also provides insight into the sources and nature of the Americanism movement. Crucial to Masons' perception of the crisis of the 1920s was an implicit assumption about America's past. They pictured a homogeneous society in which equality was real and democracy unchallenged. Native, Protestant, middle-class Americans dominated this world—politically, culturally, and economically. The society was harmonious and held together by shared values and assumptions.

This vision contrasted sharply with the America Masons faced in the 1920s. In the late nineteenth century, the increasingly national locus of economic power had shattered the relative isolation of island communities and undermined the sense of autonomy of the middle-class Americans who controlled them. Late nineteenth-century Masons had been acutely conscious of the divisiveness in their society, but by and large had chosen to retreat to the asylum of the lodge. Masons in the 1920s were more aggressive. Years of progressive reformers' agitation had helped to demonstrate how private power in the form of big business and political machines had usurped "respectable" citizens' authority over the economic and political system. Then the war, the Red Scare, and the industrial conflicts of 1919–1920 emphasized America's heterogeneity and gave it ominous overtones. For native Protestants, a new wave of immigration, as well as the rising self-consciousness of many ethnic groups, contributed to the sense of a compartmentalized society divided into conflicting groups of "radicals," "Labor," "immigrants," and "Catholics," who had no interest in assimilating into mainstream America. Viewed as having no appreciation of American ideals of democracy, equality, freedom, and justice, immigrants and Catholics were perceived as wanting to change America rather than allowing America to change them. This segmentation was disturbing because it challenged the notion of a harmonious society, but what was most alarming was that these groups appeared to be organized and able to exert their influence on the political and social life of the nation. Their unity—real or imagined—contrasted sharply with the disorganization of the native Protestant middle class—the rightful custodian of America's future.

In response to a sense that the rest of society had organized to protect its special interests, old-stock Americans turned to organizations of their own to reassert their authority by insisting upon allegiance to Americanism. In light of the historiographical emphasis on urban-rural conflict in explaining nativism, anti-Catholicism, and the rise of the Ku Klux Klan, it is important to note here that the desire to reimpose control of "real" Americans over their society could appeal to native Protestant Americans wherever they lived. As Kenneth Jackson has demonstrated, the Ku Klux Klan was not limited to rural areas, but rather had some of its strongest klaverns in urban centers. Similarly, the Masonic enthusiasm for Americanism indicates a broad-based antipathy to immigrants and Catholics. Urban dwellers could draw not only upon rural Protestant traditions of nativism and anti-Catholicism, but also on the tensions produced by actual proximity to fuel their hostility to the enemies of Americanism.

Although Masonry was less virulent in its Americanism campaign than the Ku Klux Klan, in the 1920s both organizations shared some of the same goals. Dismayed by all the factions and forces disturbing America's harmony, both groups called for unity in American life. But this unity was of a special sort. It meant conformity to their vision of American ideals, which included political and social dominance by their own kind. Here was the reason for the importance of the public school to Mason and Klansman alike. If all children were educated in the public schools, all exposed to the same values, the same language, and the same patriotic ideals, then the schools could mold America's children—immigrants, Catholics, poor, rich—into respectable, loyal citizens. Not only would America become homogeneous again, but the perpetuation of the values of native, Protestant Americans would be assured.[66]

5

"The Modern Temper": From Ritual to Service

Outsiders may think that fraternal and civic organizations exist primarily to initiate new members, to parade, hold luncheons, and listen to speeches. But such are only the superficially apparent activities.

In all such organizations there lies a firm, fine foundation of HUMAN SERVICE.

—Advertisement, *Saturday Evening Post*, 1924[1]

Masonry's involvement in the outside world, as indicated by its interest in Americanism and public education, was just one aspect of its evolution into a more secular organization. Anxieties about the threats facing American society contributed to the tendency to de-emphasize the ritualistic, religious, and moralistic qualities of the order. Equally important were the conscious efforts to modernize Masonry that arose out of the widespread sense that the order was declining. Surfacing before the war, this concern evolved as a major theme in the 1920s among worried leaders who felt that the order was losing the loyalty of its members as well as its prestigious position in the community. Searching for a solution, many Masons argued that the order's emphasis on tradition, ritual, and abstract religion had alienated younger men, who were tired of mystery and antiquity. Masonry had stagnated while the world around it had entered the modern era. Thus, prompted by fears of declining prestige and anxious to capture the waning attention of indifferent Masons, concerned leaders em-

148

barked on a path of adjusting the order to the demands of a new age.

THE STATE OF THE ORDER

At first glance, Masonic fears about the decline of the order seem misplaced. Masonry appeared to be enjoying an unprecedented popularity in the 1920s. Masons as always could point with pride to the quality of their membership. Not only did they attract the "best" men in the community, but they could also claim hundreds of famous historical figures. In addition, the list of prominent contemporary Masons was impressive and included Theodore Roosevelt, Luther Burbank, Henry Ford, Charles Lindbergh, numerous movie stars, and a vast number of local, state, and national politicians. The years of Harding's administration were particularly pleasing to Masons; in addresses to them, he continually praised Masonry, and through his initiation into numerous Masonic groups, he kept the order prominently before the public.

Other important signs of Masonry's strength were the ambitious building projects undertaken throughout the country's cities. One author estimated that in 1923 over $30 million was spent in the erection of Masonic temples. While some buildings cost a modest $60,000, nine cost over $1 million.[2] In addition, Masons were building college dormitories and clubhouses for Masons and children of Masons; several large cities boasted Masonic country clubs; many Grand Lodges were building homes for Masonic orphans and elderly; and the Shriners were constructing their hospitals for crippled children. The laying of the cornerstone and the completion of these buildings were accompanied by well-publicized ceremonials. Masons viewed the buildings, especially the temples, as impressive testimonials to Masonic strength and prestige. A 1927 report on the projected $2.5 million Oakland Masonic Temple declared, "It will ever be a source of pride to East Bay brethren and a landmark that will proclaim to the

149

world the solidarity and progressiveness of the Fraternity in Oakland."[3]

Above all, Masons could give impressive figures of membership growth as proof of the order's popularity and importance. Between 1910 and 1920, Masonry in the United States almost doubled in size, growing from 1,300,000 to 2,570,000. Masonry was also more than keeping up with the general population growth. In 1910, it claimed 7 percent of the native, white, adult males, and in 1920, 12 percent. After peak years in 1920 and 1921, Masonry continued to grow, although each year saw a declining rate of increase until in 1932 the fraternity recorded a decline in total membership (see Appendix A).

Reporting on their informal surveys of new Masons, Masonic observers offered numerous explanations why men joined Masonry. In 1924, the *Illinois Freemason* published solicited letters from ten new Masons on what induced them to join. Several mentioned fraternity, sociability, or family connections. They invariably stressed the high character associated with Masons. I. J. Hayes of Dwight, Illinois put it succinctly: "Purely a desire to be identified with the high class of men who make up the Masonic fraternity. I consider it an honor to be so identified." A. V. Aquart of Oak Park, Illinois noted his desire for good-fellowship, but explained that what most influenced him were the "unique characteristics of Masons":

I knew that not only most of the biggest and best men of this community were Masons but that men of national fame were not only members, but, in most instances, officers of a lodge. Knowing that these men, very busy, of high social, moral, and mental standing had given such a great deal of their time to the furtherance of the order made me realize that it was well worth while.[4]

Other clues as to why men joined Masonry came from the Montana Grand Master who, in 1922, reported the response of forty-six new members to the question, Why did you wish to become a Mason? The majority (thirty-seven) "promptly replied that they wanted to join for social reasons; that the

Masons had a high standing in their communities and that it was a good thing to belong; that they wanted to be eligible to attend the Masonic dances and social functions; that they might go higher and be eligible for the good times of the Shriners; that the Masonic pin was a valuable asset when among strangers, etc."[5] Other Masons complained that many men sought commercial and political benefits as well. The motives for joining Masonry in the 1920s, then, seem to have been very much the same as they had always been: fraternity, sociability, personal gain, and status.

The reasons for the rapid surge in Masonic popularity in this period are more complex. Many Masons thought that the prosperity of the 1920s had fostered the fraternity's growth. As one disapproving Mason complained, "I know we have thousands and thousands of them, men buying Masronry who could not afford it before, and it is doubtful if they will be able to afford it in a year from now."[6] Occupational data for Oakland lodges in the 1920s does suggest that the composition of Masonry was shifting toward lower-level occupational groups, a shift that may have been promoted by increased prosperity for these groups. For example, while the highest-level white-collar group showed little change in Live Oak Lodge in the 1920s, low-level white-collar workers' representation increased and the proportion of proprietors decreased. Much more than before, Live Oak was a lower-middle-class lodge (see Appendix B-1). While it is possible that this shift in occupational distribution was a result of the increased affordability of Masonry due to a general prosperity, it should be noted that the order's most spectacular growth occurred in 1920 and 1921, the years of the postwar depression. Thus, economic conditions are not in themselves obvious explanations for Masonic expansion.[7]

Perhaps a more important factor than Masonry's relative affordability in accounting for Masonic growth was the boost the postwar spirit gave to the preoccupation with the idea of "getting ahead." The end of the war, the demobilization of troops, the desire to get back to "normalcy," and excitement about technological and industrial developments gave the period an expansive quality that fostered a man-on-the-make mentality. Masonry, of course, had always fought against the notion of using the order for financial gain. In the 1920s, the same sentiment continued to dominate, especially among Grand Lodge officials who criticized "button Masons"—those men who joined the order to be able to wear the Masonic insignia in their lapels. Despite the prevalence of these traditional views, a number of Masonic magazines subtly promoted the commercial nexus of Masonry. This was reflected in part by the tendency for magazines to have extensive advertising for local goods and services. This trend had been developing for many years, but the formats of the 1920s were significantly different from their late nineteenth-century predecessors. Few 1920s ads specifically traded on the Masonic connection, although several editors made a point of noting that only advertising from Masons was printed in their magazines.[8] Other possibilities for exploiting Masonry also appeared in politics. Some magazines endorsed politicians, or more subtly, listed candidates for an office with their fraternal membership included. Thus, in the postwar period, Masonic membership may have proved to be much more materially beneficial than in the past.[9]

Masons themselves offered various explanations for their order's phenomenal growth. Many authors acknowledged the commercial motive. Others noted the increased popularity of Shrine and other auxiliary organizations and feared that a majority of new Masons joined only with the idea of going on to the "higher" bodies.[10] Observers also frequently attributed the rise in membership to the war and its aftermath. They claimed that the expansion began during the war when young men were eager to become Masons before going overseas. "These youngsters, suddenly called from the familiar associations and the settled conditions where life was secure, looked for new sources of support. They had heard from older men of the binding force of Masonry, and for self-protection sought its advantages."[11] Another source of growth attributed to the war was the opportunities soldiers had to witness Masonic friendships and clubs overseas. They were so impressed by the camaraderie of the order and the fraternal spirit it engendered that they eagerly sought Masonic affiliation when they returned from the war.[12]

The unsettled times following the war were also invoked to explain Masonic popularity. For many men, a *Trestleboard* author explained, Masonry appeared as a "beacon of safety. . . . It is a rock towards which those drifting on the sea of unstable beliefs and unsatisfactory creeds, as well as altruistic and socialistic theories, are struggling to reach."[13] This explanation has much validity. Joining a well-established traditional institution—be it a Masonic lodge or a church—could well have been an expression of a desire for "normalcy." More specifically, the appeal of Masonry in the unsettled times following the war can be traced to Masons' militant embrace of 100 percent Americanism. It is not surprising that Masonry's surge in popularity came at a time of heightened concern about radicals, Catholics, and immigrants. Highly vocal about all of these threats to Americanism, Masonry offered an opportunity of associating with a patriotic organization that provided middle-class, white, native Protestants with a means of reinforcing their own ethnic and cultural consciousness. As in the nineteenth century, Masonry was still offering a badge of respectability, but in postwar years, the definition of respectability had shifted from emphasizing the possession of moral virtues to the public qualities of patriotic Americanism.

While there are various reasons men might have been more inclined to seek out Masonry in the 1920s, perhaps the most significant source of the influx of new members was relaxed admission policies. Masonic authors reported that less stringent admissions had originated during the war years when lodges, fired by patriotism, had been eager to make men in uniform into Masons. Perhaps more significant than patriotism was the way in which Masons, much like the churches in this period, became preoccupied with numerical strength. Many Masons claimed that this enthusiasm for numbers was embraced at the expense of interest in the caliber of men seeking admission. Apparently, investigating committees became more lax than they had been in the earlier period. Recruitment of members was considered unMasonic, yet observers reported that the rule was commonly violated, particularly by lodges caught up in competition to reap the largest membership roster. Furthermore, other Masonic organizations did not have rules against recruitment, and they most certainly contributed to the solicitation of new Masons.[14]

Closely related to the general enthusiasm for building up membership rolls were the ambitious building programs that perpetuated a need for new members to finance or maintain these elaborate plants. The editor of the *Trestleboard* made the financial significance of large rosters quite clear when he encouraged lodges to be friendly to visiting unaffiliated Masons:

> A hand of welcome to the visitor within your lodge portals is not only a duty, but is good business. Your lodge exists on its income from dues and the sojourning brother, especially one from a distant jurisdiction, is a prospect for membership in your lodge if he is properly received. You need his dues. But you cannot sell him on your lodge if you do not give him a hearty welcome.[15]

A number of Masons, even those who felt that the growth of the fraternity was too rapid for its own good, rejected the idea of limiting the size of lodges on the grounds that they needed new members to meet their operating expenses.[16]

Masonry's rapid growth, then, was stimulated by a number of factors. Unsettled times, prosperity, and economic and political benefits undoubtedly contributed to the Masonic boom, but the most significant explanations seem to involve the changes in Masonry itself. Its emergence into the secular world to battle the foes of Americanism earned it much attention as a patriotic organization. And its unofficial campaigns to increase membership not only stimulated interest in Masonry, but also made it more accessible.

MODERNIZING MASONRY

Although most Masonic spokesmen could not help but take pride in the exhilarating growth of the order, at the same time there was widespread concern that the rapid expansion was not healthy. In particular, Masons worried about maintaining the loyalty of the new masses of Masons. Eager to reap whatever benefits Masonic affiliation bestowed—status, patronage, access to auxiliary organizations—most Masons apparently were not interested in taking an active part in the fraternity. Observers pointed to increasingly bleak attendance figures—some guessing that meetings averaged less than 5 percent of the roster—to suggest that Masons no longer cared about their fraternity. Furthermore, most new Masons seemed to have little interest in learning anything about Masonry or its principles. Of course, earlier leaders had expressed these same fears, but there was a major difference in the analysis of the problem in the 1920s. Formerly, leaders had primarily blamed individual Masons for Masonic apathy, criticizing them for joining for the wrong reasons and for resisting the beautiful lessons Masonry imparted. In the postwar years, many Masons continued to express this view and offered as solutions to the problem more careful selection of candidates and programs of education in Masonic principles. In contrast to this traditional response, however, a particularly vocal group of spokesmen insisted that the fault lay not with Masons, but with Masonry itself. It was too rooted in the past to be meaningful to contemporary man. To regain Masons' allegiance, the order must become progressive.

Men eager to modernize Masonry called themselves progressives or liberals. D. Frank Peffley's description of a progressive is instructive. He is "one who favors such changes in all matters pertaining to Masonry as will keep it in harmony with the culture, the taste, the spirit of the generation at any given present upon the living stage of action."[17] Masonic progressives' insistence that Masonry adapt to the times reveals the same trend that the demand for Masonry's embrace of Americanism and civic responsibility had indicated. Although the two thrusts—modernization and Americanism—were not inseparable, the two positions were frequently linked, and both shared the sense that the welfare of the order depended on its ability to respond to the changing needs and interests of its members.

This view was especially evident in the pervasive progressive theme that rank-and-file Masons, particularly young ones, were insisting upon changes. Progressives described the young men in Masonry as "typical Americans, full of energy, eager to see things happening, zealous, alive, impatient with mere routine, demanding that Masonry do something with itself."[18] A 1925 letter to the editor from a young New York Mason clearly exemplified the challenge to Masonry by its new members. He explained that he seldom went to lodge meetings. "I do begrudge an evening devoted to ritual ... We went through a lot of motions—lost motions, because they accomplished nothing. We hold to the letter of a service that was made to fit other times, different customs, outgrown habits." He continued by acknowledging that the ritual was important but that it was overemphasized, and concluded by demanding that Masonry change.

> The religious sects and fraternal societies which are progressing are those which are being adapted to Twentieth Century living. The radio, the automobile, the modern newspaper, the air-plane, the liberalization of thought are changing our life. No institution can grow as it should which does not mould itself to the new conditions.[19]

Sensitive to such criticisms and acutely conscious of the demands of modernity, progressives sought to adapt Masonry to "new conditions" by reformulating its goals and ideology. Although traditional Masonry still persisted, a new version of Masonry took its place beside the old. Minimizing the ritualistic, religious, and moralistic characteristics of the order, it offered a more secular and less sentimental Masonry aimed at appealing to the practical man in his day-to-day life.

Much of the difficulty Masons experienced in adapting the order to the needs of its members can be illuminated by first examining the very similar problems plaguing urban Protestant churches in the 1920s, for the dilemma facing both stemmed in part from the same source—the growing secularization of American society

In the late nineteenth century, the churches were being challenged from two directions. Theological disputes disrupted congregations and pointed to a diversity of faiths within the Christian fold. In addition, many liberal churches awakened to the problems of the poor and, via the Social Gospel, sought to make churches not just vehicles for salvation, but also engines of social reform. But while churches were redefining theology and broadening their goals, the late nineteenth century was nonetheless a buoyant period for American Protestants. Churchmen were optimistic about the spread and efficacy of Christianity. This optimism had not completely disappeared by the 1920s, even though contemporary observers—both inside and outside the church—took it for granted that a secular spirit pervaded much of America. While fundamentalism suggested the persistence of traditional religion, the popularity of scoffers like H. L. Mencken, the ascendancy of business, the irreverence of youth, and the disillusionment following the war strongly pointed to a decline in the importance of religion in American society. In addition, by the 1920s, a long period of scientific challenges had seriously battered religious belief, and many observers thought that science's victory was just a matter of time. They saw fundamentalism as the last gasp of a dying faith and modernism as a way station to irreligion. And, if Robert and Helen Lynds' account of Middletown's religious life is representative, there was (at least among the business classes) widespread uncertainty or indifference. Acutely aware of the "modern" quality of their time, many commentators agreed with the Lynds that secular interests—leisure, business, and consumption—had supplanted the importance of religious activities for large numbers of Americans.[20]

The predicted demise of religious faith and the churches was premature. A revival of the churches in the 1950s, as well as the continued success of evangelical religion, are evidence for the tenacity of both organized religion and personal faith.[21]

Nevertheless, religious life in America did change dramatically in the early twentieth century, and the trend was toward secularism.[22] In the private realm, scientific developments, most notably evolutionary theory and the higher criticism of the Bible, certainly altered, and perhaps undermined, the faith of millions. It is, of course, impossible to gauge accurately the extent to which private faith was shaken. Walter Lippmann in *A Preface to Morals*, however, offered a useful analysis of the significance of scientific challenges to Christian theology. He claimed, for example, that the decline in churchgoing stemmed from people's inability to be sure "that they are going to meet God when they go to church." A clever phrase, it summed up well how the undermining of the absolute certainty of Christian truths led to confusion and doubt that effectively robbed religion of its power to influence the lives of many modern people.[23]

Although the conditions of private faith are difficult to delineate, the fortunes of organized religion are more readily grasped. In the 1920s, they were undergoing an unsettling transformation.[24] The secular spirit was one index of the churches' dilemma; the low social status accorded to ministers was another. A contemporary analysis reported that ministers were "commonly supposed to be losing their influence in American life."[25] Paul Carter, in examining the declining prestige of ministers, reports that the denominational press repeatedly claimed that talented young men were avoiding the ministry "because 'the man of affairs,' who was the culture-hero of the age, seldom 'says or does anything to indicate that he regards the Christian ministry as a real challenge to a man who wants to do big worth-while things with his life.' "[26] The low salaries of ministers, according to Carter, placed the clergyman and his family in an awkward position vis-à-vis his middle-class parishioners, used to judging a man's value by his income and possessions. In Middletown, the Lynds found a similar situation and noted the demoralization of the clergy who faced an uphill battle to perform innumerable services under adverse conditions.[27]

The Lynds also reported on another problem of the churches in the 1920s. While church membership remained desirable, particularly, it seems, as a symbol of respectability, church attendance among the business classes—especially among men— was not widely valued. Whether because of irreligion or because of the competing interests of golf or Sunday motoring, ministers all over the country lamented poor attendance and the declining respect for the church and religion in general that it seemed to entail.[28]

Churchmen's response to these problems varied widely. Carter indicates that some leaders who accepted "the fact that organized Christianity in the United States was ceasing to be a part of the accepted order of things" urged concentration on preserving Christian goals among the minority committed to them. Other churchmen, however, attempted to adjust Christianity to the times. Robert Moats Miller relates that some ministers resorted to such gimmicks as attractive female ushers and giveaway items to turn out the congregation. Churches also built elaborate physical plants with cafeterias, gymnasiums, and other features to make the church a social center that would attract the youth and their elders as well. Still other ministers incorporated modern business and advertising techniques to give their message "relevance" and "pep" that would appeal to the busy "man of affairs."[29]

Although it was not merely the "modern men" who were the bane of the churches, it is their disaffection that is of particular interest here. A useful key to understanding the difficulties of the church in reaching the modern middle-class man is *The Man Nobody Knows: A Discovery of the Real Jesus*, by Bruce Barton (1924). Barton's major goal was to legitimate the pursuit of business, particularly advertising, by reinterpreting the life of Christ as a guide for business ethics and success. But Barton also criticized traditional Protestant churches, chiding them for portraying Jesus as meek and effeminate, a man who never smiled and who "went around for three years telling people not to do things." Barton argued that the theology created by churchmen had little appeal to the red-blooded active man of the day. In his account of Jesus as the life of the party ("He was the most popular dinner guest in Jerusalem!") and the creator of the most successful organization the world had ever known, Barton fashioned a role model that could have relevance to a practical man in his daily life. To do this, Barton avoided the sacred side of Christ and instead concentrated on the human aspect of his life and teachings.[30]

Barton was hardly alone in his desire to provide a practical guide for living a successful and happy life. The 1920s saw an effusion of self-help and self-improvement schemes that traded on popular interest in the new science of psychology. Richard Weiss has noted an important difference between the self-improvement trends in the 1920s and those of the late nineteenth century. He argues that the spiritual emphasis so often found in the earlier period was undermined by the secular spirit of the 1920s. There was a shift from trusting in God or some mystical force to believing in the potential power inherent in man's ability to control his subconscious. This secularism was particularly evident in the appeal of the immensely popular system of Emile Coué (whose adherents were taught to repeat, "Every day in every way I'm getting better and better"). Coué enthusiasts steadfastly denied a connection with mysticism. Weiss explains, "Mysticism was not respectable to engineers, technicians, and bureaucrats, and inspirationalists had to disguise their potions. . . . New Thought had looked to a reconciliation with science, but in the more secular atmosphere of the 1920s, inspirationalists found it necessary to eschew any connection with the avowed supernaturalism of their predecessors."[31]

The popularity of Barton and Coué, as well as the changing role of the church, suggests an important phenomenon—many people were becoming uncomfortable with the sacred. Barton and Coué were appealing because they offered a system of ideals for directing one's life that was divorced from the highly problematical issues of Christian theology—the nature of God, the divinity of Christ, and the origin of the universe. Dealing with business success, personal relationships, and mental health, they were secular guides for creating a more meaningful existence in this life.

The turn away from sacred concerns and the desire for practical guidelines for life was sharply reflected in the developments in Masonry in the 1920s. Masonry was inherently sacred. The ritual and its content, especially the emphasis on death and immortality, imparted a somber and religious tone to Masonic proceedings. In addition, the Masonic requirement of a belief in God, its prayers and ceremonies, its Bible on the altar, all contrived to make Masonry churchlike. The religious quality of Masonry may have contributed to its appeal in the late nineteenth century, but by the 1920s, it had become a hindrance rather than an asset. Given the experience of urban churches, plainly an emphasis on sacredness was not the way to secure the participation of urban middle-class males. Masonic progressives, highly conscious of the need to be "modern," recognized the necessity of de-emphasizing the religious elements of Masonry as a means of recapturing the allegiance of Masons. Although they were generally unwilling to criticize religion per se, their analysis clearly indicated that the modernization of Masonry primarily meant the secularization of Masonry.

One of the most striking indications of the trend toward secularization of Masonry was the change in the content and tone of Masonic literature in the postwar years. Although religious sentiments still persisted, references to death and immortality, so popular with early authors, all but disappeared. Similarly, the controversies over religion that had characterized nineteenth-century Masonry were largely absent. Few men continued to worry about whether Masonry was a religious or an ethical system. In addition, there was less tendency to inject Christianity into Masonry, and the conflict about sectarianism was rarely aired.

Another important secular tendency was the decreased attention given to ritual. After World War I, discussions of symbolism became rare, as did references to the beauty and majesty of the ritual. And, with the exception of a magazine devoted to Masonic research, essays delving into the fraternity's ancient past were much less evident. Masonry's role in American history, particularly its association with the glories of the American Revolution, took precedence over the more mysterious Masonic past. Similarly, discussions of Masonic secrecy and the possession of mysterious truths became far less common.

In place of an orientation toward sacred and ritualistic Masonry, magazines addressed more practical concerns. They offered accounts of local lodge activities and offered solutions for making lodges more interesting. And of course, Masonry's role in promoting Americanism and good citizenship was a major concern. To be sure, there still were many Masons who stressed the crucial link between Masonry and faith in God and who depicted the order as highly spiritual. Yet despite the persistence of traditional Masonry, it is clear that Masonry in the 1920s began to shift its emphasis from sacred to secular society.[32]

Even more indicative of the secularizing trend than the changes in Masonic literature were the overt criticisms that progressive Masons made of their organization. Although the terms employed were *to modernize* or *to make practical*, rather than *to secularize*, much of their attention was directed at modifying the sacred emphasis of Masonry. One of their key concerns was to minimize the ritualistic aspects of the order. For it was the ritual, stressing as it did Masonry's possession of ancient mysteries and veiled promises of immortality, that gave Masonry its sacred character.

Few progressives called for the elimination of ritual, but many criticized the way in which ritualistic elements had come to dominate the order. Many directed their barbs at conservative Masonic leaders, who, they claimed, had a stranglehold on the Craft and had made perfect rendition of the ritual the purpose of Masonry. The difficulties of the traditional emphasis on ritualism were compounded by the rapid growth of the order in the postwar years—the need to initiate new members resulted in a continual round of ceremonies. Thus, just at a time when the ritual was coming into disfavor, lodges' ritualistic activity was necessarily increased.

In part, the objection to ritualism was that it dominated lodge meetings to the detriment of the fraternal, educative, and altruistic purposes of Masonry. But more importantly, critics deplored the way in which the emphasis on ritual had led Masonic leaders to engage in endless—and useless—speculation about the meaning of the esoteric symbols contained in the ritual and about the ancient and sacred origin of Masonry. The result was an aura of abstraction and mysticism that was considered a major cause of the alienation of modern Masons. In 1928, the editor of the *Masonic Outlook* complained that in the past, Masonry

> was too secretive, too remote, to make itself tell deeply of the world of its time. Death, the future life, eternity, the whole funereal side of human life, and all the more abstract and farthest-removed ideals filled its mind. It drew its Tracing Board upon the dim and unattainable stretches of the sky.[33]

The somber tone of the ritual, then, placed Masonry out of step with modern times.

In their drive to undermine the preeminence of ritualism, progressives focused much of their energy on disproving the claim that Masonic rituals were ancient and sacred. They repeatedly insisted that the ritual, and Masonry itself, was man-made and of recent origin. D. Frank Peffley, for example, noted in 1921 how Masonry in the past had tended to hold itself apart from the rest of the world by virtue of its ancient origins. Masons had boasted of the "age and prestige, of the possession of mysteries peculiar to the Craft, of the light denied to the 'profane' of all ages . . . kept inviolate from at least the time of Solomon." But times had changed. "Conscientious students" of the fraternity, sorting out fact and fiction, "found that Masonry is indeed a very human organization, and subject to all the vicissitudes of time and circumstance the same as other of the works of man."[34]

In part, the aim in demonstrating that Masonry was not sacred was to support the claim that Masonry could be altered, in particular the ritual modified or shortened. In addition, demonstrating Masonry's man-made quality would permit the adjustment of the "ancient landmarks"—that body of laws which prohibited Masons from concerning themselves with religion, politics, or other profane topics—and would thus bolster attempts to make Masonry a civic organization.

Yet the critique of Masonic mythology was based on more than the need to prove Masonry's mutability. Much of the antipathy to ritualism stemmed from its unacceptability to modern thought. It seemed somehow foolish to believe in Masonry's antiquity or in its possession of eternal secret truths. Joseph Morecombe termed the stories of antiquity "as nonsensical as the tales told to children."[35] Another author pointed out that thoughtful, intelligent men found the ritual "patchwork combinations of fact, deduction, imagination, fabrication and sheer nonsense."[36] Thus, contemporary Masons, hardheaded realistic men, simply could not take the ritual very seriously. In a practical age, ritual and all that it entailed was fast becoming anachronistic.

The parallels between progressives' attempts to challenge Masonic mythology and the controversy between religious fundamentalists and modernists in the 1920s are striking. The modernist claim that the insistence upon the sacred origin and the literal meaning of the Bible had undermined the vitality of Christianity and robbed it of its practical influence was similar to the progressive contention that speculation about Masonry's origin, ritual, and symbolism had obscured the practical value of Masonry and in doing so had alienated intelligent, busy men.[37]

On occasion, progressives noted the parallel and referred to the Masonic controversy as one between fundamentalists and modernists. For the most part, however, subjects like the Scopes trial and the challenge that evolutionary theory offered to the literal interpretation of the Bible were not common topics in Masonic literature, presumably because of the desire to avoid controversial subjects that might divide the membership. When the issue was joined, Masons tended to be in the modernist camp. The fundamentalists were depicted as attempting to force their religious views on the rest of society via education laws, an attempt that went against both American and Masonic beliefs in religious toleration and freedom of thought.[38]

Masons who addressed the question also criticized the fundamentalists for their failure to appreciate modern science. As a *Masonic Digest* contributor noted,

> Judging from the public utterance of Masonic leaders and representative men, the bulk of intelligent craft sentiment is with those who hold for an ordered evolution as the plan of creation. These fail to see wherein religion is weakened because a borrowed story, recorded by a primitive people—a bit of oriental imagining—is proven inadequate to express the findings or the reasonable hypotheses of modern science.[39]

Thus, although authors made the connection between the evolution debate and Masonry's own modernist movement only infrequently, it does not take a huge leap of imagination to suggest that Masonic progressives were influenced by the religious controversy. It seems evident that Masons who challenged the importance of the ritual on the grounds that modern men could not take such stories seriously traded upon popular ideas that viewed biblical literalness as out of step with modern times.

The disaffection Masonic progressives expressed toward ritualism went beyond the sacred and abstract quality the rituals imposed on the order. They also complained that modern Masons were impatient with the teachings of the ritual, in particular the lengthy lectures about moral virtue. In 1928, for example, the *Builder* printed a private letter from a former Master of a lodge who complained that Masonry had "too many expert moralists":

The average Mason is an average good citizen, and if the members of the lodge have not violated their obligations, he is not a fool. He doesn't need to be told every meeting, under rhetorical forms, that lying is lying, stealing is stealing and all that kind of preachments. The truth is, a little horse play is much more attractive to the average business man who has to be serious during business hours than so much serious homily and commonplace moralizing.[40]

Such explicit statements of dissatisfaction with the continual Masonic injunction to moral virtue were not frequent. And indeed, Masonic literature continued to be filled with references to the Mason's responsibility to strive for high moral character. Yet a subtle change in the tone of articles and speeches suggests that sermonizing was becoming less acceptable. For example, elaboration of what Masonic morality entailed—the litany of temperance, industry, self-restraint, sobriety, and piety—became less prevalent. In addition, references to Masonic symbols to illustrate proper moral character—the plumb of rectitude or the square of morality—were increasingly rare. Although spokesmen continued to stress honesty and reliability, particularly in business transactions, the heavy emphasis on the Mason's responsibility to avoid the materialism that characterized the outside world ceased to be a major theme. In general, authors who were concerned with inculcating morality tended to be vague about what that morality entailed. They referred to "clean living" and "right thinking," implying that these standards were self-evident. This vagueness suggests an assumption that Masons were already good men and did not need—or want—continual preachments. As one author explained, a Mason is "assumed" to lead "a good clean, honest and upright life. . . . He is supposed to be moral in all that means."[41]

An excellent illustration of the shift in Masonry's emphasis on inculcating traditional morality was the disappearance of temperance as a major theme. As we have seen, in the nineteenth century, temperance was a crucial component of Masonic morality. In the 1920s, however, when Masons discussed Prohibition, it was in the context of civic responsibility, not morality. Masonic officials were dismayed not by drinking per se, but by the "wholesale law breaking." They were particularly concerned that Masons and other respectable citizens were represented among the lawbreakers. They reminded Masons that, however they felt about the law, it was their duty to support the Constitution:

> Are you doing your duty as a craftsman and citizen? Whatever your personal opinions may be, place the good of the nation before them. Support the Constitution 100%. ... The ultimate alternative is the certain disintegration of the foundations of government upon which our civilization is built.[42]

Or, as a Nevada Mason put it, "Respect for and obedience to all the laws of our country, great or small, popular or unpopular, are therefore attributes of a true Mason."[43]

The notion that Prohibition was a legal rather than a moral issue is a significant development in an organization traditionally devoted to moral self-improvement. It may be argued that the reason temperance as a moral ideal virtually disappeared in Masonic literature was that Prohibition's passage significantly changed the issues. Bootleggers, gangsters, and speakeasy denizens represented a challenge to the order of society. Massive flouting of the law of the land could be considered far more serious than individual intemperance. In addition, most earlier Masons embraced temperance, not abstinence, and for that reason Prohibition might not have been favorably received in many Masonic circles.

The reticence about emphasizing temperance may also have stemmed from the desire of Masonic progressives to be modern. The decreasing emphasis on inculcating traditional morality indicates their recognition that by the 1920s the Masonic virtues of frugality, self-restraint, piety, industry, and temperance were ceasing to be the dominant motifs for many

Americans. While many Masons may have eagerly embraced Prohibition as the fruition of a moral ideal, Masonic officials' tendency to soft-pedal the temperance theme suggests that they were conscious that many Masons were not sympathetic to an interdiction of drinking on moral grounds. Joseph Gusfield has argued in his study of Prohibition that for many Americans in the twentieth century, especially the urban middle class, temperance was an old-fashioned and increasingly disrespected ethic.[44] Just as antievolution was considered to represent an outdated mode of thinking, temperance was becoming identified with a backward, religiously fanatical segment of American society. It is not surprising, then, that progressives, eager to have Masonry appeal to "modern" men, would couch their objections to violations of Prohibition in legal terms instead of moral ones. Many Masons might object to considering moderate drinking immoral, but few could openly deny the desirability of obeying the Constitution in principle (if not in fact) without forfeiting their claim to good citizenship.

The attitude toward Prohibition is a paradigm for the general tendency of Masonry in the postwar years. There is no doubt that Masonic leaders were still committed to the ideal of having men of high moral character associated with Masonry. However, it is also clear that authors were much less inclined to harp on the personal traits and habits of Masons, turning instead to inculcating the Mason's civic duties. In this context, the emphasis on Masons as citizens explored in the preceding chapter gains new importance. Certainly the secularizing trend that stressed civic responsibility stemmed in large measure from the perception that American society was being threatened by pernicious forces that could be met only by the concerted efforts of the responsible elements of the population. However, citizenship also filled an important role in Masonic progressives' efforts to win the allegiance of rank-and-file Masons. Compared to morality, citizenship was "modern," and it had the advantage of being "practical." One hundred percent Americanism, voting, and public education gave Ma-

sons the sense of pursuing concrete programs for civic betterment. Part of the appeal of identifying Masonry with citizenship was that it offered Masonry the means of substituting
secular goals for sacred ones.

Providing new purposes and goals was an important corollary of the progressives' critique of ritualism and the sacred
aspects of Masonry. Above all, they hoped to make Masonry
practical. An *Illinois Freemason* author offered a typical call for
practicality:

> We talk about Freemasonry being a beautiful system
> of morality, veiled in allegory, but what the devil is the
> value of such a system if some practical use is not made
> of it.
>
> The time is fast approaching when men are going to
> discard the useless things of life. The question is, will
> Freemasonry stand the test. It will not unless it can be
> shown that it has a definite purpose and a practical rela-
> tion to the world in which we live.[45]

Practicality was generally tied to modernity and was perceived
as requiring action rather than theorizing and speculation. In
addition, practicality was quite often linked with masculinity.
Denman Wagstaff, a prominent San Francisco Mason, was
particularly adamant about practical Masonry's virility. Under
the provocative title, "A Real Man's Organization—Freemasonry Not a Thing of Dreaminess and Namby-Pambyism," he
explained that Masonry was not "sloppy sentimentalism" or
"a ladies' sewing circle or a church pink tea." Rather, it was a
"practical, workaday system."[46]

The Masonic clamor for practicality bears striking resem-
blance to Bruce Barton's attempt to make the life of Jesus
relevant to the modern man. Progressives were anxious to show
that Masonry could help men in their day-to-day lives, could
provide a set of ethical guidelines for daily living.

One aspect of the practical application of Masonry involved
explaining how Masonic principles could be applied to one's
work. In particular, Masons noted that the fraternity's belief

in treating men "on the square" (that is, honestly), if widely implemented, could improve business ethics and minimize labor tensions. Much less frequently, authors suggested that Masonry would be more practical if it encouraged Masons to stick together in terms of employment and patronage. In this context, the widespread establishment of Masonic employment agencies for Masons and their families was heralded for its practicality as well as its adherence to Masonic principles of relief and fraternity. Other indications of "workaday" practicality included calling for lodges to offer speeches on business conditions and contemporary events, which would serve a useful educative function. Stocks and bonds were a popular topic for Masonic speeches in this period, and regular columns on investments appeared in a number of Masonic magazines.[47]

SERVICE

Although practicality was occasionally interpreted to mean aiding Masons in their business life, far more often Masonic spokesmen criticized the selfishness of traditional Masonry that aided Masons and their families, but cared nothing for the problems of the outside world. The major thrust in the calls for practicality in the 1920s was the demand that Masonry justify its existence by extending its principles beyond the walls of its temples. It must show that it had practical plans for the betterment of humanity. Modern Masonry, if it was to earn the respect of society and its members, must dedicate itself to Service.

Much of the new secular spirit in Masonry was captured by the term *Service*. It became the alternative to sacred Masonry. Permeating Masonic literature, as well as American society in general, the term's popularity was a significant phenomenon of the 1920s. In 1922, Herbert Hoover discussed Service as a vital component of American individualism:

There is developing in our people a new valuation of individuals and of groups and of nations. It is a rising vision of service. Indeed if I were to select the social force that above all others has advanced sharply during these past years of suffering, it is that of service—service to those with whom we come in contact, service to the nation, and service to the world itself. If we examine the great mystical forces of the past several years we find this great spiritual force poured out by our people as never before in the history of the world—the ideal of Service.[48]

For Hoover, Service and the sense of sacrifice and civic responsibility that it entailed prevented the American spirit of individualism from becoming rapacious. Significantly, Hoover's discussion of Service came under the chapter heading of "Spiritual Phases." He saw the desire to be of service as akin to religious feeling and claimed that it reflected man's need to be guided by idealistic principles.[49]

The ideals embodied in Service—the concepts of sacrifice and responsibility—were hardly new in the 1920s. Undoubtedly the years of inculcation of moral and civic duty by Progressives and proponents of the Social Gospel had helped to shape the tone of Service. In addition, the enthusiasm for Service in the postwar years can be seen in part as an outgrowth of war propaganda and rhetoric, as the Great Cause glorified the prospect of group effort and sacrifice.[50] Developing from several sources, by the 1920s, *Service* had become a ubiquitous term covering a variety of ideas.

Although Service was closely related to idea of social betterment, perhaps its most typical characteristic in the 1920s was its use in the business world. *Service* was a popular advertising slogan: "Armour and Company seeks public good will. Its business is to serve."[51] But its business meaning had more substance than that. In a study of the business community's sense of social responsibility in the 1920s, Morrell Heald has traced the link between Service and business. He claims that corporate leaders, concerned about the public image of business, were anxious to demonstrate that their firms pursued a policy of social responsibility. To this end they pursued philanthropy as well as welfare capitalism. They claimed that Service, to their customers and to the public at large, and not profits, was the major purpose of business.[52]

This definition of *Service* was an important part of the ideology of the Rotary Club, the oldest and most famous service, or civic, club. Rotary originated in 1905 with the goals of providing fellowship for businessmen as well as forming a basis for business cooperation. In a very few years, this rather bald appeal to self-interest was supplemented by incorporating the idea of service into the official slogan, He Profits Most Who Serves Best.[53] The other aspect of Rotary's commitment to Service was its desire to contribute to the well-being of the community. It prided itself on its civic activities, especially youth work. A particularly apt illustration of the desirability of a club's being identified with civic Service is provided in a 1924 *Saturday Evening Post* advertisement for the Grinnell Company's sprinkler system (Figure 7). By suggesting that installation of the sprinkler system in some worthy institution would be an ideal activity for a civic or fraternal organization, the ad indicates the popularity of community service projects. Perhaps most striking, however, is the attention given to the lapel emblems of the various orders—Rotary, Kiwanis, Elks, Masons, Macabees, Knights of Columbus, and others. The ad asks, "Which are you?" By linking these lapel pins to the issue of "HUMAN SERVICE," the ad makes it clear that the pin of a service-oriented club was a badge that testified to the wearer's altruism and community participation.

However, the other side to Service was the legitimation of profits and success. Moneymaking should not be the Rotarian's only concern; he must also be motivated by high ideals. The historian of Rotary's ideology attributed the emphasis on Service to a concern for public opinion and a need for improved prestige. As one Rotarian put it, Service "placed the business man on the level with the professional man, the scientist, or the artist—men whose avowed object was service—the business man was no longer a profit-maker or even a bread-winner, he was a public servant. . . . The Rotarian serves the people daily through the channel of his business or profession."[54] Service, then, was a means of underlining the businessman's respectability and assuring himself and others that he possessed idealistic purposes.

Although the concept of Service may be analyzed in terms of its civic and business orientations, contemporary references to the ideal—whether by Masons or civic-club members—tended to be somewhat vague. Joseph Wood Krutch in *The Modern Temper* described *Service* as a "characteristically American nebulosity."[55] Sinclair Lewis caught the cliché-ridden quality of the term perfectly in *Babbitt*. On a place card at a Boosters' Club luncheon appeared the message:

SERVICE AND BOOSTERISM

Service finds its finest opportunity and development only in its broadest and deepest application and the consideration of its perpetual action upon reaction. I believe the highest type of SERVICE, like the most progressive tenets of ethics, senses unceasingly and is motived by active adherence and loyalty to that which is the essential principle of Boosterism—Good Citizenship in all its factors and aspects.

Dad Peterson

Compliments of Dadbury Peterson Advertising Corp.
"Ads not Fads, at Dad's"

Lewis observed that "the Boosters all read Mr. Peterson's aphorism and said they understood it perfectly."[56] They *did* understand it perfectly. *Service* was so widely bruited about that it needed little definition. It was inextricably tied up with a belief in progress and prosperity and a delight in the expansion of modern life. It legitimated individual success by connecting that success to the well-being of the community. Membership in a service organization allowed the individual to feel that he was contributing to shaping the quality of life in his community. Above all, he was a good citizen and motivated by higher ideals—not just the pursuit of wealth.

Thus, when Masons drew upon the idea of Service, they invoked a wide range of ideals. Service was perfectly suited to the goal of modernizing Masonry. On the one hand, Service was free from sentimentality and mysticism; its call for doing something practical would correct traditional Masonry's tendency toward abstraction and speculation. On the other hand, by emphasizing public responsibilities, Service allowed Masonry to adopt an idealism grounded in secular rather than sacred values. Instead of serving God, the new Masonry served the community.

In many instances, Masonic discussions of Service were quite general and merely reiterated the need for the uplift of mankind. They reflected a grandiose vision of Masonry serving the world and promoting the ideals of truth and justice. Traditionalists as well as progressives called for this variety of Service. But for the most part, authors who called for Masonic Service tended to be progressives. They linked the concept with the demand that Masonry be practical, that it have concrete goals. And in particular, they called for specific projects that would benefit society, especially the local community. Progressives continually used the term *community* in connection with Service. As an *Exchange* author asked:

What place ought a Masonic lodge to fill in the civic life of a community? The most intimate and closest possible, varying only with different conditions and wants of that community. The lodge which works under the idea that it is accomplishing the work prescribed under its charter by conferring a degree now and then, in a cloister-cell seclusion, and neglecting its duty to its community, is neither a Masonic lodge nor any other thing which is worthy of respect or consideration. The highest honor

which can be conferred on a Masonic lodge is the civic
crown of leaves and the highest aim in existence is to
make such Masons as can go out into their community
and make their lodge become a civic asset.[57]

This stress on community, which was common among civic
clubs as well, suggests a desire to recreate a real sense of community that was perceived to be ebbing in the wake of increased urbanization. These calls for Service reveal a sincere
belief that community activities could make a substantial difference in the quality of life in the local community.[58]

The means suggested for Masonry to implement practical
service varied. Certainly one of the most important vehicles
for Service was expressed in the demand that Masons take an
active role in political and civic affairs. Thus most Masonic
pronouncements involving Americanism and public education
were generally linked to the concept of Service. A related field
of service was Masonic support of youth groups. Not only
were Masons involved in originating De Molay, an organization for boys aged sixteen through twenty-one, but they also
participated in Boy Scout activities. Both organizations served
as models for good citizenship and clean manhood. As a rule,
Masonic magazines did not devote much attention to the
"youth" problem that captivated public interest in this period,
but clearly, work with boys was seen as a contribution to the
boys' well-being as well as to the stability of society.[59]

Charitable activities formed another aspect of Service, an
apt field of endeavor for an organization dedicated to relief.
The Shriners' hospital system for crippled children, started in
1920, was continually held up for emulation. Other organizations pursued somewhat less ambitious projects. The Scottish Rite Masons were particularly active. In 1910 in Duluth,
they organized an infant-care clinic that continued to flourish
into the 1920s. Maryland Scottish Rite Masons had a similar
program, and in San Francisco, the Scottish Rite organized a
free milk distribution program.[60]

The Grand Lodges of Blue Lodge Masonry rarely participated in large-scale charitable activities beyond the realm of relief for Masons and their families, undoubtedly because of the considerable expenditure and administration necessary to maintain Grand Lodge Masonic homes and other facilities already in operation. Nonetheless, they continually encouraged individual lodges to pursue general charitable projects that included milk funds, Christmas trees, summer camps, and educational scholarships and loans, as well as emergency aid to disaster-struck areas. Although many lodges responded to the call for Service, their activities, both in the civic and charitable realm, tended to be unsystematic, sporadic, and dependent upon the interests and energies of lodge officers. Service became a widely accepted ideal, but an incompletely implemented one.[61]

One aspect of Service that Masonic progressives did not seem to accept was its business-and-profit motif. They did not urge Masons to serve others because he who serves best profits most. This reticence undoubtedly stemmed from the fact that one of Masonry's strongest traditions was its lack of commercialism. Although the nineteenth-century refrain of criticism of the crass materialism of the outside world became significantly muted in this period, Masonic leaders did not actively embrace the glorification of business success in the way that civic clubs and popular culture did.

The reasons for this hesitancy are numerous. The diverse occupational makeup of Masonry would make a clear business orientation awkward, for it would have been difficult to find a common ground for skilled workers, clerks, and attorneys. A second important reason may have been that the critics themselves were moved by Masonry's ideals concerning materialism. For all their emphasis on practicality, Masonic progressives were in fact idealists. They felt that if Masonry could be wrenched away from its emphasis on ritualism and its members made to recognize its potential, Masonry could become a living force to make the world a better place. But they desired to adapt Masonry only within certain restricted limits. In their attempt to modernize Masonry, they were hampered not only by conservatives who opposed them, the difficulties of altering ingrained practices, and the apathy of rank-and-file members, but also by their own commitment to traditional ideals.

Masonic progressives' enthusiasm for Service reveals their desire to make Masonry practical without sacrificing idealism. Their embrace of Service also indicates how closely their agitation for adaptation to modern times was linked to their fears about impending Masonic decline. Most of the Service projects had a dual purpose—to improve the community and to give Masonry goals. Progressives were often quite specific in offering Service as a means of curing Masonic apathy. In an article entitled "The Master as a Social Engineer," for example, an Illinois Master offered efficient ways to improve attendance. He suggested that the Master's first step should be to analyze the needs of his town. There might be unemployment, poverty, or health problems. The town "politics may be of the dirty variety; or it may lack a chamber of commerce, or what not." Whatever the problem, "each and every one of these conditions constitutes an opportunity for a lodge imbued with Masonic spirit." What is so significant about this Master's assessment is that his subject was not primarily community improvement, but rather, Masonic indifference.

Men are very much averse to wearisome repetition, to idly sitting about doing nothing; they take pleasure in activity, they like to see difficult things attempted, and they enjoy the zest of a conflict. It is not to be expected—for it is not in keeping with human nature—that grown men will attend a lodge night after night that does nothing but grind at the degree mill. Moreover, such a lodge becomes selfish, inbred, and seclusive, and that is the flattest contradiction to the spirit of Masonry, and every real man in the membership will have the half-repressed feeling that his lodge (as a lodge) is a hypocrite, professing as it does an ideal of unselfish service but DOING nothing for the community which it professes to serve.[62]

177

This theme appeared repeatedly. Community projects could offset the tedium of the ritual. Moreover, by giving Masons something concrete to do, dedication to Service could create new interest in Masonry. As H. L. Haywood of Iowa put it, "Social Service is necessary for Masonic health."[63]

But the relationship of Service to Masonic health went beyond giving Masons projects to accomplish. In all the calls to Service there was the sense that Masonry needed to justify itself, that somehow the organization's prestige was tied to its claim to being a service organization. For example, in 1927, a South Dakota Grand Master spoke about the importance of the community's knowledge of Masonic service: "Masonry in South Dakota must continue to justify its existence and impress itself upon each community as a social agency of surpassing worth. Each lodge should be known as a distinct asset in the life of the community."[64] A dissatisfied Mason's letter to the editor of the *Builder* reveals the same demand that Masonry somehow justify its existence. Contrasting the activities of churches, luncheon clubs, and other groups, he asked why Masonry, "an organization of such great size, such large influence, and with such tremendous potentialities for accomplishment is doing nothing to which we as Freemasons can point with any pride."[65] In the past, Masons concerned about the fraternity's public image directed their energies to promoting Masonry as a highly religious and moral institution. In the 1920s, the public image rested on Masonry's civic characteristics.

Masonic leaders' interest in maintaining the fraternity's prestige in the community stemmed in part from their concern about the competition provided by the increasingly popular civic clubs such as Rotary, Kiwanis, and Lions. They continually aired their fears that the "best" men in the fraternity were transferring their interest from Masonry to the new clubs.

Civic clubs were indeed enjoying great popularity in the 1920s. Rotary started in 1905; by 1915, it had 19,000 members in 186 clubs, and by the 1920s, it had expanded to 54,000 members in 758 clubs. Other clubs, such as Kiwanis and Lions, experienced similar growth.[66] But it was not merely the growth of civic clubs that was threatening to Masons, for they, too, could point to impressive membership figures. What disconcerted Masonic leaders was the way in which civic clubs were able to maintain the loyalty and interest of their members. Civic clubs made committee work and attendance at their weekly luncheon meetings mandatory. But more than compulsion made men interested in these clubs. Compared to lodges, the clubs were small and limited to high-status business and professional men, characteristics that encouraged fraternal exchange among members.[67] Their lunches included speeches—frequently about the profession of the speaker—yet tended to be characterized by informality and the joviality of friendly banter and communal singing. While meetings might include prayer or silent grace, civic clubs were distinctly secular.[68]

In 1930, a *Trestleboard* author captured the secular-sacred contrast between civic clubs and Masonry perfectly when he compared the gloom of the Masonic atmosphere with the progressive tone of the civic club:

> The civic club has stolen nothing from fraternalism. Fraternalism, Masonry, is standing still; it is resting on its oars, it is living in a past age and a past generation. Young men, active men, repel from the thought of breaking into the sepulchre-like quietness, the Infinite drama, the sedate dignification of mortality, and the metaphorcation of immortality. He likes it, finds something of value in it, then takes a deep breath and seeks the sunshine, fills his lungs with fresh air and turns to his civic club men, and into the discourse of the events of this age.[69]

In addition to noting the secular and modern spirit of clubs, progressives also pointed to their practicality and compared Masonry unfavorably. All civic clubs participated in some form of well-publicized service—usually related to promotion of good citizenship, youth work, or charitable activity. While a contemporary sociologist observed that this activity was sporadic, he also noted that it tended to be face-to-face philanthropy

179

that dealt directly with the needy or disadvantaged. Thus, civic clubs' programs provided a measurable sense of satisfaction to the individual club member—it was concrete, practical service that gave him a sense that he was contributing to the welfare of his community.[70]

The community-service aspect of civic organizations was also instrumental in keeping them before the public eye and contributing to their community prestige. The composition of civic clubs further heightened their prestige. Their policy was to select one or two representatives of each type of business and professional occupation. Thus, membership was drawn not only from the high-status middle class, but also presumably from the "best" of that group. The careful selection policy and limited membership conveyed the sense of a highly select organization.[71]

In the late nineteenth century, Masonry had enjoyed a similarly prestigious position. It had gained its status in part from its representations about the quality of men who entered its temples. They were the "best" men, both in virtue and in social prestige. In the 1920s, Masonry continued to attract men of high social status, and it still maintained that its members possessed exceptional character. Yet Masonry had inadvertently sacrificed much of its claim to exclusiveness. With such an influx of new members and the rapidity with which they were selected and initiated, it was hard pressed to maintain the image of selectivity. Thus, ironically, Masonic growth contributed to its declining prestige, especially vis-à-vis the civic club.

Another part of Masonry's success in the past had been that it had expressed the contemporary cultural values of the Protestant middle class: piety, industry, sobriety, and self-restraint. Men saw in Masonry the opportunity to associate with leading citizens, but they also sought Masonry as a badge of respectability. Masonic progressives could do little about the fraternity's fading aura of exclusiveness, but they could try to bring Masonry in line with contemporary ideals by minimizing the sacred and moralistic qualities of Masonry in favor of becoming more like the popular civic club—practical and service oriented. Service, then, promised to meet many of Masonry's needs. It would contribute to regaining the interest of rank-and-file members; it could reestablish the order's community status as a prestigious middle-class organization; and, by directing Masonry's emphasis away from personal morality and traditional ritualism and toward civic responsibility, Service would secularize Masonry while permitting it to retain its sense of idealistic purpose.

To some extent, progressives' fears about Masonry's future were well founded. The Lynds, in *Middletown*, and the President's Research Council on Social Trends described fraternal orders as old-fashioned societies whose heyday had passed.[72] By the mid-1920s, Masonry's growth had leveled off, and even before the Great Depression drastically cut membership rolls, Masonic leaders were noting an ominous decline in new membership. Periodicals and official transactions reverberated with intense anxiety about Masonry's future.[73] Although Masons offered numerous reasons for apathy and decreased prestige, perhaps the most important was the one seized upon by Masonic progressives: Masonry was not modern.

The decade's secular spirit was one aspect of its modernness. But there were other changes in cultural values that contributed to its modern quality. A number of observers have offered schemata for understanding the change in values that accompanied the development of modern mass society. David Riesman has posited inner- and other-directed personality types, and Leo Lowenthal has suggested a shift from a production- to a consumption-oriented society. Both of these analyses suggest that the Horatio Alger vision of frugality, hard work, and virtue as the path to personal success had become much less meaningful in the increasingly bureaucratic corporate world of the twentieth century.[74] Both models are helpful for understanding the modern quality of the 1920s. Prosperous citizens, with the aid of mass communications and the advertising industry, were intent on enjoying the rapidly expanding world of consumption and leisure. And in the business and social worlds, it was personality and style more than character that brought success. The virtues of cooperation and affability seemed more viable than self-restraint and piety.[75]

The developments in Masonry are excellent illustrations of the value changes accompanying America's modernization. Masonic progressives clearly recognized that modern society had new standards to which Masonry must adapt if it was to survive as an important organization. In striving for a more secular and less moralistic society, these leaders undoubtedly proceeded in the correct direction. They succeeded to some extent in identifying Masonry with civic concerns, and Masonic literature did become far less religious and moralistic than it had been in the past. This updating of Masonry most certainly contributed to its ability to survive in the twentieth century. It remained an idealistic, patriotic order that conveyed a sense of higher purpose without the mystical and sentimental quality of nineteenth-century Masonry.

Progressives were not successful in reestablishing Masonry as a prestigious and vital organization. Ultimately there were limits to how modern Masonry could become. Part of the progressives' dilemma in their struggle to maintain Masonry's preeminence as a middle-class male organization stemmed from their apparent unwillingness to embrace the ethos of business that seemed such an important part of the middle-class world of the 1920s. In addition, progressives faced another major difficulty. However much they might succeed in identifying Masonry as a civic organization, the obstacle of the ritual seemed insurmountable. Speeches about practicality and service projects could not erase the fact that initiation into Masonry entailed three separate ceremonies that were imbued with mysticism and, as Joseph Morecombe put it, "abstract philosophical cobwebs" and "Egyptian rites, now mummified."[76] The Masonic lodge room with its prescribed formalities and sacred symbols defied complete secularization. As even progressives realized, ritualism was too intrinsic a part of Masonry to be jettisoned. As will be seen in the next chapter, Masters of lodges attempted to undermine the importance of the religious element in the lodge room in order to improve attendance, but here, too, they met with only partial success in their attempt to secularize Masonry and enhance its appeal to modern men.

Despite their limited success in maintaining Masonry's position, the efforts of Masonic progressives to modernize their society are significant. As in the case of the enthusiasm for Americanism, the thrust for modernization reveals something about the dynamics of institutional change. Both movements help to convey the leaders' sense that the well-being of their organization depended on its ability to reflect the interests and concerns of its members. As such, Masonic progressives had to be sensitive to the changes taking place in American society. Thus, the progressives' struggle to prevent the decline of Masonry by modernizing it provides insight into the changes in cultural values that had accompanied America's own modernization. The attempt to identify Masonry as primarily a civic institution suggests the eclipse of traditional Horatio Alger virtues. Men may still have sought respectability in identifying with Masonry and other organizations, but what respectability entailed had been modified. It was now the assumption of high moral character without the constant injunctions to temperance, self-restraint, piety, and other virtues. Citizenship became the badge of the good Mason and the good man. More emphatically, Masonic experience illuminates the nature and importance of the secular spirit of the 1920s. For although the sacred appears to have become an embarrassment for the urban, middle-class male, the alternatives to traditional religion were not blatant materialism and hedonism. As the idea of Service indicates, men were still eager for ideals and guidelines with which to order their lives.

Masonic developments in the 1920s also highlight something of the special spirit of that decade, best characterized as its preoccupation with modernity. Historians have long recognized that changes in America that created a mass society began well before the 1920s, and that developments frequently associated with that decade—secularism and consumerism, among others—belonged to an earlier era as well. Yet sources for the 1920s teem with a consciousness of modernity. Krutch's *Modern Temper* and Lippmann's "acids of modernity" suggest the perception of fundamental changes in the society. Of a different sort were the advertisements of the period, which vibrated with the excitement over modernness. Masonry reveals this self-conscious modernity particularly well. There were in Masonry many traditionalists who were dismayed not only by changes in Masonry, but also by changes in the culture. They lamented the age of jazz and immorality. This side of the response to change in the 1920s is well known and has been extensively analyzed. What is striking about Masonic progressives is that they provide the opportunity to investigate a group of people who were enthusiastic about change. Certainly Masonic progressives, especially in their concern for Americanism, reveal dismay over the encroaching pluralism of the society; but as their embrace of modernism suggests, their response to change was complex and ambivalent. While ethnic and religious pluralism was an unwanted development, they were able to embrace other changes in their society more readily. Progressives were infected with the popular spirit that had been fueled by prosperity and such exciting technological developments as movies, automobiles, airplanes, and radios. They were certain that practical guidelines for living could be found, that modern man could adapt to the changes in his society. What remained to be seen was whether Masonry would have a role in the rapidly evolving modern world.

6

Social Activities and Auxiliary Organizations: From Temple to Club

In the Lodge room, an unadulterated diet of ceremony and symbolism is apt to surfeit the normal man and kill his interest. Man is but the boy full grown; he prefers his pills of Masonic wisdom sugar-coated. The wise Master of a Lodge ensures that the sugar is supplied in full quantity. . . . To get the most out of Masonry, to hold the interest and keep up the attendance of members of Lodges, we must bring entertainment into Masonry.

—Ernest L. West, *The Masonic World*[1]

The reformulation of Masonic ideology to create a more modern and secular order was accompanied by parallel developments in lodge activities and auxiliary organizations. The efforts of Blue Lodge officials to make meetings more entertaining and convivial, and the expansion of a wide variety of Masonic organizations designed to make Masonry more fun and more practical, reflect the growing importance of the pursuit of leisure in the 1920s as well as Masons' attempts to adjust their order to the needs and values of a secular and consumption-oriented society.

SOCIAL ACTIVITIES

While progressives worried about declining prestige and the need to give Masonry a worthwhile purpose, other Masons were concerned about poor attendance and Masonry's failure

185

to offer the men the fraternity it had promised. These fears led many officials and observers to concentrate on schemes for revitalizing Blue Lodge Masonry. For the most part, they called for a de-emphasis on ritual in favor of a wide range of carefully organized social activities.

Attendance had always been a source of concern to Masonic leaders, but in the twentieth century, especially the 1920s, poor attendance became a major theme in Masonic literature as officials and authors tried to assess the problem and offer solutions. As Joseph Morecombe noted in 1928, "In monthly bulletins of the lodges harassed Masters recur with almost every issue to the problems of nonattendance. They plead with the brethren to turn out, and are at their wits' end to devise attractions calculated to increase the number of those present."[2] The *Shawnee Light Bulletin* editor's lament was typical: "There must be something radically wrong in Shawnee Lodge, but what is it? Can anyone solve the question? If there is something wrong the lodge should know it so if there is a possible way to correct the wrong, we wish to do so."[3]

Observers were convinced that attendance had become much worse than in the past. The estimates they offered in the 1920s for average turnout varied from 5 percent to 20 percent.[4] It is difficult to judge how much leaders' perception of declining participation was based on nostalgia, for in the nineteenth century, although there were complaints about attendance, there were no large-scale attempts to estimate average attendance. Records for Live Oak Lodge in Oakland reveal a sharp decline after 1880. In 1880, the average lodge attendance was 26 percent of its 105 members, but in 1885, only 13 percent of its 135 members came to the monthly scheduled meetings. By 1900, the figure had dropped to 9 percent. In the late 1920s, attendance improved somewhat. In 1920, for a lodge of 913, 11 percent was the average figure, and by 1928 (1,128 members), attendance had improved to 15 percent. Live Oak figures substantiate the vision of better-attended meetings in an earlier era, but also suggest that severe attendance problems may have begun before they became such a major theme in the 1920s.[5]

Records compiled for Minnesota in 1911 and Indiana in 1929 offer a more systematic view of lodge turnout. The Minnesota Grand Lodge report reveals that only 5 percent of the lodges had an average attendance of less than 10 percent. Fifty-nine percent of the lodges had an attendance of better than 20 percent. In 1911, then, Minnesota lodges were by and large well attended. The 1929 Indiana statistics for its 332 lodges reveal significantly poorer attendance. For 61 percent of the lodges, the average turnout was less than 10 percent. Only 4 percent of the lodges averaged more than 20 percent of its membership. Although these figures are for different states, they support Masons' perception of declining interest in lodge activity in the 1920s.[6]

In assessing attendance problems, many observers concluded that the rapid influx of new members was a major factor. In particular, they pointed to "degree mills"—lodges that seemed to do nothing but confer degrees—and to the increase in average lodge membership that accompanied growth and made lodge meetings boring and impersonal.[7] Masonic experts pinpointed several evils stemming from the degree mills. One was that in the frenzied rush to process applications to add to the membership roll, lodges were not felt to be scrutinizing applicants zealously enough. This laxity became particularly serious because, in the haste to put a candidate through his paces, it was felt that few Masters took time to make sure that he truly understood the Masonic principles being imparted.[8] Not only did the new Mason not learn the nature of Masonry when he was processed through the mill, but the mass-production quality of the procedure was also felt to militate against the ritual's instilling a commitment to Masonry. As one observer complained, "The nightly grinding out of candidates may make numbers, but it will never make Masons."[9]

The major difficulty inherent in the degree mill, however, was its emphasis on the ritual. Not only did the sacred quality of the ritual seem increasingly anachronistic in the context of modernizing Masonry, but the ceremony, so often repeated, was boring. The nightly rendition of the same material could become monotonous, even to the most loyal Mason. As the *Illinois Freemason*'s editor explained:

> When we stop to consider that the average lodge does nothing but confer degrees and that some lodges hold as many as three or four special meetings per week, that candidates are hurried through the degrees with a rapidity that is astounding, it is no wonder that men become tired of seeing the same thing over and over again. The average person does not care to see a play more than once.[10]

Interestingly, in light of the pervasive fears about declining Masonic prestige, authors frequently specified that the "best" men were the ones most alienated by the constant repetition of the degrees. "We have tried to fool ourselves into believing that the conferring of the degrees should attract intelligent busy men as a regular thing. Thoughtful men will not waste their time on Blue Lodge meetings as they are now conducted."[11] Concerned observers feared that if the lodge degenerated into nothing but a parrotlike ritualistic exercise, lodges would become the "patrons of the mediocre."[12]

Another major problem surrounding the degree mill was that officers were so preoccupied with the rendition of the ritual that they neglected to promote the social and fraternal aspects of Masonry. The Grand Master of California, in 1919, recognized the "pronounced undercurrent of dissatisfaction at undue emphasis placed upon ritualistic activities" and recommended social and educational programs.[13] Unofficial observers were much more emphatic. Paul R. Clark, writing in *The Square and Compass*, explained, "Just as the church cannot afford to spend too much time on theological discussions, so no Blue Lodge can hope to grip its members if it continually devotes the major part of the time on Masonic Symbolism and Ritual. Men must have recreations. We need to relax."[14]

Thus, the demand that Masonry develop its social side became a persistent corollary of the criticism of the degree mill: "If the Masonic lodges are to be well attended the meetings must be made attractive. Men are not going up to a Masonic lodge to hear a lot of half-baked officers mumble through a lot of ritual, and the sooner lodges find this out the better off they are going to be."[15]

Low attendance and general indifference appeared also to stem from another problem related to Masonry's growth—the large lodge that characterized urban Masonry.[16] Large lodges were not new. As early as 1905, observers began to sound the alarm about the problems presented by lodges with more than 300 people.[17] The postwar expansion led to many more large lodges, and the numbers they reached were unprecedented. A survey of California lodge size for the years 1880, 1900, and 1920 reveals a striking increase in the number of large lodges. Lodges with under 100 members predominated for both 1880 and 1900 (88.3 percent and 78 percent, respectively), and there was only one lodge with more than 300 members in 1880. By 1920, however, 23 percent of California lodges had over 300 members. Even more striking evidence for the proliferation of large lodges is indicated by a comparison of the number of Masons in large lodges in 1900 and 1920. In 1900, 17 percent of all California Masons were in lodges of over 300 members; by 1920, the proportion had grown to over one-half. The correlation between attendance and lodge size may also be seen in the Minnesota and Indiana attendance reports. Both reveal that attendance decreased as lodge size increased.[18]

The major difficulty of the large urban lodge was its lack of fraternity. Spokesmen questioned how the Mason could experience brotherhood when he could know so few of his brethren. As William Rhodes Hervey, a California Grand Lodge official, noted:

When a lodge becomes so large that its members are unacquainted and, in the very condition of things cannot cultivate the social amenities and fraternal relations, then the Lodge is failing in one of the high and important purposes for which it was called into existence. *It is not possible for a man to love a name in a roster* nor pour out the royalties and generosities of friendship and human brotherhood to one he has never seen and does not know.[19]

Instead of a community, it was feared, large lodges were cold, sophisticated business machines, concerned with administrative details and ritualistic work. Equally serious was the way in which large lodges limited the ability of members to participate, with the result that the "individual member therefore feels a very small sense of responsibility for either the Lodge or Masonry in general."[20]

Part of the critique of large lodges was the glorification of small ones. In this connection, Masons frequently praised English lodges that generally had fewer than 100 men and that were noted for high attendance (80-90 percent, Masonic authors claimed) and a high degree of sociability and fraternal good will.[21] In addition, Masonic fiction of this period glorified lodges in small towns while generally neglecting urban settings. An advertisement for P. W. George's *Lodge in Friendship Village* captures the essence of that book and illustrates the nostalgia surrounding Masonry in the small town. "It is a book about a friendly village and the influence of the Masonic Lodge on the peace and prosperity of the life there. A series of thrilling episodes follow one another with breathless rapidity, and there arise interesting problems and situations which the Masons of the village solve and handle in a masterful way." This same advertisement pointed out how humble the lodge was, with an implicit comparison to the well-outfitted urban lodges. The lodge room is "not luxurious." "The roof is tin. The carpet worn by the tread of heavy boots shows a dim pattern of squares and compasses. . . . There are no tailored clothes or gleaming shirt fronts to be seen." Yet it is clear that the Masonry in Friendship Village is of the highest type—intimate, with a strong sense of fraternal responsibility.[22]

Similarly, sentimental accounts of actual rural lodges occurred frequently in the literature. Small-town lodges were praised for their friendliness to visiting Masons, their readiness to provide personal charity, and their genuine fraternal concern for brethren and Masonic widows and orphans.[23] Although an occasional reference suggested that small-town lodges were stagnating from lack of new members and energetic leadership, in general small-town lodges were depicted as much more Masonic than their city counterparts. "The light of Masonry burns as brightly in the country as it does in the city. Indeed we are tempted to remark that away from the multifarious distractions of city life the true spirit of Masonic brotherhood and ideals develops to its fullest extent."[24]

It is difficult to determine whether small lodges were more "Masonic" than large ones. Nostalgia obviously must be considered a factor in the accounts of the loss of fraternal commitment seemingly fostered by the degree mill and the anonymity of the large lodge. Attendance and lack of fraternal spirit had been a theme of writers in the nineteenth century as well. They, too, had worried about the need to combine ritualism with social activity. And they, too, romanticized small-town lodges and a golden age of Masonry in the immediate past. To caution against Masonic observers' sense of a dramatic decline in Masonic spirit in the 1920s, however, is not to deny their assessment. While apprehension about the quality of Masonic loyalty and fraternity was a theme in earlier years, it had been only a minor one. In the postwar years it was one of serious concern. The sense of urgency in the later years, underlined by the existence of concerted efforts to solve the dilemma, further indicates that Blue Lodge Masonry was in fact undergoing a serious challenge.

There were some attempts to deal with the rush of degree work and large-lodge problems legislatively. In many states, Grand Lodges modified or shortened rituals.[25] A number of Grand Lodges also passed laws fixing minimum times between degrees to slow the pace and give initiates time to reflect upon what was being taught. There were also laws that prohibited Masons from joining other Masonic organizations until three months to one year after their initiation. It was hoped that these laws would discourage those men who were joining for such "improper" reasons as commercial benefits or a desire for the "higher" degrees of Masonry.[26] Some Grand Lodges also tackled the problem of large lodges. Nebraska, for example, limited lodges to 400 members.[27] Although the journals were filled with concern about the detrimental effects of large lodges, restrictions generally met with little favor. While in theory small lodges were superior, in practice large lodges would hardly be willing to split up, particularly those with expensive physical plants to maintain.[28] On a different note, the California Grand Lodge enacted legislation to improve the quality of lodge meetings. In 1919, it changed its rule limiting lodge expenditures for social activities from 10 percent of the total lodge dues to 20 percent.[29]

In addition to legislative efforts to make better Masons, many officials embraced the idea of Masonic education. They felt that lack of involvement on the part of newer members stemmed from the failure of large lodges to assimilate new Masons. In the rush of the degree mill, it was impossible for a candidate to understand Masonry sufficiently to insure his continued interest. Masonic education schemes were linked to concerns over Americanism and consisted in part of urging lodges to address civic questions. Equally important was their implicit purpose of making lodges more appealing to members. Indeed, as the theme of Americanism receded, Masonic education committees focused on the problem of lodge attendance and lodge vitality. In 1928, for example, the Grand Master of California decreed a plan of education for all lodges. Masters received a list of topics around which they were to organize monthly meetings. Grand Master Fisher claimed that his educational program was successful and that Masters who took pains to secure good speakers were rewarded with improved attendance and vitality. Thus, in addition to their interest in civic questions, education committees in the various Grand

Lodges sought ways to develop interesting programs that would increase attendance while simultaneously teaching the principles and traditions of Masonry.[30]

It is difficult to evaluate the success of the various Masonic education plans. Programs that dealt strictly with Masonry apparently met with a lukewarm response. As Joseph Morecombe noted in 1928, most Masons were unconcerned about "the origins of ritual or the trivial points of Craft history. They will not give attention to the many guesses as to symbolic meanings nor to the intricacies of ceremonial development."[31] In contrast, programs dealing with the more practical aspects of Masonry—its relationship to business, citizenship, or community affairs—may have met with more approval.[32]

Much more successful than Masonic education in stimulating lodge interest were the efforts of individual lodge Masters who devised elaborate methods to improve attendance and fraternal spirit. These Masters' attempts to rejuvenate their lodges clearly reflect the belief that a major function of the Masonic lodge was to entertain its members. Many Masters were convinced that men would only turn out for meetings if they were sure of having a good time. And, because of the competition provided by the modern amusements of movies, radios, and automobiles, providing a good time in the lodge had become a particularly urgent matter. The simple sociability of Masonry in the past no longer sufficed. As one man explained in 1924, "The average Mason will not give up his evening radio entertainment, a favorite book, a prize collection of phonograph records or evening drive with his automobile unless a greater and more attractive feature is promised."[33] A letter to the editor from a Scottish Rite Mason who called himself "Pep" reflects the rank-and-file's desire for entertainment. Although he was referring to Scottish Rite meetings, the sentiment seems applicable to Blue Lodge Masonry as well:

> The difficulty [poor attendance] is that there is not enough certainty of an attractive program to be furnished us at the suppers. The meals are fine, but why can't we have a

good musical program and a good peppy speaker every Thursday night. Occasionally we have a forceful speaker . . . but it's just good luck when there is a program, and we never know whether there will be worthwhile entertainment or not. If the members were sure to be entertained at supper there would be a big attendance every Thursday night, and most of those who attended the suppers would stay for the meetings.[34]

Agreeing with "Pep," many Masters made providing social features their major goal in office. Compared to social activities, the ritualistic and charitable concerns of Masonry received comparatively little attention. Increasingly, the definition of a good Master depended less on his ability as a ritualist and more on his skills in organizing social functions. Interesting talks about civic affairs, contemporary events, travel, and business were part of the new attractions. Dinners, parties, movies, and other entertainment formed the other half of a good Master's scheme to cultivate the interest of his members.[35]

The most common method of making lodges more interesting was the institution of a carefully organized schedule of events well publicized by monthly bulletins sent out to the membership. Some of these bulletins were quite lengthy, with a magazine format; others were only one page. All served to inform members of coming meetings and the highlights of past events. There was usually a "personal" column with accounts of marriages, deaths, illness, funerals, and vacations. Invariably bulletins strove for a warm, chatty tone and promised members an interesting or fun time at the upcoming events.[36]

The bulletins of Live Oak Lodge for the 1920s reveal energetic attempts to enliven the lodge and promote fellowship. Obviously the Masters were not concerned about keeping business or politics out of the lodge room. For example, one speaker in 1928 discussed "Keeping Up with the Times," an analysis of changes in the business and commercial world. In

1921, Brother Squier addressed the lodge on the need to make public-school attendance compulsory, and in 1928, a prominent banker discussed "Credits: Their Meaning and Use."[37]

In addition to offering men an opportunity to be enlightened on issues of importance to them, Live Oak had a less serious side. The bulletins also tell of well-attended parties, dances, and stag parties at which "Wooers of Lady Nicotine burned much incense at her shrine over keenly contested card games."[38] A special feature of Live Oak was its own orchestra and quartet, which graced most functions and were known throughout the area. The *Masonic World* reported in 1928 that Live Oak featured music at every meeting: "Whether it be coupled with degree work or some form of entertainment it seems that the brothers are always regaled with melody. It must have been found attractive, and likely had an influence in arousing and maintaining interest."[39]

At Pacific Lodge in San Francisco, Harry Wolff, the Master for 1923, was determined to improve attendance and apparently succeeded, for his lodge averaged 200 of the 500 members residing in the city. His success stemmed from his plan of having "something doing" at every meeting: "lectures, parties, club night entertainments—in fact every type of intellectual, social and educational program imaginable."[40]

The lodge's eight-page bulletin gives ample evidence that Pacific continued to be active. A 1927 list of its standing committees indicates the weight given to social aspects as well as the degree of specialization needed to coordinate lodge social activities. The Finance Committee and Board of Trustees were administrative; the Coaching Committee and Ritual Assistants were concerned with ritualistic work. The rest were geared toward enlivening the lodge: Commissary Assistants, Publication Committee, Pacific Luncheon Club, Pacific Players, Informal Entertainment Committee, Latch String Committee, and Speaker's Committee. Almost every month during the period from 1927 to 1930, the lodge offered an instructional talk (such as "The Automobile in American Life" or "Insurance: Safeguarding the Future"). The several degree meetings a month were usually followed by a "club" night that featured "smokes, eats, cards." Frequent parties—dinner dances and the like—included wives and sweethearts. Often, Pacific featured "ladies' night," which was under the direction of a standing committee of hostesses. Pacific occasionally showed movies such as the "fast and furious war-time movie, 'The Fighting Sap,'" with Reginald Denny. In addition, the lodge frequently visited other lodges in California and made an annual New Year's trip to nearby Lake Tahoe.[41]

Perhaps one of the most entertainment-oriented lodges was Detroit's Palestine Lodge, with the largest membership in the United States: 4,000 men. Its bulletin, the *Palestiner*, offered accounts of parties, bowling leagues, baseball teams, women's auxiliary organizations, trips, dinners, and other functions. Its numerous festive occasions featured both amateur and professional entertainment.[42] In 1921, the bulletin included an entertainment questionnaire, which indicates how extensively the lodge had devoted itself to the entertainment of its members:

> Are you interested in Palestine's annual—Thanksgiving party? ... Theater party? ... Children's Xmas party? ... New Year's party? ... House party? ... Formal Ball? ... Masque Ball? ... Arcadia dance? ... Moonlight party? ... Day Boat Excursions? ... U. of M. football special? ...
>
> Do you enjoy—smokers? ... cards? ... concerts? ... picnics? ... barbecues? ... festivals? ... auto parties? ... informal dances? ... dinner dances? ... Performances? ...
>
> Do you, or members of your family, attend Palestine's private dancing classes—(1) for adults? ... (2) for children? ... Would you care to attend such classes? ...
>
> Would you, or members of your family, attend card parties at Palestine lodge houses to play—Pedro? ... Euchre? ... Five Hundred? ... Bridge? ... Pinochle? ... Dominoes?

The questionnaire also asked about interest in baseball, basketball, football, golf, and other sports, and about musical and acting talents.[43]

The extent of Palestine social activities may have been exceptional, yet they indicate the trend among urban lodges to offer their members a wide range of leisure-time activities in the hopes of improved attendance and renewed vitality. Palestine functions also suggest an important innovation in lodges—the inclusion of women in their activities. Throughout the country more and more lodges found room for wives and girlfriends. In the nineteenth century, Masons invited women only occasionally to their functions. In the 1920s, Masonic leaders apparently assumed that men were eager to share much of their leisure-time with women. As Paul R. Clark put it, "One of the most interesting developments of the growth of club life in America is the very important part our wives, mothers and sweethearts are playing. The club that doesn't find a place for our women is doomed."[44] Clark was quite perceptive; the line dividing the separate spheres of men and women had blurred considerably. While sex-segregated leisure-time pursuits proliferated (luncheon clubs, study clubs, and sports), couple- and family-oriented group activities were an important characteristic of the leisure time of the 1920s as well.[45]

The erosion of the all-male quality of Masonry is important not only because it reveals, once again, how Masonry mirrored the trends of the profane world, but also because it indicates how far Masonry had moved from the notion of a sacred asylum. The inclusion of women is striking evidence of Masonry's increasingly public and secular character.

In addition to revealing the importance of secular entertainment, social activities of lodges such as Palestine also indicate the emphasis on lodge organization. Masters were striving to create an interesting and sociable atmosphere that would encourage attendance and involvement in Masonry. To do so, they had to become adroit managers. This was in striking contrast to nineteenth-century Masonry. Then, the banquet was a yearly or semiyearly affair; occasional outings and parties including wives and sweethearts were exceptional events. Although the lodge might have had refreshments and a social hour after the closing of the lodge in the nineteenth century, this was a far cry from the well-organized, systematic efforts of later lodges.[46]

Another example from Palestine lodge provides an excellent illustration of the organizational bent of lodges in the 1920s. A. G. Pitts, Secretary for 1920, offered a detailed plan of how his lodge of 4,000 operated successfully and maintained that fraternal feeling so essential to Masonry. The lodge met on Tuesday for conferring the first degree, on Thursday for the first and second alternatively, and on Fridays for the third degree. Meetings lasted from 5 p.m. until 10 p.m., but members were not expected to be in the lodge room at all times. Dinner was served in the lodge's own restaurant from 5:30 to 7:30, with workers and candidates taking turns. "A Palestine man spending the evening at lodge puts in a third of the time in the lodge room. Another third in the dining-room where he is surrounded by the family and takes a leisurely meal, sweetened by social intercourse. Very likely his wife dines with him and both with half a dozen other like couples." His other one-third of the evening was spent in the billiard room, reading room, or ballroom. Palestine's attendance ranged from 300 to 800, and Pitts felt the system worked splendidly.[47]

This account of Palestine is significant for a number of reasons. Clearly, it indicates the way in which elaborate organization and efficiency were understood to facilitate fraternity. It also illustrates how the ritual tended to become something to dispatch efficiently so that the members could enjoy themselves.[48] In addition, the obvious importance of the physical plant of Palestine is a significant feature. The lodge room where the ritual was performed was just one small part; the club-room, dining room, and ballroom point to a trend in Masonic buildings. While only the largest metropolitan areas could boast of such impressive facilities, smaller cities kept pace within their means. Noting the interest in new buildings, the *Builder* remarked that the question of how to build a Masonic Temple for $50,000 had become a frequently asked question. In 1915, the magazine ran an article on a particularly successful, although modest, temple: Kenwood Lodge in Wisconsin. In addition to separate facilities for the various Masonic orders, in the basement was a banquet room for 400 with an ample kitchen. There was also a billiard room, dance hall, and various other rooms that could be devoted to social purposes.[49] Here once again, Masonry parallels developments in the churches. The churches' elaborate physical plants designed to meet the social needs of their parishioners pointed to a secularization tendency within the church.[50] Similarly, Masonic buildings, by reflecting Masons' desires to be entertained, suggest the fraternity's increased secularity. These building innovations provide graphic illustration of the way in which Masonry was being transformed from temple to club.

Other indications of the clublike quality, as well as the organizational impetus of modern lodges, are provided by the careful schemes of Masters to promote fraternity and social exchange among members. Rockridge Lodge in Oakland, with a membership of 336, was faced with increased enrollment but declining attendance. The Master, A. C. Peterson, responded by dividing the membership alphabetically into twelve groups. Each group was assigned a captain who appointed four subcaptains. They were responsible for contacting specific men in their group to urge their attendance. When the plan was implemented, attendance immediately doubled. These groups continued to hold meetings in individual's homes and were given specific responsibilities for lodge activities. They might be in charge of "the entertainment, eats, dances, card parties or other lodge activities." As part of their duties, two members from each group agreed to be present at each meeting during the month, which guaranteed twenty-four men in attendance. They were the greeters and were supposed to make everyone, especially visitors, feel at home. Lodge visitors wore big buttons of a specified color so that they could be spotted easily and welcomed accordingly. Peterson explained that the success of the program stemmed from its ability to make the individual Mason feel that he was making a contribution to lodge life.[51]

James Hamilton Rothberg, the 1924 Master of Fellowship Lodge in Oakland, had a similar plan for integrating new members into the lodge. He felt that after the initial excitement of lodge attendance wore off, and new members continued to sit idly by on the sidelines as mere spectators, they lost interest and ceased coming. Thus in midyear he organized the new members into a "coterie." The new members elected a president and met regularly to gain proficiency in the degree work. They also had social gatherings at each other's homes. "Whatever they do they are held together by a common bond, a common aim, a feeling that they are actually 'one of the bunch.' " At the end of the year, the officers of the lodge stepped down and allowed the class to confer a degree. Importantly, the association did not stop after the end of the year, but continued to meet for social, charitable, and other purposes.[52]

The ways in which Masons turned to efficient organization to promote sociability, as well as fraternity, may also be seen in the proliferation of lodge social clubs. These clubs started around the turn of the century and grew rapidly after World War I, so that by the 1920s, they were an important component of Masonry.[53] One of the purposes of the clubs was to provide entertainment. A representative of the Senators Club of Culver City (California) Lodge No. 467 explained that its purpose was "hilarity," noting that "at the club a continuous round of laughter and joy may be heard."[54] Similarly, the Acacia Club of Shawnee Light Lodge in Louisville, Kentucky promised "an evening of solid enjoyment" where you could "be among your own brethren, whom you know and with whom you are familiar and can slap on the back with a hearty 'hello' and feel at home."[55]

In addition to "hilarity," proponents of social clubs stressed that they provided the fraternity so difficult to find in the formal atmosphere of the large urban lodge. A 1909 account of Masonic clubs explained that large lodges hindered intimacy not only because they were formal and anonymous, but also because they were composed of men of such diverse "tastes, education, means and social position." In contrast, the social club was small, more homogeneous, and more informal. The result was fraternity.

> To supply the lack, to remedy such conditions and to promote a friendly and brotherly spirit among Masons— these are the functions of the Masonic Club. Those will be attracted who would lay aside all stiffness and reserve, who would meet intimately with their brethren on occasions of ease and relaxation. Without the distraction of lodge work and formality of behavior acquaintanceship speedily ripens into friendship, and brotherhood becomes with men thus drawn together a meaningful word.[56]

There are several detailed accounts of the operations of lodge clubs. The Fellow Craft Association of Bridgeport, Connecticut, for example, established a club called a quarry with its own ritual, which "instructs and amuses at the same time." The club's goal was to develop the social side of Masonry, and it was so successful that it spread all over Connecticut. A committee planned fraternal visits throughout the state. In 1923, a "monster" Field Day was being planned for all the Blue Lodge Masons in Connecticut. It was generally agreed that every lodge that had a quarry had seen a revival in interest in Blue Lodge Masonry.[57]

A New York club, the Jamestown Fellow Craft Club, was formed in direct response to the large membership and constant degree work. It performed the third degree for the lodge, but like the quarry, had a "fourth degree"—an amusing ritual that presumably contained a fair amount of horseplay. This group recognized that degree work could not maintain the interest of busy men and that what was needed was an "emphasis on the social features which make gatherings of men attractive." Thus the club also planned numerous social activities to enliven lodge life. Observers felt that the club was highly successful in awakening interest and in giving men something to do with their organization.[58]

Between the clubs and other attempts by Masters to enliven meetings, the quality of Masonic lodge experience changed significantly in the twentieth century. That the tendency toward entertainment and "fun" was widespread is indicated not only by the accounts of individual lodge programs and schemes, but also by the frequent criticism offered this development by conservative Masons. In 1926, an author writing in the New Hampshire *Bulletin* expressed disdain for the decision of a recent conference of New Hampshire Masons to prevent the stagnation of Masonry by emphasizing social activities. The critic asked why the social side of the fraternity must be developed to insure attendance: "Has Masonry reached the state that it is necessary to establish the card games, bowling alleys, opera bouffe, or the banquet table to keep something that has stood the test of hundreds of years?"[59] Another critic of the entertainment trend, Herbert Hungerford, suggested in 1929 that the efforts to transform Masonry into a club had had little effect in solving attendance problems.

> And this ebbing tide of interest in routine Masonic meetings has not been stemmed by the frantic efforts of many Lodges to introduce vaudeville stunts, moving pictures, minstrel shows and other entertaining features to compete with similar outside attractions, which, it is assumed, are drawing members away from their Lodge meetings.[60]

Hungerford's observation is an important one, suggesting the uphill struggle Masters faced in making Masonry an important part of the social life of its members. Although Masters with energy and skill were apparently able to inject vitality into their lodges, their successes were within narrow limits. Their efforts evidently made the fraternity more appealing than traditional Masonry may have been, but it seems clear from the low attendance at even successful lodges, such as Live Oak, that the vast majority of the membership viewed Masonry more as a symbolic than a participatory organization.

Whatever the measure of their success, all of the schemes to improve the quality of lodge life illustrate the importance of the careful organization needed to coordinate the many activities vital to a lodge's success. They also reveal how Masons were embracing secular entertainment at the expense of sacred activities. The secularizing and organizational tendencies of the schemes for rejuvenating the lodges were particularly well demonstrated in the subtle transformation of the idea of fraternity. The struggles of Masters to create an environment more conducive to fraternal exchange indicate that Masonry was plagued not only by its old-fashioned and sacred quality, but also by its failure to provide men with one of its central tenets: fraternity. Its ideals promised brotherhood, yet its expansive growth militated against the possibility of intimacy. The Masters responded with elaborate schemes, clubs, and entertainment. Thus, organization and shared leisure time, rather than the symbolic bond forged by ritual and shared secrets, became the basis of fraternity. Fraternity was increasingly defined as the sharing of good times with good fellows. This perception of fraternity indicates that the secularization of the lodge went beyond the de-emphasis on ritual in favor of social features and permeated a major component of Masonic ideology. Fraternity shed its sacred connotations and became a secular ideal.

Auxiliary Organizations

While Masters and other officials were attempting to reinvigorate Blue Lodge Masonry by secularizing it, a variety of auxiliary organizations were offering Masons alternatives to the lodge. Predicated on membership in the Blue Lodge, these organizations help explain the dichotomy of increased numbers and declining attendance. For while interest in participating in Blue Lodge Masonry was waning, the Shrine, Sciots, and a host of other groups, unhampered by the sacred and ritualistic characteristics of Blue Lodge Masonry, were flourishing. With their emphasis on entertainment, sociability, and practicality, they deflected interest from the lodge by offering a version of Masonry better suited to the needs of men in a secularized, consumption- and business-oriented society.

In the late nineteenth century, Masonic observers frequently complained that men joined Blue Lodge as a means of gaining admission to the higher orders. By World War I, the problem had become more severe. There was a multiplication of auxiliary groups as well as a tremendous expansion of already existing organizations. Both Scottish and York Rites were still considered elite and prestigious. However, while York Rite held its own and Scottish Rite expanded tremendously, both groups suffered problems similar to those of the Blue Lodge in the 1920s. Leaders in both Rites complained of serious attendance problems. They traced the difficulty in part to their Rites' emphasis on ritual and formality. In addition, leaders attributed these problems to men joining the Rites in order to have access to the Shrine, one of the most desirable men's groups of the decade.[61]

The Shrine had always had a reputation as the playground of Masonry, and in the 1920s, this orientation persisted. It offered banquets, parades, entertainments, circuses, and conventions. Its ceremonial ritual, in striking contrast to Blue Lodge degrees, was an amusing and entertaining ceremony. Shriners' love of a good time led many Masonic officials to criticize them for their buffoonery, particularly their public demeanor in parades and conventions. In 1923, for example, an Idaho Grand Master complained that the Shrine in his state undermined the dignity of Masonry:

> For many years in this State it has been a common practice at the periodical ceremonial gatherings of the Shrine for certain members to seize upon the occasion as a fitting time to throw off all restraint and to indulge in drunken debauches and other unseemly conduct, much to the disgrace of themselves and to the chagrin of others who are themselves helpless to protect the good name of Masonry.[62]

Shriners agreed that their proceedings lacked dignity, but claimed that their fun was clean, and more than that, essen-

tial—men needed relaxation and amusements. Shriners articulated a creed of amiable good-fellowship. As Julian D. Harries, a San Francisco Shriner, explained, man is perpetually
beset with difficulties, yet if he faces life with the right spirit
he will persevere. To do this, you should "be a good fellow
yourself, cultivate the 'Hello' spirit and a cheery smile." Good-
fellowship was crucial, Harries explained, because, "almost all
our experiences in life come from contact with the 'other fellow,' and he will surely react to us in exactly the same way in
which we affect him."[63] Similarly, Shriners repeatedly emphasized outward signs of good-fellowship: "A congenial countenance and a hearty handshake contribute so much toward
the joy and real pleasure of life."[64]

This same cult of the good fellow dominated another popular Masonic playground, the Grotto. Founded in 1889, the
Grotto was especially popular in the Midwest, but not well
known on the West Coast. It admitted all third-degree Masons, thus the Scottish or York Rites were not prerequisites.
Like the Shrine, the Grotto was criticized for its horseplay and
lack of decorum. Also like the Shriners, the Grotto's "Proph-
ets" justified their mirth as positive and necessary. The joviality and good times provided by their ceremonials, smokers,
stag parties, entertainments, and picnics allowed men to relax
and forget business cares and the drudgery of everyday life.
And by giving men the opportunity to let their dignity slip a
bit, the revelry of the Grotto broke down the barriers between
men and promoted the spirit of friendship. For those not already adept at good-fellowship, the Kentuck Grotto of Louisville, Kentucky promised to teach them.

Kentuck Grotto supplies that opposite to worry: revelry.
If you see a brother who has forgotten to smile because
his daily vocation demands concentration and energy, go
after him, he is a good prospect. A brother who lets his
dignity get the best of him and is losing firm ground
from under his feet is a good prospect. He needs to be
brought down among us mortals and be taught that life
with all work and no play degenerates into drudgery, and

the price paid is happiness. A brother who is too timid to come out with a smile and assert his personality must be taken by the hand and shown how to make his bow.[65]

The Shrine and the Grotto's emphasis on revelry as a cement to fellowship is significant and very similar to the lodge's adoption of sociability as a means to foster brotherhood. In the past, shared moral virtue and the experience of the ritual linked men together as brothers; what was primarily needed now was shared amusements and informal behavior. Both the Shrine and the Grotto elevated to a philosophy of life, however vaguely expressed, many of the characteristics of Riesman's other-directed man. Sensitivity to one's interaction with others, emphasis on an outgoing and friendly personality, and praise for cooperation and sincerity, coupled with a preoccupation with entertainment and leisure, were the Shriner and the Prophet's ideal characteristics. As both Riesman and Lowenthal argue, the values of production were becoming less valuable in a bureaucratic world. Success in one's job depended as much on style and personal interaction as it did on hard work and skill. And the emphasis went beyond the world of work; to be a successful person, one needed to cultivate cooperation and personality, must know "how to win friends and influence people." The Shrine and the Grotto gave expression to these newer values and, perhaps more importantly, required them. Group pressure within the organization demanded joviality and "personality." The Shrine and the Grotto were thus perfectly suited to an emerging consumer culture.

Although the values espoused by the Shrine and the Grotto were easily adapted to the business world, neither of these organizations placed very much explicit emphasis on the commercial benefits accruing to their members.[66] In striking contrast was the attitude of the Ancient Egyptian Order of Sciots, a West Coast organization of third-degree Masons similar to the Grotto. Although Sciots was open to all Masons in good standing, they freely described themselves as businessmen. The Sciots' business orientation was evident in their motto, B.O.A., or "Boost One Another." One Sciot compared the organization to Rotary, explaining that its "main objective was to patronize the members of the organization in their business and professional life, everything else being equal."[67] Members of local "pyramids" were continually urged to consult their roster's classified directories.[68] Moreover, Sciots had insignia that identified them and, in addition, had decals for their cars and for displays in office windows. And, as part of their emphasis on business, they stressed practical Masonry. Sciots aimed to apply Masonic principles to "everyday life," for "as business men, we place no value upon a philosophy which does not help us in all of the daily relations of life."[69]

In addition to its emphasis on practicality, Sciots, like the Shrine and the Grotto, offered entertainment and fraternal camaraderie, without, one Sciot put it, "the restrictions of the lodge room."[70] However, while these groups were successful in filling many of the voids left by the Blue Lodge, they undoubtedly had difficulty in establishing a sense of intimacy, for all these organizations were large ones, ranging from several hundred to a few thousand members.

There were, however, a number of organizations, small in size, that offered entertainment and practicality, as well as the promise of a more intimate fraternity. Preeminent among them was High Twelve International, a conscious attempt to provide a Masonic alternative to civic clubs. High Twelve started in 1921 in Sioux City, Iowa, when a group of young businessmen, unable to gain admission to the restricted, trade-based civic clubs such as Rotary, sought to organize a club of their own. When they realized that they were all Masons, a luncheon club for Masons seemed the obvious conclusion. The idea quickly spread throughout the country, and by the mid-1920s, the High Twelve clubs were flourishing.[71]

No precise information is available on the occupational breakdown of High Twelve clubs. High Twelve literature suggests that members were primarily businessmen, although there may have been a wide range of white-collar workers.[72] Although patronage networks may have operated informally, High

Twelve officials, unlike Sciots, were anxious from the start to de-emphasize the financial benefits that might accrue to High Twelvers. To underscore the point, its first motto, reminiscent of Rotary, was Service without Profit.[73]

In addition to sharing the goal of Service with civic clubs, High Twelve also promoted sociability and entertainment typical of Rotary and other businessmen's luncheon clubs. High Twelve clubs were small compared to Masonic lodges (117 members was the average size of thirteen representative lodges in 1927).[74] High Twelvers attributed their excellent attendance figures (in the range of 75–90 percent) to their ability to provide a relaxing and enjoyable time.[75] Short talks on business, civic affairs, and general-interest topics were one aspect of the program. But accounts of club life in the magazine, the *High-Twelvian*, stressed the boisterous good times, with much entertainment, community singing, and joking. As an Aberdeen, Washington High Twelver explained, "We have a stunt committee whose mission in life is to provoke hilarity, either by the presentation of some special entertainment, or by making life miserable for some certain member during the duration of the meeting."[76] Invariably, in discussing the joviality and "peppy" atmosphere of High Twelve meetings, observers compared them to the solemnity of Blue Lodge meetings.

> The High Twelve Club is a place for making friends worth while, for doing something to put cheer into other folks' hearts and is a recreational ground for members of the Masonic fraternity. The social features of life, of necessity, cannot be enjoyed to any large degree in the Lodge room. The work in the Lodge room is of a serious ritualistic nature. . . . A Mason would fight for the Order and its principles and yet very many of us do not enjoy social intercourse in any large degree among our brethren, nor the development of one of the greatest things in life— friendships. The High Twelve Club is trying to cultivate this fellowship by bringing together a selected company

of the best men from the greatest order that has ever been devised by the human mind.[77]

High Twelve was successful in part because it provided a smaller, more homogeneous group than the Blue Lodge, and thus enhanced the possibilities for fraternal exchange. The small size and the informal luncheon format promoted an atmosphere of good-fellowship. In addition, High Twelve seems to have been able to offer Masons what progressives had hoped to provide in Blue Lodge Masonry—a secularized and modernized version of Masonry that emphasized the practicality and Service that had made civic clubs popular and prestigious.

Although High Twelve was the only federated Masonic luncheon-club organization, local clubs proliferated throughout the country. Many lodges had their own clubs, and in a number of communities there were luncheon clubs that encompassed all the Masonic orders. Los Angeles's citywide club, for example, had its own "luxurious" clubhouse and offered lunches daily and prominent speakers twice a week. The club also had a stag smoker once a month with professional vaudeville entertainment, as well as a monthly dance.[78]

Sciots, High Twelve, and luncheon clubs, although they probably included low-level white-collar and skilled workers, were oriented toward businessmen. More specifically defined occupational groups proliferated among Masons in this period. One major form was the degree team. The practice of having men from the same company learn the ritualistic parts and visit various lodges to confer a degree on a fellow employee began in the early twentieth century. By 1925, the practice was so widespread that California Grand Master Charles Reese claimed that there was one in "every industrial association, in every professional occupation, in every government and public association."[79] The degree team was a particularly important phenomenon in California. There were dozens of them in the San Francisco Bay area alone, including ones in the San Francisco Fire Department, Bank of Italy, Matson

Navigation, Pacific Gas and Electric, and the Southern Pacific Railroad.[80]

Although some Masonic officials had reservations about the suitability of degree teams, most commentators praised the teams because they fostered Masonic interest, encouraged attendance, and allowed more people to participate. The good attendance did not seem to stem so much from any special skill in rendering the rituals as from the general spirit of camaraderie that degree teams brought to their activity. When a candidate was initiated, other Masons working for the same company generally attended in large numbers. As the *Trestleboard* reported on a 1924 postal workers' degree-team effort, "The unusual interest that is always manifested when a fellow of the worker—a fellow in the daily life—is advanced through the grades of Masonry did not fail in this instance."[81] Although in a big company not everyone would know everyone else, degree teams and an audience of many fellow workers made it more likely that the initiate would be well acquainted with many of the witnesses of his experience. Thus, a special spirit of fellowship was possible among the degree team, initiate, and audience that was not usually available in a large-lodge environment. Masonic officials maintained that this "undefinable spirit of one-ness" in the conferring of the degree could facilitate a stronger commitment to Masonry.[82] More importantly, perhaps, it seems evident that it could strengthen bonds between fellow workers.

Similar to degree teams, although more emphatically social and much less concerned with ritualistic Masonry, were the clubs organized on the basis of occupation. Unfortunately, no statistics exist for the number of occupational clubs, although commentators considered their spread epidemic. One of the most prevalent types of occupational club brought together Masons working for a particular corporation or government agency. Clubs for railroad workers and civil servants were quite numerous, but a wide variety of companies was represented among the clubs.[83]

These clubs apparently encompassed a broad spectrum of

employees and, much like Masonry itself, were generally extolled for the way in which they mitigated distinctions of rank or class. A Cleveland Club of New York Central Railroad Line workers urged any Mason working for the line to come to one of the monthly meetings "to determine for yourself that there is a common level upon which all fellow workers in one of the greatest industrial organizations in the country can meet."[84] Similarly, thirty-eight Los Angeles industrial clubs were praised for the equality and brotherhood they encouraged. As one club member explained, "There [are] usually entertainment features along with a banquet at a moderate cost giving the Brethren opportunity to put their feet under the table and usually get acquainted with the fellow at his elbow, where Presidents, Vice-Presidents, Managers come down from their lofty seats and fraternize."[85]

Although Masonic occupational clubs offered contact between company officials and workers, their practical advantages were considered much broader than this connection. By drawing together men of similar work experience and providing them with entertainment and opportunities for socializing, these clubs enhanced fraternity. For example, a member of a club of Los Angeles postal workers described it as "a social organization whose purpose is to . . . provide means of bringing together, periodically, the Masons employed in the local post office, to the end that they may become better acquainted and drawn more closely together by the joys of fraternalism."[86]

What was particularly important about this fraternity was that by facilitating more intimate association with fellow workers, it promised to produce a more pleasant working environment. The Doric Club, composed of 150 Masons working for Barker Brothers furniture company in Los Angeles, was praised because it helped to "create a greater spirit of fraternalism and places Masonry into practical use in the daily work of those who are fortunate enough to belong to it."[87] Similarly, Cyril DeWyrall commenting in the *Kraftsman* on the esprit de corps of Masons in industrial clubs, explained that "men in industrial life have far greater confidence in each other after their Masonic relations have been brought to light, and are more ready to help each other, which makes for better service, and both employee and employer benefit."[88] Thus, Masonic occupational clubs offered sociability and entertainment. In addition, they held out the implied promise of practical goals such as work advancement, while at the same time creating a fraternal atmosphere more pleasant and less anonymous than the work environment.

Although numerous comments were made about the benefits accruing to a firm where a Masonic club was organized, there is no evidence to suggest that companies themselves originated clubs as a form of welfare capitalism or company unionism. Although undoubtedly companies had little objection to such organizations, the clubs appear to have been far more spontaneous than this. They were the work of groups of Masons eager to form their own club.[89]

These clubs' purposes of fraternity, entertainment, and practicality were also evident in organizations based on specific trades. Clubs consisting of plasterers, accountants, printers, carpenters, building supervisors, and salesmen proliferated with the aims of providing social activities and mutual benefits.[90] The New York Printers' Square Club's purpose was typical—"to foster the knowledge of the entire allied trade [of printing], and to expand socially, good fellowship among its members, to extend pleasure gatherings and to uphold and cultivate the principles of Masonry."[91]

Many clubs of this type affiliated with the National League of Masonic Clubs; for engineers, however, there was a separate organization, the Council of Engineers. This federation of Masonic engineers originated in Cincinnati in 1903. By 1915, the original four councils had expanded to forty-nine councils with 6,000 active members throughout the United States. By 1929, there were fifty-four councils with 12,000 members.[92]

Councils had three main functions. One was to provide "clean" entertainment for Craftsmen and their families—dinners, parties, and outings were frequently reported in the journals. The sociability offered by councils was held to be conducive to improving the sense of fraternity among Masons because it brought together a "group of brothers who have a community of interests and like work and needs."[93]

Another important aspect of the councils was their educational feature. Council monthly or bimonthly meetings featured talks on technical problems; council officers repeatedly urged members to bring their technical difficulties to the meetings. They explained that the educational aspects of the councils promoted that efficiency or skill which could assure the craftsman of advancement. As one official put it, the council "is a body of Masonic engineers who meet . . . to talk over their troubles and to enjoy each others' pleasures. When in trouble come and let it be known. I assure you that there is some brother who will be able to help you. Sometimes a little help along the line of engineering means a big lot to a man who is trying to get up the ladder to that place they call the chief."[94]

The third function of the councils was employment. All councils were required to have an employment committee, and were apparently successful in finding work for their members. Most proudly reported that they had few men out of work. The Cleveland Council of Engineers, for example, had placed fifty-four men in jobs during the first six months of 1915. Of its 331 men, only two were out of work.[95] Their success stemmed in part from the reputation Masonic craftsmen achieved for both their professional and personal merit. In addition, councils apparently were able to keep their members employed by dint of their numbers and organizational strength. A Council of Engineers official, O. N. Pomeroy, described his organization in the *Builder* in 1922 as "powerful enough to enable Masonic engineers to hold their own in the competitive market."[96]

In their formal commitment to employment benefits, craft councils were unique among Masonic occupational groups, yet there were many similarities among the various types of occupationally defined clubs. With the exception of the degree teams, all were secular adaptations of Masonry. All tried to imbue the fraternity with practical value in the world of work. And all reveal the combination of an interest in practicality with the desire to find sociability and fraternity with men of similar occupations. All suggest that men were seeking in Mason-related groups much of what Blue Lodge Masonry had promised, but had had increasing difficulty in delivering in the impersonal atmosphere of the large urban lodge.[97]

It is impossible to estimate how many Masons became involved in subgroups based upon occupation; however, it seems clear that the proliferation of these groups represents a significant structural development in Masonry, which became formally subdivided on the basis of occupation. This specialization is an intriguing phenomenon. Masons were already assumed to be a group of chosen men—the respectable elements of the population, sharing the same ideals and values. Yet the existence of subgroups suggests a desire for a more specific group identification within Masonry. High Twelve, Sciots, and luncheon clubs self-consciously catered to the businessman. The degree teams and other clubs had more specific definitions, catering to various levels of white-collar and skilled blue-collar workers.

What can be concluded from these groupings? Obviously, they suggest a type of occupational consciousness developing within Masonry that, if it existed before, was never formally recognized. Masonry's expansion in the late nineteenth century may be viewed as an attempt to create a homogeneous community of men of shared values and experiences. But now men were apparently finding the lodges themselves too heterogeneous for meaningful participation. As the lodge became larger, the variety of men one encountered there became much more pronounced, encompassing many occupational groups as well as men of diverse interests. Specialization was needed to find a more concrete basis for fraternity and socializing, and the means employed were formal organizations with the men one worked with.

Masonic auxiliary organizations—the playgrounds, the luncheon clubs, the occupational clubs—are significant for a number of reasons. Because many appear to have originated from the ranks rather than from concerted efforts of Masonic officials, they are excellent examples of the way in which individuals found means of participating in the shaping of their institutions. Whatever the origins of the groups, they all reflect attempts to change the nature of Masonic activity. In part, their success helps to explain the dichotomy between Masonic growth and Masonic apathy. While Blue Lodge waned, Masons developed other organizations within the Masonic network more suited to their needs and interests. For many men these organizations probably supplanted the lodge in their allegiance.

Clubs and other organizations seem to have had few of the problems that plagued the Blue Lodge. The reason is not hard to find: They created more homogeneous groups and offered greater possibilities for fraternity. The Shrine, the Grotto, and Sciots, while large groups, seem to have been able to impart a sense of fraternity, if not intimacy, by insisting upon camaraderie and informality. And occupationally defined groups provided sociability with fellow workers to promote the sense of fraternity that was lacking in many Blue Lodges. These organizations not only offered sociability as a facilitator of fraternity, but also provided practical and work-related advantages. Masons were supposed to help one another. Groups like the craftsmen councils made that type of brotherliness a reality. Finally, the success of these organizations stemmed from the fact that they were less bound than Blue Lodges by traditions and regulations; they could jettison those elements of Masonry which proved cumbersome and substitute more congenial, modern ones. By stressing business, occupation, Service, or leisure activities, they broke down the walls of the Masonic asylum. While still maintaining a traditional emphasis on fraternity, they dropped the more sacred and ritualistic characteristics of Masonry to create a secular club.

Like the modernizing efforts of progressives, the schemes

215

to make Blue Lodges more entertaining and the appeal of auxiliary organizations that created a more practical and convivial version of Masonry stemmed from the recognition that the fraternity must adapt itself to the changed concerns, interests, and values of modern Masons. The new social emphasis in Masonry thus illuminates broader patterns in American culture, more specifically, America's evolution toward a consumer society. The Lynds and other observers have pinpointed the generally increased standard of living and increased leisure time in the 1920s as part of the stimulus for the wide variety and importance of leisure-time pursuits so noticeable in that decade. In addition, the technological innovations of the radio, mass-produced automobiles, and motion pictures dramatically transformed the possibilities for leisure and lent new excitement and specialization to entertainment. More leisure, more money to enjoy it, and remarkable strides in technology made Americans—and Masons—more demanding. The simpler social times of nineteenth-century Masonic lodges no longer satisfied. In particular, the ritual, which at one time may have served as a form of entertainment as well as a symbolic, spiritual activity, declined in popularity in the more secular and more amusement-sophisticated times of the 1920s. Masonry and the many other organizations offering opportunities to spend leisure turned to careful and elaborate planning of social functions.[98]

These changes in Masonry not only indicate an emphasis on leisure, but also something of its contours. The occupational specialization in Masonry reflects the increasing role one's job could play in organizing one's social life. In *Middletown*, the Lynds noted that members of the business class tended to combine their leisure-time activities with their careers. The evidence of Masonry suggests that there was a whole range of lower-level white-collar and blue-collar workers in the twentieth century who sought to combine work and leisure time. What is striking about the mingling of social functions and fraternal exchange with the world of work is the way in which it demonstrates the importance of good-fellowship and cooperation in both work and play environments. Fraternalizing Masonically with co-workers indicates that men found it more comfortable to socialize with those in similar employment because of the assurance of a major source of shared interests. It also suggests that men expected the cooperation and friendliness fostered by shared leisure pursuits to improve the conditions of work; they not only made the job more pleasant, but also influenced possibilities for patronage and advancement. Thus, the attributes that contributed to both a happy life and a successful career—sociability, personality, and cooperation—could be developed in the occupational club.

These developments in Masonry indicate the time, money, and energy Americans channeled into their pursuit of leisure, and reflect a move away from the values of production inculcated by late nineteenth-century Masons and an embrace of those associated with a consumer culture. Lodge social activities and auxiliary groups aimed to develop a bond of fraternity based on shared good times—a bond cemented by sociability and cooperation. Above all, they sought to cultivate the "good fellow," the man with the "congenial countenance and . . . hearty handshake." Once an institution dedicated to religion and morality, Masonry's emphasis on piety, industry, sobriety, and self-restraint receded in the 1920s. Masonry changed because modern men wanted an organization more suited to their consumer-oriented society—more secular, more practical, more fun. Instead of emphasizing religion and morality, they wanted to stress patriotism and service. Instead of ritual and solemnity, they sought entertainment and practicality. As in the nineteenth century, Masonry in the 1920s was a microcosm of the male middle-class world; the drive to transform Masonry from temple to club mirrored the cultural and social transformations taking place in the world outside the temple.

Conclusion

No matter how much attendance may have suffered and officials may have worried about Masonic decline, for much of the 1920s the desire to be affiliated with Masonry persisted. Masonry's traditional reputation as a prestigious organization composed of the best men in the community may have been undergoing a transformation in this period, as civic clubs and Masonry's own growth undercut its claim to exclusivity. Yet Masonry still had symbolic importance for many men. As evidenced by auxiliary groups' emphasis on fraternity, that ideal continued to be important. In addition, as Masonry modified its ideology to include Service, as well as an emphasis on the good citizen and the good fellow, it kept pace to some extent with the values of the middle-class men who formed its constituency. Thus, as it had in the late nineteenth century, Masonry could still offer prestige and respectability. It continued to stand for respected values and provided the opportunity of claiming Masonry's ideals as one's own.

The innovations in Masonry in the 1920s helped the organization to survive, but not thrive. It suffered heavy losses during the Depression, as many men dropped out or were suspended and few new members joined. The 1950s saw a slight resurgence, but not a permanent reinvigoration. Masonry never again achieved the popularity and prestige it had enjoyed in the late nineteenth and early twentieth centuries.

The order's decline may be traced to a variety of factors. Masonry's phenomenal growth in the wake of World War I affected its ability to live up to its elite image. Its very popularity hurt its claim to be a prestigious order. In contrast to the civic clubs, for example, Masonry was clearly less selective. Similarly, the large size of urban lodges precluded the sense

218

of fraternity that earlier lodge life may have been able to establish. The development of subgroups within Masonry suggests dissatisfaction with the large, impersonal lodge. Moreover, the occupational emphasis of many of the new auxiliary groups indicates the desire to create a more homogeneous group than could be found in the large heterogeneous lodge.

While internal institutional dynamics such as the rapid growth in membership and the proliferation of large lodges undoubtedly shaped the future of the fraternity, external changes seem by far the most significant. Masonry was well suited to late nineteenth-century America. Although it offered sociability and relief in times of distress, as well as possible financial and political advantages, the most important aspect of the fraternity was the way in which it expressed the religious and moral values of the Victorian middle class. By the 1920s, however, society had changed. The decade had a "modern" tone, as the culture became more secularized and more consumer oriented. None were more aware of these changes than the Masonic leaders who sought to modernize the fraternity in a variety of ways. The Americanization thrust revealed attempts to alter the asylum quality of Masonry and have the fraternity emulate groups like the American Legion that sought to enhance the political power of the native middle class. The efforts to minimize the ritual and religious aspects of the fraternity and model it after civic clubs with their emphasis on Service also indicate a desire to make the fraternity more modern by making it more practical and less sacred. Similarly, the social activities and the auxiliary organizations reveal the drive to bring Masonry up-to-date with the spirit of the times. All led to a deemphasis on the sacred and moralistic. While the efforts to modernize the fraternity met with limited success, they are extremely important: the process of institutional change in Masonry illuminates the process of cultural and social change in American society.

Masonry, then, provides a window on the middle-class world and the process of modernization. But the order is also significant as an archetype of a secret society. According to anthropologist Noel Gist, who studied secret societies in the 1940s, most fraternal orders evidence a striking degree of "cultural patterning."[1] Masonry appears to have been the model for the structure, ritual, government, and function of other orders. Among the major fraternal orders, the Knights of Pythias and the Odd Fellows were most similar to Masonry. Societies such as the Ancient Order of United Workmen and the Knights of Columbus, which were insurance fraternities, paralleled much of Masonry's structure and features and may have functioned for the working-class and immigrant groups in much the same way as Masonry served its middle-class clientele. They could, of course, provide charity, but they also offered rituals, officeholding, secrecy, contacts, entertainment, and fraternity. Moreover, like Masonry, they undoubtedly provided their members with the opportunity to identify with an organization that articulated their values.[2]

Historians have traditionally seen the multiplication of fraternal orders as a result of urban anomie or the breakdown of the family. As was argued in Chapter 3, these are not very satisfactory explanations. Another common analysis has rested upon the concept of Americans as joiners. This view emphasizes the American character and finds the American genius for association linked to the leveling influence of democracy. Charles and Mary Beard, for example, borrowing from Alexis de Tocqueville, stated that in a "democracy which professes equality, the individual without special titles, riches, distinctions, or gifts feels an oppressive sense of weakness alone in a vast mass of general averages; and thus bewildered he seeks strength and confidence in an affiliation with kindred spirits."[3] Undoubtedly, conditions in America contributed to the habit of voluntarism, but the search for the elusive American character as shaped by democracy does not seem particularly productive in this instance. One of its many difficulties is the assumption of a sameness, of "general averages." What should be emphasized is not the leveling of American society, but its diversification and specialization. Fraternities and other organizations in the late nineteenth century multiplied because of the increasing complexity, and in particular, the heterogeneity of American society. Fraternal orders reflected that diversity, providing parallel institutions for men and women of different class, ethnicity, religion, and race. While fraternities were not substitutes for the family, they were psychic communities that brought together men (and women) of shared beliefs and experiences.

Once major institutions, fraternal orders' heyday has long since passed. Many fraternities, like the Masons, still exist and are important to their members. For historians, who have given all too little attention to fraternal orders, their importance is of a different kind. Fraternal orders are vehicles for exploring the experiences and values of specific groups. Moreover, as institutions flourishing in the late nineteenth and early twentieth centuries, they enhance our understanding of the changes accompanying America's industrialization, urbanization, and modernization. Thus, Masonry reveals the nineteenth-century middle-class emphasis on religion and morality, its hostility to materialism, and its fear of change. Masonry provided an asylum, an escape from a disordered world, as well as a means of reaffirming traditional values. By the 1920s, however, the preoccupations of Masons indicate not resistance to change but adaptation. The attempts to modernize the fraternity in the 1920s highlight the contours of an increasingly secular, consumption-oriented middle-class world. But while historians may view Masonry as a vehicle for understanding historical change, Masons themselves used their order as a means of coping with and adjusting to change. In providing brotherhood and defining respectability, Masonry exemplifies the way in which individuals used organizations to develop meaningful ways of interpreting their society and ordering their lives.

Appendixes

Appendix A

TABLE A: Masonic Membership and United States
Native, White, Adult, Male Population, 1850–1970

Year	Masons[a]	Masons as % of native, white, adult, male population[b]
1850	66,000[c]	not available
1860	221,000	not available
1870	446,000	7.3
1880	537,000	6.2
1890	609,000	5.3
1900	854,000	5.9
1910	1,317,000	7.2
1920	2,238,000	10.1
1930	3,303,000	12.0
1940	2,490,000	7.5
1950	3,511,000	8.9
1960	4,099,000	9.3
1970	3,763,000	7.6

SOURCES: Data on Masonry came from Leon Hyneman, *World's Masonic Register* (Philadelphia, 1860); *Proceedings of the Grand Lodge of California*; *Proceedings of the Grand Lodge of Ohio*, 1890, appendix C, pp. 359–360; and from personal communication from California Grand Lodge officials. U.S. population figures are from United States Department of Commerce, *Historical Statistics of the United States: Colonial Times to 1970*, pt. 1 (Washington, D.C., 1975), pp. 16–17.

[a] Rounded to the nearest thousand
[b] Over age 20; 21 was the minimum age for joining Masonry
[c] Estimate

225

Appendix B: Occupations

Occupations for Live Oak Masons were obtained from applications and the secretary's ledger. Since an individual's occupation was only given for the year he joined, the Oakland City Directory was used to determine his occupation for the specific years used in this study—1880, 1890, 1900, 1920, and 1930. Not all Masons could be traced. Occupations were not known for 18.1 percent of 105 men in 1880; 7.7 percent of 183 in 1890; 10.6 percent of 379 men in 1900; 16.2 percent of 987 men in 1920; and 28.8 percent of 1,131 men in 1930. These "unknowns" were either not listed in the directory or listed without occupations. On the one hand, it seemed unwarranted to assume the same occupation for a man who joined, for example, in 1910, but could not be traced to 1920. On the other hand, leaving out unknowns from the distribution seemed likely to skew the data more heavily toward higher occupational groups, assuming that these groups might be most likely to stay in Oakland and be listed in the directories. To evaluate the extent to which these unknowns might skew results, I drew up two tables—one with unknowns omitted, another with unknowns included under their last known occupation. With the exception of 1880, when no previous occupation was available for most unknowns, the occupation distributions that included unknowns did not vary appreciably from those that did not. These comparison tables are available in my dissertation, "Brotherhood and Respectability: Freemasonry and American Culture, 1880–1930" (University of California, Berkeley, 1981), appendix B. Table B-1, below, omits unknowns.

Material for Durant Lodge was drawn from a printed roster list that included occupations (available at the Bancroft Library, University of California, Berkeley). All other occupational information came from the records of the Grand Lodge of Free and Accepted Masons of California.

Eight categories have been used for occupations: (1) high-level white collar (professionals, manufacturers, etc.); (2) proprietors; (3) low-level white collar; (4) skilled workers; (5) semiskilled workers; (6) unskilled workers; (7) students; and (8) retired. Except for category 2 (proprietors), these categories were adapted from Stephan Thernstrom, *The Other Bostonians: Poverty and Progress in the American City* (Cambridge, Mass., 1973), appendix B, pp. 240–272. Thernstrom uses property values of $5,000 to divide proprietors into high-level and low-level white collar. There are several reasons that I chose to use a separate category for proprietors. One is the

TABLE B-1: Live Oak Lodge Occupation Distribution
1880, 1890, 1900, 1920, 1930

Category[a]	1880 (%)	1890 (%)	1900 (%)	1920 (%)	1930 (%)
1. High-level white collar	14.0	19.5	21.2	19.8	19.6
2. Proprietor	31.4	25.5	20.3	10.9	8.3
3. Low-level white collar	29.1	33.1	38.1	46.6	48.8
4. Skilled worker	20.8	14.2	14.5	16.4	14.3
5. Semiskilled worker	1.2	4.7	3.5	1.6	3.2
6. Unskilled worker	3.5	1.2	0.6	0	0
7. Student	0	0.6	0.3	0.7	0.4
8. Retired	0	1.2	1.5	4.0	5.4
Number known	86	169	339	827	805
Number unknown	19	14	40	160	326
Total	105	183	379	987	1,131

[a] See the introduction to Appendix B for description and discussion of occupation categories.

difficulty of determining property values; another is the arbitrariness of assuming a set valuation of property through time. More importantly, it seemed useful for this study to keep proprietors separate, because of the patronage possibilities of Masonic membership. Category 2 includes small businessmen—florists, restaurateurs, carpet merchants, auto dealers, etc. It also contains a small number of skilled workers who operated their own businesses, such as contractors and butchers. Category 2 may contain some "big" merchants who belong in category 1. Similarly, category 4 may contain some self-employed craftsmen who belong in category 2. Such misgroupings are inevitable. In general, however, I feel that the tables provide an accurate sense of the Live Oak membership's occupational distribution.

Category 8 (retired) includes men who stated that they were retired, as well as Masons who were listed in the Oakland directory without occupations who were over 65. In addition, any man over 80 was included in category 8.

TABLE B-2: 1919 Occupation Distribution for Oakland
No. 188, Brooklyn, and Alcatraz Lodges

Category[a]	Oakland No. 188 (%)	Alcatraz (%)	Brooklyn (%)
1. High-level white collar	22.2	8.7	10.0
2. Proprietors	13.3	7.3	13.0
3. Low-level white collar	38.2	28.1	44.0
4. Skilled workers	18.2	43.3	23.4
5. Semiskilled workers	2.3	11.8	6.2
6. Unskilled workers	0.2	0.6	0.3
7. Students	1.0	0	2.8
8. Retired	4.6	0.2	0.3
Number known	518	356	291
Number unknown	23	6	8
Total	541	362	299

SOURCE: California Grand Lodge Records. As in the case of Live Oak Lodge, there may be a number of skilled craftsmen in category 4 who owned their own businesses and should more properly be in category 2. Moreover, the occupation data for these lodges may be more problematical than Live Oak's, since they were not refined by consulting city directories or application forms.

[a] See the introduction to Appendix B for a discussion of occupation categories.

Appendix C: Attendance

Attendance figures for Live Oak Lodge were obtained from the Tyler's register—an attendance book signed as members entered the lodge—for the years 1880, 1885, 1890, 1895, 1900, 1920, and 1928. The table provides the yearly average number of the total lodge membership attending stated (monthly) and called (special) meetings. The average attendance dropped sharply after 1880 and continued to decline steadily until 1920, when it improved slightly. There is no discernible reason for the sharp drop between 1880 and 1885. (The attendance figures for another Oakland lodge, Oakland No. 188, were obtained for 1890, and they show the same poor attendance.) While these figures indicate the percentage of membership attending lodge meetings, it should be noted that lodges had visitors from other lodges; in many instances there were as many visitors as members, so the lodge was not quite so empty as the lodge membership percentage would indicate. For a detailed study of individual attendance patterns, see my dissertation, "Brotherhood and Respectability: Freemasonry and American Culture, 1880–1930" (University of California, Berkeley, 1981), appendix C.

TABLE C: Live Oak Lodge Average Attendance

Year	Total Membership	Average Percentage of Members Attending[a]		
		Stated[b]	Called	All Meetings
1880	105	26.0	18.0	22.0
1885	135	13.0	14.5	11.4
1890	183	12.4	13.7	12.9
1895	242	10.6	12.2	11.9
1900	379	9.0	9.6	4.0
1920	913	10.6	4.4	5.4
1928	1,131	14.8	5.0	5.6

[a] For a discussion of data for attendance, see the introduction to Appendix C.

[b] Twelve meetings yearly. For each year, the total number of meetings (stated and called) was: *1880*, 44; *1885*, 32; *1890*, 38; *1895*, 49; *1900*, 74; *1920*, 88; and *1928*, 44.

Notes

ABBREVIATIONS: *Journals of Proceedings* from the various states are listed by an abbreviation of the state name, followed by "*Proc.*"

PREFACE

1. Charles A. Beard and Mary Beard, *The Rise of American Civilization* (New York, 1927), 2: 761.
2. Dorothy Ann Lipson has provided an excellent account of early American Masonry in *Freemasonry in Federalist Connecticut, 1789–1835* (Princeton, N.J., 1977). There are two major studies on black Masonry: see William Alan Muraskin, *Middle-Class Blacks in a White Society: Prince Hall Freemasonry in America* (Berkeley, Calif., 1975); Loretta J. Williams, *Black Freemasonry and Middle-Class Realities* (Columbia, Mo., 1980). For a study of a Catholic fraternal order, see Christopher Kauffman, *Faith and Fraternalism: The History of the Knights of Columbus, 1882–1982* (New York, 1982). Brian Greenberg offers a brief account of the Odd Fellows in "Worker and Community: Fraternal Orders in Albany, New York, 1845–1885," *Maryland Historian* 8 (Fall 1977): 38–53. See also Greenberg's dissertation, "Worker and Community: The Social Structure of a Nineteenth-Century American City, Albany, New York, 1850–1884" (Princeton University, 1981), chap. 5. Another important study of fraternalism is anthropologist Noel Pitts Gist's "Secret Societies: A Cultural Study of Fraternalism in the United States," *University of Missouri Studies* 15 (October 1940). Gist examined a variety of secret societies to explore the "cultural patterning" existing among them. In their organizational structure, ritual, and ideology, he found striking similarities. Although Gist provided valuable information on fraternal organizations in 1940, he did not study any single group in depth nor examine how these societies changed over time. Fraternal orders are given passing attention in such

classic works as Charles Beard and Mary Beard, *The Rise of American Civilization*, 2 vols. (New York, 1927); Arthur M. Schlesinger, *The Rise of the City 1879–1898* (New York, 1933) and "Biography of a Nation of Joiners," in *Paths to the Present* (Boston, 1949). Roland Berthoff offers a brief analysis of fraternal orders in *An Unsettled People: Social Order and Disorder in American History* (New York, 1971); see especially pp. 270–274, 444–454. There is, of course, a wealth of sociological literature on voluntary associations. Little of it is theoretical and few sociologists have addressed fraternal orders specifically. An exception is Alvin J. Schmidt, *Oligarchy in Fraternal Organizations: A Study in Organizational Leadership* (Detroit, Mich., 1973). For a basic introduction to the literature of voluntary associations, see Constance Smith and Anne Freedman, eds., *Voluntary Associations: Perspectives in the Literature* (Cambridge, Mass., 1972).

3. B. H. Meyer, "Fraternal Beneficiary Societies in the United States," *American Journal of Sociology* 6 (March 1901): 650. Freemasons, Odd Fellows, and Knights of Pythias accounted for two and one-quarter million; forty-seven other national organizations had two and one-half million, with the remainder scattered in smaller societies.

4. There are many typologies of voluntary associations. Arnold Rose coined the term *expressive*, and C. Wayne Gordon and Nicholas Babchuk added *instrumental* and *instrumental-expressive* (see Smith and Freedman, *Voluntary Associations*, pp. 2–10).

CHAPTER 1

1. Samuel W. Dexter in David Brion Davis, ed., *The Fear of Conspiracy: Images of Un-American Subversion from the Revolution to the Present* (Ithaca, N.Y., 1971), p. 80.

2. Dorothy Ann Lipson, *Freemasonry in Federalist Connecticut, 1789–1835* (Princeton, N.J., 1977), pp. 1–45; Ronald Formisano and Kathleen Smith Kutolowski, "Antimasonry and Masonry: The Genesis of Protest, 1826–1827," *American Quarterly* 29, no. 2 (Summer 1977): 139–165.

3. Lipson, *Freemasonry in Federalist Connecticut*, passim.

4. On anti-Masonry, see Formisano and Kutolowski, "Antimasonry and Masonry"; Lipson, *Freemasonry in Federalist Connect-*

icut, pp. 267–311; David Brion Davis, "Some Themes of Counter-Subversion: An Analysis of Anti-Masonic, Anti-Catholic, and Anti-Mormonism Literature," *Mississippi Valley Historical Review* 47, no. 2 (September 1960): 205–224; Ronald Formisano, *The Birth of Mass Political Parties: Michigan, 1827–1861* (Princeton, N.J., 1971), pp. 60–71; Lorman Ratner, *Antimasonry: The Crusade and the Party* (Englewood Cliffs, N.J., 1969).

5. For the damage done to Masonry during the 1820s and 1830s, see Ralph J. Pollard, *Freemasonry in Maine, 1726–1945* (Portland, Maine, n.d.), pp. 47-53; Thomas Sherrard Roy, *Stalwart Builders: A History of the Grand Lodge of Masons in Massachusetts, 1733–1970* (Boston, 1971), p. 149. For a discussion of the expansion of another fraternal order, the Odd Fellows, see Brian Greenberg, "Worker and Community: Fraternal Orders in Albany, New York, 1845–1885," *Maryland Historian* 8 (Fall 1977): 38–53. For a detailed discussion of changes in the religious climate and their impact on Masonry, see the following chapter.

6. *Chicago Tribune*, 23 June 1874, 25 June 1874. *N.Y. Proc.*, 1885, pp. 48–57. Between 1866 and 1912, for example, Iowa's Grand Lodge laid the cornerstones for ninety-four buildings, which included twenty courthouses, twenty-seven Masonic buildings, and thirteen churches: Episcopalian, Methodist, Universalist, Christian, and African Methodist Episcopalian (William F. Cleveland, *History of the Grand Lodge of Iowa, A.F.&A.M.* [Cedar Rapids, Iowa? 1913], vol. 2, pt. 1, pp. 362-365). Both the *Oakland Tribune* and *Chicago Tribune* offered fraternal columns. The *Fraternal Monitor*, a journal directed primarily at fraternities with insurance features, was delighted with the attention given secret societies. In an 1890 article entitled "Fraternal Power," the editor noted, "The fraternal departments of the live, progressive publications of the day are as important and necessary as the political, the financial, or the religious" (*Fraternal Monitor* 1 [1 December 1890]: 6–7).

7. California Grand Lodge, *The California Digest of Masonic Law* (San Francisco, 1867), pp. 5–7, 106.

8. For white Masonic response to Prince Hall, see *Pacific Mason* 4 (August 1898): 200–209; ibid., 4 (October/November 1898): 248–264. For an account of Prince Hall Masonry, see William Alan Muraskin, *Middle-Class Blacks in a White Society: Prince Hall*

Freemasonry in America (Berkeley, Calif., 1975); Loretta J. Williams, *Black Freemasonry and Middle-Class Realities* (Columbia, Mo., 1980).

9. Live Oak Lodge records do not contain place of birth; however, birthplaces for 72 out of 506 men are available. This sample, drawn from an account of Live Oak Lodge officers and from Oakland Scottish Rite records, is highly skewed toward the Masonic elite. Of these 72 men, 80 percent were born in the United States, 12 percent in the British Isles and Canada, 4 percent in Germany, and 4 percent in other countries. If what obtained for these officers and Scottish Rite Masons obtained for the membership as a whole, Live Oak contained a far greater percentage of native-born men than Oakland as a whole. In 1890, for example, 55.6 percent of Oakland's adult white males were native born (*Souvenir: Fortieth Anniversary Celebration of Live Oak Lodge* [Oakland, Calif., 1896], passim; Secretary's Ledger, Oakland A&ASR Scottish Rite; U.S. Bureau of the Census, *Eleventh Census, 1890: Population*, pt. 1 [Washington, D.C., 1895], p. 790).

Records for two other Oakland lodges for 1912 were available and reveal a high percentage of native-born Masons. Alcatraz Lodge had a total of 362 members. For 61 of these men, no birthplace is recorded. Of the remainder, 69 percent were native born, and of the foreign born, 71 percent were from Canada and the British Isles. Oakland Lodge No. 188, had 541 members. For 21 of these no birthplace is recorded. Of the remainder, 75 percent were native born and of the foreign born, 61 percent were from Canada and the British Isles (California Grand Lodge archives).

Roy Rosenzweig, in a study of Boston Masons for 1900–1935, found them to be predominantly native born. "In a systematic sample of seventy members drawn from a 1901 list of members of Boston's Joseph Webb Lodge, and traced to the 1900 U.S. Manuscript Census, eighty-six percent were American-born. And of these native Americans, ninety percent were sons of New England. The few foreign-born came almost exclusively from English Canada and Scotland" (Rosenzweig, "Boston Masons, 1900–1935: The Lower Middle-Class in a Divided Society," *Journal of Voluntary Action Research* 6 [July–October

1977]: 120). Anthony Fels, however, who is working on a dissertation (Stanford University) on San Francisco's Masons in the late nineteenth century, has told me that his preliminary findings indicate that immigrants were well represented in San Francisco Masonry, and that they were not isolated in ethnic lodges.

10. In 1900, Oakland's four lodges (Live Oak, Brooklyn, Alcatraz, and Oakland) contained 989 men. Of these, 11 names were clearly Jewish; another 4 may well have been. Including the 4 "possibles," the percentage of men with Jewish names in Oakland Masonry was 1.5. Anthony Fels has told me that his research indicates that Jews were much more numerous in San Francisco lodges (see *Calif. Proc.*, 1900, passim). I am indebted to Susan Glenn for assistance in identifying Jewish names.

11. *Trestleboard* 9 (November 1895): 527–528. Rosenzweig notes the existence of Jews in Boston, but claims that it was not until the late 1920s that many Jews joined Boston Masonry. Even then, they tended to join Jewish lodges (Rosenzweig, "Boston Masons, 1900–1935," p. 120).

In 1918, Norman Frederick de Clifford, a non-Jewish Mason, published a book in which he chastised Masons for their anti-Semitism, and claimed that it had long been an unwritten rule in many lodges to exclude Jews (de Clifford, *The Jew and Masonry*, Lion's Paw Series, vol. 2 [Brooklyn, N.Y., 1918], pp. 4–20).

12. *Trestleboard* 9 (November 1893): 516–517, reprinted from *American Tyler*; see also ibid., 7 (February 1893): 49; ibid., 7 (December 1893): 567; ibid., 6 (October 1892): 438–447. The *Trestleboard* and the *American Tyler* were so shrill in their protestations against Catholicism that they echoed the viewpoints of the rabidly anti-Catholic American Protective Association.

13. *Masonic Advocate* 38 (December 1905): 460–462; *American Tyler* 2 (5 December 1889): 130. For a personal account of one well-known Catholic who joined Masonry, see Terrence V. Powderly, *The Path I Trod: The Autobiography of Terrence V. Powderly*, edited by Harry J. Carman, Henry David, and Paul N. Guthrie (New York, 1968). Powderly had been denied entrance into a cathedral because he was wearing a lapel emblem of the Machinist and Blacksmiths' International Union, which

resembled the Mason's square and compass. He remembered this when he was asked to join the Knights of Columbus, a Catholic secret society. He based his decision to join Masonry instead on his favorable impressions of Masons. He recalled that when visiting a scene of labor strife, he generally asked Masons for information. "That day, holding the petition of the Knights of Columbus in my hand, I recalled that fact that never once was I misled or misinformed as to local conditions by a man who wore the Masonic emblem. . . . Often I had said to myself, 'That organization must be based on sound principles to attract such men to it.' " Powderly became a Mason in 1901 (pp. 318–319, 370–371). For a Catholic account of Catholicism and secret societies, see Fergus MacDonald, *The Catholic Church and the Secret Societies in the United States*, United States Catholic Historical Series, monograph 22 (New York, 1946), pp. 3, 97, and passim.

14. See, for example, W. Lloyd Warner, *Democracy in Jonesville* (New York, 1949), pp. 118–119. Rosenzweig found Boston Masons to be primarily lower middle class. In a sample of 573 Masons in six lodges, he found that 77 percent were white-collar workers, as compared with 36 percent for Boston's entire labor force. Half of the sample was lower middle class—salesmen, clerks, and petty proprietors. This average includes data from 1899, 1901, 1930, 1933, and 1934 (Rosenzweig, "Boston Masons, 1900–1935," pp. 121–122).

15. Live Oak's proportion of white-collar workers was high compared to Oakland as a whole, whose white-collar workers comprised only 38.7 percent of all Oakland workers in 1900. I am indebted to Michael Griffith for the breakdown of the 1900 occupational census.

16. Lodge initiation fees for any year may be found in the Grand Lodge proceedings of most states. For Oakland wages, see U.S. Bureau of the Census, *Tenth Census, 1880: Social Statistics of Cities*, pt. 2 (Washington, D.C., 1887), pp. 783–788. It is likely that the workingmen who had the means to invest in lodge membership joined fraternal orders that had contractual insurance features, such as the International Order of Redmen or the Ancient Order of United Workmen. For a brief discussion of other fraternal orders, see Albert C. Stevens, *The Cyclopaedia of Fraternities* (New York, 1907). For a more recent account, see

Charles Wright Ferguson, *Fifty Million Brothers: A Panorama of American Lodges and Clubs* (New York, 1937). For insurance features of fraternal societies, see Abb Landis, "Life Insurance by Fraternal Orders," *American Academy of Political and Social Science Annals* 24 (1904): 475–488; B. H. Meyer, "Fraternal Beneficiary Societies in the United States," *American Journal of Sociology* 6 (March 1901): 646–661; and Walter Basye, *History and Operation of Fraternal Insurance* (Rochester, N.Y., 1919). The *Fraternal Monitor* is a useful primary source for fraternal societies with insurance features.

17. For a detailed breakdown of California and Texas Masons in urban and rural lodges, see my dissertation, "Brotherhood and Respectability: Freemasonry and American Culture, 1880–1930" (University of California, Berkeley, 1981), appendixes A-2 and A-3. California and Texas Masonry, for example, reflected the degree of urbanization in these states. In 1880, 39.8 percent of Californians lived in cities of 4,000 or more, while 36 percent of the state's Masons were in urban lodges. Texas was a far more rural state, and Masonic membership reflects this. In 1880, 7.25 percent of Texans lived in cities of 4,000 or more, and 8.34 percent of Masons were in urban lodges.

18. Comparative occupational statistics for Oakland lodges in the late nineteenth century are not available. However, records for three Oakland lodges in 1912 do exist, and they reveal significant differences. Oakland Lodge No. 188, which according to its historian was a prestigious lodge, had 73.7 percent white-collar workers. Brooklyn Lodge was slightly less white collar, with 67.0 percent in this category. Alcatraz Lodge, which was noted for being a railroad workers' lodge, had only 44.1 percent white-collar workers (see Appendix B-2).

19. See, for example, Walter B. Hill, "The Great American Safety-Valve," *Century* 44 (July 1892): 383–384; Charles Beard and Mary Beard, *The Rise of American Civilization* (New York, 1927), 2: 763; Arthur M. Schlesinger, "Biography of a Nation of Joiners," in *Paths to the Present* (Boston, 1949), p. 39.

20. Robert Macoy, *Worshipful Master's Assistant: The Encyclopedia of Useful Knowledge* (New York, 1885), p. 19; Albert G. Mackey, *A Manual of the Lodge; or, Monitorial Instructions in the Degrees of Entered Apprentice, Fellow Craft, and Master Mason* (New York, 1871), passim. The appointment procedure and the automatic

rotation was frequently criticized by Masonic spokesmen. The former gave the appearance that a "clique" dominated the lodge. The latter meant that officers might be advanced automatically without regard for their ability to rule the lodge. See, for example, *Calif. Proc.*, 1879, p. 141; *Trestleboard* 13 (January 1899): 109–110; ibid., 9 (March 1895): 120; *American Tyler* 20 (1 September 1905): 94.

21. For a breakdown of Live Oak officeholding patterns, see my dissertation, appendix B-6. Similar officeholding patterns were found in five other California lodges for the period from 1880 to 1900. See the rosters in *Calif. Proc.* for California Lodge No. 1 (San Francisco), Clay Lodge No. 101 (Dutch Flat, Placer County), Hallenbeck Lodge No. 319 (Los Angeles), Silbeyville Lodge No. 201 (Solano), and Redlands Lodge No. 300 (San Bernardino). Oligarchy was also evident in the California Grand Lodge offices. Between 1880 and 1900, 185 men filled 441 positions; 34 men occupied the 126 most important Grand Lodge offices. For a sociological study of the oligarchy in fraternal orders, see Alvin J. Schmidt, *Oligarchy in Fraternal Organizations: A Study in Organizational Leadership* (Detroit, Mich., 1973).

22. Mackey, *Manual of the Lodge*, pp. 10–11.

23. For an account of the various Masonic orders, see Stevens, *Cyclopaedia of Fraternities*, pp. 1–6, 17–55.

24. *Chicago Tribune*, 7 November 1890.

25. *Trestleboard* 2 (1888): 306–307; see also pp. 6, 179.

26. Ibid., 17 (September 1904): 114.

27. Ibid., 12 (December 1898): 557; Oakland A&ASR Scottish Rite Records. According to an M. C. Lilley Company ad, a Knights Templar uniform cost $71 (*Masonic Chronicle* 3 [April 1884]: 88).

28. In 1880, for the United States as a whole, 22.1 percent of all Masons pursued York Rite, and only 8.9 percent were in Knights Templar. By 1900, the ratio had become smaller, and Knights Templar were more prevalent (26.5 and 14.9 percent, respectively). Scottish Rite was even more exclusive—only 1.6 percent of all Masons were Scottish Rite Masons in 1880, with the percentage rising to 4.6 in 1900. Complete figures are not available for the Shrine. In 1892, the order had approximately 23,000 members or less than 4 percent of all Masons (George M. Saunders, *A Short History of the Shrine* [Chicago, n.d.], p. 2). For

details on Live Oak membership in "higher orders," see my dissertation, appendix B-5.

29. *Trestleboard* 26 (May 1913): 327.

30. *Voice of Masonry* 28 (October 1890): 775.

31. Arthur R. Andersen, *How Sturdy an Oak: A Centennial History, Live Oak Lodge No. 61, Free and Accepted Masons in California* (Oakland, Calif., 1954), p. 41.

32. *Oakland Tribune*, 22 February 1881; "Special Edition of Fifty Thousand Copies," *Oakland Tribune*, January 1887, p. 42 (this fifty-page celebration of Oakland included a sketch of the temple and one-and-a-half columns on Masonry in Oakland); Oakland Board of Trade, *Oakland, California* (Oakland, 1886); *Chicago Tribune*, 7 November 1890; Carl W. Condit, *The Chicago School of Architecture: A History of Commercial and Public Building in the Chicago Area, 1875–1925* (Chicago, 1965), p. 104.

33. The extent of the charitable activities of boards of relief varied. Financed by contributions from city lodges, between 1881 and 1890, New York's board dispensed $14,408 to 1,682 applicants, the majority of whom were from foreign countries (*N.Y. Proc.*, 1890, p. 17). In California, all major cities had boards of relief to meet the problems caused by a large influx of Masons migrating from other jurisdictions. The boards were quite active. In 1890 alone, the San Francisco board dispensed $10,481 to 157 cases, for an average of $66.76 (*Calif. Proc.*, 1890, pp. 478–488).

34. Iowa's Leighton Lodge No. 387, for example, had a forty-seven-year-old Mason in poor health with dependents. In 1893, the lodge furnished $85. The lodge's Senior Warden personally provided some aid, and the Grand Lodge contributed $300 (Cleveland, *History of the Grand Lodge of Iowa*, vol. 2, pt. 1, pp. 205–229).

35. Ibid., vol. 2, pt. 1, pp. 222–230. See also *Trestleboard* 5 (October 1891): 433–437. For a discussion of the operation of California's Masonic home, see *Trestleboard* 4 (September 1890): 268; *Calif. Proc.*, 1899, pp. 208–218.

36. [California Grand Lodge of Free and Accepted Masons], *A History of the Masonic Widows' and Orphans' Home of California* (San Francisco, 1898), p. 21.

37. Frederic H. Kent to Live Oak Lodge, 2 February 1883, Live

Oak letters; Samuel Gompers, *Seventy Years of Life and Labor* (New York, 1925), 2: 204.

38. Of these 506 Masons, no occupational information was available for 4.2 percent. Salesmen, proprietors, and service professionals comprised 48.6 percent. Compared to the city of Oakland as a whole, this is a high percentage. For example, in 1900, only 19.6 percent of Oakland's labor force was engaged in sales, service professions, or as merchants (U.S. Bureau of the Census, *Twelfth Census, 1900: Population*, pt. 2 [Washington, D.C., 1902], p. 582). The remaining 47.2 percent of the lodge had both white- and blue-collar occupations, in which the usefulness of a Masonic connection was not readily apparent. However, Masonry may have been useful in obtaining jobs and perhaps promotions, so the range of occupations for which Masonry was beneficial may have been quite large.

39. *Trestleboard* 9 (December 1895): 583; ibid., 11 (June 1897): 252–253; ibid., 6 (December 1903): 561.

40. See, for example, John Stewart Ross, ed., *Digest and Compilation of Approved Decisions and Regulations by the Grand Lodge of Free and Accepted Masons of California, 1850 to and including the Annual Communication, October 1931* (San Francisco, 1932), pp. 340–395; *Revised Constitution, General Regulations and Grand Lodge Standing Resolutions with Annotated Decisions of the Grand Lodge of Free and Accepted Masons of Minnesota* (Saint Paul, Minn., 1915).

41. Edwin A. Sherman, Fifty Years of Masonry in California (San Francisco, 1898), 1: 211, 366.

42. Lodges generally welcomed visiting Masons, but Masonic law required them to satisfy a committee on credentials as to their Masonic bona fides. If the visitor had no one of that lodge to vouch for him, he had to demonstrate knowledge of the fraternity's secrets and answer a series of standardized questions designed to prove his brotherhood.

43. Macoy, *Worshipful Master's Assistant*, pp. 14, 15, 25, 50; Albert G. Mackey, *The Symbolism of Freemasonry* (New York, 1869), pp. 136–141.

44. For an account of secret-society rituals, including those of Masonry, see Noel Pitts Gist, "Secret Societies: A Cultural Study of Fraternalism in the United States," *University of Missouri Studies* 15 (October 1940).

45. *Calif. Proc.*, 1883, p. 161.
46. *Texas Masonic Journal* 1 (November 1886): 411–412, reprinted from the *Freemason's Journal*.
47. Lipson, *Freemasonry in Federalist Connecticut*, pp. 187–197, 329–338. Though the Eastern Star was predominantly a women's organization, men could be members. For a brief account of the Order of the Eastern Star, see Stevens, *Cyclopaedia of Fraternities*, pp. 98–99. For a typical Masonic account, see *Texas Masonic Journal* 2 (May 1887): 175–176.
48. Arthur W. Calhoun, *A Social History of the American Family*, vol. 3, *From 1865 to 1919* (New York, 1919), pp. 161, 192. On the separate spheres, see Carl N. Degler, *At Odds: Women and the Family from the Revolution to the Present* (New York, 1980), pp. 26–51; Peter Gabriel Filene, *Him/Her/Self: Sex Roles in Modern America* (New York, 1974), pp. 3–104.
49. James Pettibone, ed., *The Lodge Goat, Goat Rides, Butts, and Goat Hairs: Gathered from the Lodge Rooms of Every Fraternal Order* (Cincinnati, Ohio, 1902), p. 206. This is an interesting collection. Lodge humor among fraternal orders seems interchangeable.
50. *Trestleboard* 1 (November 1887): 321. See also ibid., 13 (November 1899): 578; ibid., 7 (March 1893): 111, 133; *Masonic Record* 7 (June 1887): 4.
51. In *Men in Groups*, Lionel Tiger has investigated the phenomenon of male bonding and argues that it is an evolutionary remnant of primate hunting patterns. While Tiger's biological determinism is not a particularly convincing argument for the source of male bonding, his book does address an important aspect of human association. It seems evident that male bonding does and did exist, and that it was an important component of the dynamics of Masonry (Lionel Tiger, *Men in Groups* [New York, 1969]).
52. To give a clearer sense of participation in the lodge, individual attendance records for Live Oak were tabulated for these years. The percentage of men who never attended a meeting ranged from 25 to 41 percent. With the exception of 1880, there were relatively few years with consistent attenders. For the other four years, no more than 8 percent attended more than one-half of the meetings. To some extent, attendance may be correlated to occupation. If attendance at 0–10 percent of the meetings is considered poor attendance, then for all years studied, the high-

level white-collar workers were consistently poor attenders. With the exception of one year (1885), when they were the worst, low-level white-collar workers were the best attenders, with skilled workers running them a close second. As the membership in higher bodies and officeholding indicate, the backbone of Live Oak Lodge was lower-middle-class men. While occupation may be correlated to attendance, other variables are clearer. Attendance was highest among men who had been in the craft less than five years and among the younger members. Membership in other Masonic bodies does not appear to have affected attendance. Live Oak Masons in Scottish and York Rites did not have lower attendance than other members of the lodge. For a detailed breakdown of these data, see my dissertation, appendixes C-2, C-3, C-4, and C-5.

53. See, for example, *American Tyler* 3 (17 May 1890): 1; *Masonic Home Journal* 4 (14 June 1886): 20; *Trestleboard* 2 (June 1888): 16; ibid., 5 (November 1892): inset pp. [1–6]; *Masonic Advocate* 13 (September 1880): 139.

54. *Trestleboard* 10 (October 1897): 495–496; ibid., 11 (November 1899): 556–557; ibid., 13 (January 1889): 47.

55. See chap. 6, p. 187.

56. Robert Michels, *Political Parties* (Glencoe, Ill., 1949); Bernard Barber, "Participation and Mass Apathy in Associations," in *Studies in Leadership: Leadership in Democratic Action*, edited by Alvin W. Gouldner (New York, 1950), pp. 477–504; David Sills, *The Volunteers: Means and Ends in a National Organization* (New York, 1957), pp. 32–35, 62–68; idem, "Voluntary Associations: Sociological Aspects," in *International Encylopedia of the Social Sciences* (New York, 1968), 16: 362–379; Robert K. Merton, *Social Theory and Social Structure* (Glencoe, Ill., 1949), pp. 153–157.

57. Of course, not all men stayed in the fraternity. Suspension for nonpayment of dues was a major source of attrition. California's yearly average for suspensions for nonpayment for the period from 1880 to 1900 was 326, compared to an average of 818 new members each year. Another sign of disaffection was nonaffiliation. A Mason in good standing became a nonaffiliate when he obtained a "demit" from his lodge. Theoretically, a demit allowed him to transfer to another lodge by paying an affiliation fee and submitting to a ballot by the new lodge. The difficulty

was that many thousands of men demitted without reaffiliating. In 1890, for example, Masons estimated that there were 500,000 nonaffiliates in the United States and Canada (*Trestleboard* 13 [May 1890]: 67).

58. Joseph Cairn Simpson to Live Oak Lodge, December 1885, Live Oak letters.

CHAPTER 2

1. *Trestleboard* 3 (May 1889): 131.
2. *American Tyler* 3 (5 June 1890): 1–2.
3. *Calif. Proc.*, 1899, p. 280 (italics added).
4. Robert Macoy, *The True Masonic Guide* (New York, 1870), p. ix. Other monitors, or guides to the ritual, consulted were James Wright Anderson, *A Masonic Manual* (San Francisco, 1893); Albert G. Mackey, *A Manual of the Lodge; or, Monitorial Instructions in the Degrees of Entered Apprentice, Fellow Craft, and Master Mason* (New York, 1871); [California Grand Lodge of Free and Accepted Masons], *The Monitorial Work of the Three Degrees of Masonry: Revised and Approved by the Grand Lodge of California* ([San Francisco], 1899).
5. See, for example, *Texas Freemason* 3 (February 1897): 4; *Masonic Review* 64 (August 1885): 22; *Wash. Proc.*, 1895, correspondence, p. 47. For an account of the Masonic legends of origin, see Albert C. Stevens, *The Cyclopaedia of Fraternities* (New York, 1907), pp. 18–25.
6. *Trestleboard* 8 (January 1894): 29, reprinted from *Masonic Constellation*. See also ibid., 1 (November 1887): 232–233; *Masonic Advocate* 19 (March 1896): 42.
7. *Masonic Chronicle* 15 (February 1896): 78. See also ibid., 10 (August 1891): 172; *Trestleboard* 12 (April 1898): 172–173.
8. Mackey, *Manual of the Lodge*, p. 49 and passim.
9. Anderson, *A Masonic Manual*, pp. 227, 238.
10. Ibid., p. 227.
11. Mackey, *Manual of the Lodge*, pp. 58–61.
12. Ibid., pp. 88–90.
13. Anderson, *A Masonic Manual*, pp. 242–243.
14. Mackey, *Manual of the Lodge*, p. 40.
15. Ibid.
16. Noel Pitts Gist, "Secret Societies: A Cultural Study of Frater-

nalism in the United States," *University of Missouri Studies* 15 (October 1940).

17. One monitor explained that the dedication to these saints stemmed from the fact that they were "eminent patrons of Masonry" (Anderson, *A Masonic Manual*, p. 232). But a different monitor revealed that ancient brethren had decided that all lodges "whose members acknowledged the divinity of Christ should be dedicated to St. John the Baptist, and St. John the Evangelist . . . reserving to our Jewish brethren the right of dedicating their lodges to King Solomon" (Macoy, *The True Masonic Guide*, p. 31).

18. Macoy, *The True Masonic Guide*, p. 74.

19. Gist, "Secret Societies," p. 95.

20. *Trestleboard* 1 (December 1887): 258.

21. See, for example, Georg Simmel, *The Sociology of Georg Simmel*, trans. Kurt H. Wolff (Glencoe, Ill., 1950), p. 358.

22. Mackey, *Manual of the Lodge*, p. 20.

23. On the rights of Master Masons, see Albert G. Mackey, *A Textbook of Masonic Jurisprudence: Illustrating the Written and Unwritten Laws of Freemasonry* (New York, 1872), pp. 180–252.

24. *Oakland Tribune*, 22 February 1881 [p. 2].

25. *Wash. Proc.*, 1895, correspondence, p. 35; *Trestleboard* 3 (September 1889): 257–259; *Freemason* 5 (February 1901): 105–108; *Ind. Proc.*, 1876, p. 46; Robert Macoy, *Worshipful Master's Assistant: The Encyclopedia of Useful Knowledge* (New York, 1885), p. 127.

26. Mackey, *Manual of the Lodge*, pp. 205–206. The salute resembled the Nazi salute.

27. Bronislaw Malinowski, "Magic, Science and Religion," in *Magic, Science and Religion and Other Essays* (Glencoe, Ill., 1948), p. 23.

28. Mircea Eliade, *Rites and Symbols of Initiation: The Mysteries of Birth and Rebirth* (New York, 1965), pp. 135–136.

29. A typical example was the *Masonic Review*, which, in 1894, ran a series of articles on whether the saints John had been Masons.

30. *Trestleboard* 3 (May 1889): 131.

31. Aaron Ignatius Abell, *The Urban Impact on American Protestantism, 1865–1900*, Harvard Historical Studies, vol. 54 (Cambridge, Mass., 1943); Paul Boyer, *Urban Masses and Moral Order in America, 1820–1920* (Cambridge, Mass., 1978), pp. 132–

134; Henry F. May, *Protestant Churches and Industrial America* (New York, 1967).

32. Judaism and Catholicism were affected by controversies prompted by scientific discoveries, but Protestantism appears to have been the most profoundly affected. For example, because of the ultimate authority of the pope, Catholics were somewhat less dependent upon the authority of the Bible (Paul A. Carter, *The Spiritual Crisis of the Gilded Age* [De Kalb, Ill., 1971], p. 39). Catholics and Jews were both preoccupied to some extent with questions concerning Americanization (see Winthrop S. Hudson, *Religion in America* [New York, 1965], pp. 253–258, 331–335).

33. For accounts of the scientific and historical challenges to traditional religion, see Carter, *The Spiritual Crisis*, pp. 3–61; Sydney E. Ahlstrom, *A Religious History of the American People* (New Haven, Conn., 1972), pp. 763–774; Sidney Warren, *American Freethought, 1860–1914* (New York, 1966), pp. 45–74.

34. See Carter, *The Spiritual Crisis*, pp. 3–61; Robert T. Handy, *A Christian American: Protestant Hopes and Historical Realities* (New York, 1971), p. 73; William R. Hutchison, *The Modernist Impulse in American Protestantism* (Cambridge, Mass., 1976), pp. 76–110; Kenneth Cauthen, *The Impact of American Religious Liberalism* (New York, 1962).

35. For the strength of liberalism, see Hutchison, *The Modernist Impulse*, p. 3; Ahlstrom, *A Religious History*, p. 775; Warren, *American Freethought*, p. 59.

36. On Liberal Protestantism, see especially Hutchison, *The Modernist Impulse*; Cauthen, *The Impact of American Religious Liberalism*.

37. Carter, *The Spiritual Crisis*, pp. 30–34; Warren, *American Freethought*, pp. 45–74, 81–89; Martin E. Marty, *The Infidel: Freethought and American Religion* (Cleveland, Ohio, 1961), pp. 152–176.

38. *New York Daily Tribune*, 18 March 1895, in Warren, *American Freethought*, p. 101. See also Hutchison, *The Modernist Impulse*, pp. 97–104.

39. Between 1860 and 1900, the total of the nine major denominations rose from four and one-half million to twelve and one-half million (Handy, *A Christian America*, p. 79). For an account of the popularity of religious themes in fiction, see Carter, *The Spiritual Crisis*, pp. 65–107; Winthrop Thorp, "The Reli-

gious Novel as Best Seller in America," in *Religious Perspectives in American Culture* edited by James Ward Smith and A. Leland Jamison, 2: 195–242 (Princeton, N.J., 1961). For the general triumph of Christianity, see Marty, *The Infidel*, p. 139.

40. Carter, *The Spiritual Crisis*, see especially pp. 8–20.
41. Ruth Miller Elson, *Guardians of Tradition: American Schoolbooks of the Nineteenth Century* (Lincoln, Nebr., 1964), pp. 41–62; Handy, *A Christian America*, pp. 110–119.
42. Sidney E. Mead, *The Lively Experiment: The Shaping of Christianity in America* (New York, 1963), p. 134.
43. Handy, *A Christian America*, pp. 95–116; Ahlstrom, *A Religious History*, pp. 842–854.
44. The attention Ingersoll garnered is a good gauge of the popularity (or notoriety) of freethinkers (see Warren, *American Freethought*, pp. 83–95).
45. *Masonic Monthly* 1 (February 1879): 323.
46. *Freemason* 5 (November 1900): 39. See also *Masonic Review* 82 (December 1894): 309; *Trestleboard* 29 (September 1915): 76.
47. *Masonic Review* 82 (September 1894): 97.
48. *American Tyler* 2 (18 July 1889): 6.
49. *Trestleboard* 2 (September 1888): 277.
50. *Masonic Record* 7 (June 1887): 4. See also *American Tyler* 7 (18 November 1894): [8–9]; *Trestleboard* 2 (September 1888): 274; *Masonic Monthly* 1 (February 1879): 343.
51. *Pacific Mason* 2 (March 1896): 76.
52. *American Tyler* 11 (2 November 1896): 8.
53. *Masonic Advocate* 39 (March 1906): 83–88, reprinted from *New England Craftsman*.
54. *Voice of Masonry* 28 (August 1890): 618.
55. *Masonic Review* 81 (April 1894): 171.
56. See, for example, *Trestleboard* 18 (August 1904): 80; ibid., 7 (March 1893): 133; *Masonic Advocate* 27 (February 1895): 65; *American Tyler* 14 (15 March 1900): 511; *Masonic Home Journal* 29 (23 November 1911): 11.
57. *N.Y. Proc.*, 1885, correspondence, p. 21.
58. *Trestleboard* 10 (January 1896): 39–40, reprinted from *Repository*.
59. Handy, *A Christian America*, pp. 115–119. Handy notes that in 1892, even the Supreme Court held "that the Christian religion

was part of the common law." See also Mead, *The Lively Experiment*, pp. 135–136.

60. Will Herberg, "Religion and Education in America" in *Religious Perspectives*, 2: 21–22.

61. David Edwin Harrell, Jr., *The Social Sources of Division in the Disciples of Christ, 1865–1900* (Atlanta, Ga., 1973), 2: 288–289. One important Christian group that was militantly anti-Masonic was the National Christian Association, which was founded by Johnathan Blanchard, a Congregationalist. Blanchard established the American Party and ran for President in 1892 on a plank that included withdrawal of the charters of secret societies, acknowledgment of God as the author of civil government, use of the Bible in public schools, legislation against monopolies, and justice to the Indians. Blanchard and his followers were vocal opponents, but they do not appear to have seriously threatened the popularity or prestige of Masonry or other fraternal orders. For a biography of Blanchard, see Clyde S. Kilby, *Minority of One: The Biography of Johnathan Blanchard* (Grand Rapids, Mich., 1959).

62. *American Tyler* 15 (1 December 1900): 269.

63. *Calif. Proc.*, 1889, correspondence, p. 5.

64. *N.Y. Proc.*, 1890, p. 37. The breakdown of denominations was: Methodist, 288; Episcopalian, 146; Baptist, 112; Presbyterian, 59; Universalist, 31; Congregationalist, 21; Dutch Reformed, 13; Christian, 13; Lutheran, 11; Jewish, 7; Unitarian, 1; and Reform Jewish, 1.

65. *N.Y. Proc.*, 1896, correspondence, p. 118.

66. *Ind. Proc.*, 1888, p. 27.

67. *Oreg. Proc.*, 1889, correspondence, p. 163.

68. *Trestleboard* 2 (April 1889): 178.

69. *Masonic Home Journal* 29 (28 December 1911): 30.

70. *Trestleboard* 9 (May 1895): 227–228.

71. *Masonic Advocate* 43 (February 1910): 69. See also *Tyler-Keystone* 24 (August 1909): 81; *Masonic Home Journal* 4 (20 September 1886): 76.

72. *American Tyler* 7 (1 July 1893): 6.

73. Ibid., 4 (3 October 1890): 772–773.

74. Ibid., 10 (August 1896): 611–612.

75. *Trestleboard* 12 (December 1898): 567.

76. *Voice of Masonry* 28 (February 1890): 139–140.

77. *Texas Freemason* 4 (September 1897): 5.
78. *N.Y. Proc.*, 1884, correspondence, p. 31.
79. *Masonic Advocate* 38 (February 1905): 20.
80. *Masonic Review* 64 (August 1885): 23. No attempt was made here at a detailed, systematic study of regional variations of religious belief. However, Grand Lodge officials in Midwestern and Southern states (Texas, Arkansas, Kentucky, Kansas, and Indiana) seem well represented among those Masons who insisted that the fraternity was Christian and that Masons must believe in the literal interpretation of the Bible. The most militant opponents to Christianizing trends came from California, Washington, Arizona, Oregon, Illinois, Ohio, and Michigan. Trials concerning religious beliefs were found in Texas, Arkansas, New Mexico, Arizona, Illinois, and Missouri. For trials, see *Voice of Masonry* 26 (November 1888): 1120–1123 (Missouri); ibid., 26 (December 1888): 1094–1096 (Illinois); *Vt. Proc.*, 1887, correspondence, p. 3 (Arkansas); *Ariz. Proc.*, 1889, correspondence, p. 54 (New Mexico); *Calif. Proc.*, 1889, correspondence, p. 10 (Arizona); *Tex. Proc.*, 1888, p. 117 (Texas).
81. *Tex. Proc.*, 1888, p. 117.
82. *Voice of Masonry* 26 (November 1888): 1120–1121.
83. *Ill. Proc.*, 1887, pp. 48, 157–158.
84. *Ariz. Proc.*, 1889, correspondence, p. 23. See also *Masonic Advocate* 23 (September 1890): 133.
85. *Masonic Review* 82 (January 1895): 350.
86. *Masonic Chronicle* 15 (March 1898): 81–82, reprinted from *Kansas Freemason*.
87. *Masonic Advocate* 24 (January 1891): 6.
88. *Trestleboard* 4 (June 1890): 165.
89. Ibid., 10 (April 1896): 172–173. See also *Masonic Advocate* 27 (April 1895): 132–133.
90. *Trestleboard* 5 (April 1891): 189.
91. Ibid., p. 151. See also *N.Y. Proc.*, 1884, correspondence, pp. 73–74.
92. *Trestleboard* 6 (April 1897): 172.
93. Ibid., 10 (March 1896): 156.
94. Ibid., 9 (October 1895): 435.
95. Ibid., 1 (November 1887): 237–238. See also *Pacific Mason* 4 (March 1898): 78–79. It is tempting to suggest that Masonic efforts to establish Sunday services in lodges would have cre-

ated all-male churches and hence could be interpreted as reactions against what Ann Douglas has called the "feminization of American culture." If Masons were influenced by the desire to provide a religious environment free from the interference of women and effeminate ministers, however, it must have been a highly subconscious motivation. Although organized religion received frequent criticism in Masonry, the theme that the religion of the churches was too sentimental or feminine never surfaced (Ann Douglas, *The Feminization of American Culture* [New York, 1977]).

96. *Calif. Proc.*, 1894, p. 737. For the movement for a "pure Christianity," see Mead, *The Lively Experiment*, p. 108.
97. *Calif. Proc.*, 1896, p. 581.
98. *Trestleboard* 2 (September 1888): 259.
99. *Pacific Mason* 2 (December 1896): 369–373.
100. *Trestleboard* 3 (February 1889): 44, reprinted from *Masonic Tidings*. See also *American Tyler* 15 (1 August 1900): 740.
101. *Masonic Advocate* 43 (March 1910): 109, reprinted from *Freemason*.
102. *Pacific Mason* 14 (January 1898): 19.
103. *N.C. Proc.*, 1900, p. 39.
104. *Trestleboard* 8 (November 1894): 1.

CHAPTER 3

1. William F. Cleveland, *History of the Grand Lodge of Iowa, A.F. & A.M.* (Cedar Rapids, Iowa? 1913), vol. 2, pt. 1, p. 339.
2. *Calif. Proc.*, 1885, p. 114.
3. Robert Macoy, *The True Masonic Guide* (New York, 1870), pp. 27–28.
4. *Trestleboard* 1 (October 1887): 203.
5. Ibid., 2 (June 1888): 191. See also ibid., 17 (August 1903): 80; *Masonic Advocate* 23 (May 1890): 71.
6. *Chicago Tribune*, 11 March 1877.
7. *Trestleboard* 11 (May 1897): 213–214.
8. For other fraternal orders, see Royal B. Melendy, "The Saloon in Chicago," *American Journal of Sociology* 6 (January 1901): 435. Melendy discusses lodges as potential substitutes for the saloon.
9. For a study of Prohibition as a symbolic reform aimed at re-

affirming the cultural and political dominance of the native middle class, see Joseph R. Gusfield, *Symbolic Crusade: Status Politics and the American Temperance Movement* (Urbana, Ill., 1963), p. 4. For hostility to the saloons and the prohibition movement, see Peter H. Odegard, *Pressure Politics: The Story of the Anti-Saloon League* (New York, 1928), pp. 36–77. For an excellent example of popular treatment of the saloon, see Charles M. Sheldon, *In His Steps* (Chicago, 1897).

10. In the late nineteenth century, the WCTU split over the prohibition issue, with the more conservative wing insisting upon persuasion as a means to abstinence, and the more radical wing supporting Prohibition (see Gusfield, *Symbolic Crusade*, pp. 61–86). For an account of the Anti-Saloon League, see Odegard, *Pressure Politics*. For a general account of antisaloon agitation, see Andrew Sinclair, *Era of Excess: A Social History of the Prohibition Movement* (New York, 1962), pp. 1–128. For an account of Prohibition as a form of social control, see Paul Boyer, *Urban Masses and Moral Order in America, 1820–1920* (Cambridge, Mass., 1978), pp. 189–204.

11. *Trestleboard* 17 (June 1904): 480. See also *N.Y. Proc.*, 1884, correspondence, p. 43; *Iowa Proc.*, 1905, appendix, p. 141; *Calif. Proc.*, 1894, p. 719.

12. *Voice of Masonry* 28 (November 1890): 867–868.

13. *Ariz. Proc.*, 1893, p. 253.

14. Ibid., p. 269.

15. *American Tyler* 2 (5 December 1889): 5. Further evidence that anti-saloonkeeper legislation was aimed at making a symbolic stand on temperance, rather than correcting a serious evil, may be found in the case of Missouri, one of the few states to make the legislation retroactive and demand indefinite suspension or expulsion of saloonkeepers. Apparently the law was strictly enforced; yet between 1885 and 1890, only 339 men were expelled or suspended for all causes. Even in the unlikely event that these cases all concerned saloonkeepers, they represent only 1.3 percent of all the Masons in Missouri (*Mo. Proc.*, 1887, p. 9; *N.Y. Proc.*, 1890, correspondence, pp. 63–65).

16. *Masonic Advocate* 38 (November 1898): 378. See also *Trestleboard* 6 (March 1892): 119.

17. *New York Times*, 14 September 1887.

18. John H. Brownell, ed., *Gems from the Quarry and Sparks from the*

Gavel (Detroit, Mich., 1893), 2: 311. A different type of indication that Masonry did not officially disapprove of liquor per se was the official souvenir printed to publicize the California Widows' and Orphans' Home in 1888. The program was filled with advertisements for beer, champagne, whiskey, and gin ([California Grand Lodge], *A History of the Masonic Widows' and Orphans' Home of California* [San Francisco, 1898], passim).

19. *Pacific Mason* 10 (16 April 1904): 3.

20. *Calif. Proc.*, 1891, p. 13.

21. *Calif. Proc.*, 1883, pp. 70–71. In 1904, Arizona's Grand Master's request that liquor be banned from Arizona lodges met the same fate (*Iowa Proc.*, 1905, appendix, p. 8). The issue in Utah developed somewhat differently. In 1910, a resolution to prohibit lodges from serving intoxicants was "hotly debated and voted down." Opponents of the measure claimed that the "large majority" of Utah Masons were temperate and that the issue was a matter of lodge rights. One Utah Mason maintained that the bill had been defeated in the belief that lodges "should have the right to say for themselves that they don't want the damnable stuff without being dictated to by the Grand Lodge" (*Utah Proc.*, 1911, pp. 40–41; *Ill. Proc.*, 1911, appendix, p. 225).

In contrast to the antisaloonkeeper legislation, Southern states did not pass laws against liquor at Masonic functions.

In some jurisdictions, Grand Lodges prohibited Masons from sharing buildings with saloons or other places where liquor was sold (*Ill. Proc.*, 1913, appendix, pp. 35, 155). In "The Saloon in Chicago," Melendy reported that fraternal orders in general tended to have lodges near saloons. He also noted, however, that in localities where there were many lodges, saloons were relatively scarce (p. 435).

22. The fourteen states were California, Colorado, Delaware, Idaho, Indiana, Minnesota, Mississippi, Montana, New York, Oklahoma, Pennsylvania, Texas, Washington, and Wisconsin.

23. Gusfield, *Symbolic Crusade*, pp. 117–138.

24. *Voice of Masonry* 28 (March 1890): 194.

25. *N.Y. Proc.*, 1890, pp. 34–35.

26. For an example of Masonic jurisprudence, see John Stewart Ross, ed., *Digest and Compilation of Approved Decisions and Regulations by the Grand Lodge of Free and Accepted Masons of California,*

1850 to and including the Annual Communication, October 1931 (San Francisco, 1932).

27. *Calif. Proc..* 1900, pp. 904–906. See also *Masonic Advocate* 13 (May 1880): 6.

28. *Calif. Proc.*, 1883, p. 170.

29. Ibid., 1884–1891, passim. Massachusetts figures for 1880, 1885, 1890, 1895, and 1900, show a range of 24, 22, 18, 12, and 18 percent, respectively. Missouri had a similar pattern with larger rejections in the 1880s of 27 and 22 percent, with a decline to 14 percent in 1900. Not all Grand Lodges published rejection data, making a systematic study for the entire country impossible (*Mass. Proc.*, 1880, 1885, 1890, 1895, 1900; *Mo. Proc.*, 1880, 1885, 1890, 1895, 1900). An example of personal pique affecting a lodge vote was revealed by a California Grand Lodge inspector who reported a "spirit of contention" in Buckeye Lodge No. 195, stemming from the objectionable fact that "several good men have been rejected simply because they are friends of one or the other faction of the lodge" (*Calif. Proc.*, 1887, p. 44).

30. *Mo. Proc.*, 1887, pp. 41–47.

31. *Tex. Proc.*, 1893, pp. 132, 86, 92; ibid., 1896, pp. 75–78.

32. Ibid., 1895, p. 63.

33. Los Angeles, San Francisco, Sacramento, San Jose, Stockton, and Oakland accounted for less than 24 percent of the disciplinary measures (*Calif. Proc.*, 1880–1900).

34. Undated letter, Live Oak Lodge letters. Luelling was expelled in 1878 and restored in 1884 (*Calif. Proc.*, 1884, p. 706).

35. *Calif. Proc.*, 1880–1900; *Mo. Proc.*, 1880, 1885, 1890, 1895, 1900. These figures may be somewhat misleading, for they do not reveal how many men were brought to trial and found not guilty, nor indicate those men who were merely reprimanded.

36. See, for example, *Mo. Proc.*, 1886, pp. 8–9, 46–47.

37. *Calif. Proc.*, 1883, p. 71.

38. *N.Y. Proc.*, 1884, correspondence, p. 23.

39. *Mo. Proc.*, 1887, appendix, pp. 186–187. See also *N.Y. Proc.*, 1890, p. 201; *Calif. Proc.*, 1885, p. 138.

40. *Tex. Proc.*, 1895, p. 43.

41. Edwin A. Sherman, *Fifty Years of Masonry in California* (San

42. *American Tyler* 14 (1 April 1900): 544. Newspaper coverage appears to have been either neutral or accepting of the order's rhetoric. Thus the *Chicago Tribune* could report of a specific

lodge that it contained some of the "best young men in the city," and the *New York Times* could be bitingly sarcastic about anti-Masons' claims that Masons were immoral (*Chicago Tribune*, 11 March 1877; *New York Times*, 15 September 1882).

43. *Calif. Proc.*, 1881, p. 23.
44. *N.C. Proc.*, 1895, p. 32.
45. *Calif. Proc.*, 1885, p. 106.
46. [California Grand Lodge], *The Masonic Widows' and Orphans' Home*, p. 34.
47. Brownell, *Gems from the Quarry*, 2: 380.
48. Robert H. Wiebe, *The Search for Order, 1877–1920* (New York, 1967), pp. 1–75, 4.
49. The classic account of the transformation of the middle class is C. Wright Mills, *White Collar: The American Middle Classes* (New York, 1951). For a more recent treatment, see Jurgen Köcka, *White Collar Workers in America, 1890–1940: A Social-Political History in International Perspective* (London, 1980). For an account of the impact of industrialization on ideas about work, see Daniel T. Rodgers, *The Work Ethic in Industrial America, 1850–1920* (Chicago, 1978).
50. For nativist sentiment in the 1880s and 1890s, see John Higham, *Strangers in the Land: Patterns of American Nativism, 1860–1925* (New York, 1969), pp. 35–105.
51. May, *Protestant Churches*, pp. 91–124. For an interesting account of the middle-class response to disorder in urban life, see Boyer, *Urban Masses*, especially chap. 8, "The Ragged Edge of Anarchy."
52. For a discussion of the tensions produced by economic expansion and egalitarianism in the Jacksonian period, see Marvin Meyers, *The Jacksonian Persuasion: Politics and Belief* (Stanford, Calif., 1957), especially chaps. 4–6. For social reform in this period, see Clifford S. Griffin, "Religious Benevolence as Social Control, 1815–1860," in *Ante-Bellum Reform*, edited by David Brion Davis, pp. 81–107 (New York, 1967); David J. Rothman, *The Discovery of the Asylum: Social Order and Disorder in the New Republic* (Boston, 1971). For the persistence of the belief in individual morality as a means of achieving social order, see Boyer, *Urban Masses*; Richard Weiss, *The American Myth of Success: From Horatio Alger to Norman Vincent Peale* (New York, 1969), pp. 48–121.

53. Brownell, *Gems from the Quarry*, 1: 216. For a discussion of the World's Fair, see Mark Sullivan, *Our Times: The United States, 1900–1925* (New York, 1926), 1: 189–193.

54. *Calif. Proc.*, 1883, pp. 29–43. See also ibid., 1885, p. 121; *Mo. Proc.*, 1887, appendix, p. 121; Brownell, *Gems from the Quarry*, 1: 351–352.

55. *Trestleboard* 8 (October 1894): 458–459. See also ibid., 6 (October 1892): 473; ibid., 7 (March 1893): 103.

56. *New England Craftsman* 1 (March 1906): 194–196.

57. *Texas Masonic Journal* 1 (November 1886): 399–400, reprinted from *Dispatch*. See also *Voice of Masonry* 29 (May 1891): 327.

58. *American Tyler* 14 (1 January 1900): 669–670. See also *Trestleboard* 11 (July 1897): 29–34.

59. *Trestleboard* 6 (March 1892): 107.

60. *Oakland Tribune*, 22 February 1881.

61. *Trestleboard* 10 (April 1896): 173.

62. Ibid., 2 (August 1888): 228–231.

63. Ibid., 1 (June 1887): 65–70.

64. [California Grand Lodge], *Masonic Widows' and Orphans' Home*, pp. 30, 45.

65. [California Commandery Knights Templar No. 1], *Itinerary of California Commandery No. 1, K.T., Twenty-eighth Triennial Conclave at Louisville, Kentucky* (San Francisco, 1901), n.p.

66. See Weiss, *Myth of Success*, pp. 48–121; John Cawelti, *Apostles of the Self-Made Man: Changing Concepts of Success in America* (Chicago, 1965), pp. 101–163.

67. *Voice of Masonry* 38 (April 1890): 290.

68. *Ohio Proc.*, 1890, p. 12.

69. *Masonic Advocate* 38 (June 1905): 218–219.

70. *Trestleboard* 18 (February 1905): 509–510.

71. [Live Oak Lodge], *Souvenir: 40th Anniversary Celebration of Live Oak Lodge* (Oakland, Calif., 1896), p. 60.

72. *Trestleboard* 2 (August 1888): 248.

73. Brownell, *Gems from the Quarry*, 2: 255.

74. For eighty-five officeholders between 1880 and 1900, the occupational breakdown was as follows: high-level white collar, 22.9 percent; proprietors, 22.9 percent; low-level white collar, 44.6 percent; skilled workers, 8.4 percent; and semiskilled workers, 1.2 percent. For more details, see my dissertation, appendix B-6.

75. *Trestleboard* 13 (December 1889): 602.
76. *Trestleboard* 1 (June 1887): 110, reprinted from *Freemason's Repository*. See also *Calif. Proc.*, 1891, p. 89.
77. See Paul Kleppner, *The Cross of Culture: A Social Analysis of Midwestern Politics, 1850–1900* (New York, 1970), especially chaps. 3, 4.
78. *Masonic Advocate* 13 (November 1880): 171, reprinted from *Freemason's Repository*. See also *Calif. Proc.*, 1885, p. 132; *Trestleboard* 4 (December 1890): 370; *N.Y. Proc.*, 1883, p. 52.
79. *Trestleboard* 5 (July 1891): 299.
80. *N.Y. Proc.*, 1883, pp. 51–52; ibid., 1890, p. 41.
81. *Trestleboard* 49 (September 1890): 68.
82. Ibid., 3 (June 1889): 170–172, reprinted from *American Tyler*.
83. Ibid., 12 (February 1889): 57–59. See also ibid., 2 (July 1888): 196–197.
84. Brownell, *Gems from the Quarry*, 2: 340. See also ibid., 1: 165.
85. *Masonic Advocate* 13 (March 1880): 33–39. See also ibid., 27 (February 1895): 37; *Trestleboard* 7 (March 1893): 127.
86. *New England Craftsman* 1 (March 1906): 194–196.
87. *Trestleboard* 10 (August 1896): 37, reprinted from *Dispatch*.
88. Ibid., 10 (August 1896): 406–407.
89. Wiebe argues that organizational development in the late nineteenth and early twentieth centuries was a means of reordering a "distended" society. As a partial antidote to the erosion of community autonomy, it gave group members networks for achieving status and political and economic power (Wiebe, *The Search for Order*, pp. 111–132).
90. For the Farmers Alliance and the creation of community, see Lawrence Goodwyn, *The Populist Moment* (New York, 1978), pp. 32–35. Goodwyn argues that the Alliance movement went beyond creating a sense of community to forge a "movement culture" that encompassed a "new political vision." For the creation of community in a black fraternal order, see William Alan Muraskin, *Middle-Class Blacks in a White Society: Prince Hall Freemasonry in America* (Berkeley, Calif., 1975), pp. 25–27. Muraskin views Masonry as one of the major institutional devices for forging the group self-consciousness of middle-class blacks.
91. Louis Wirth, "Urbanism as a Way of Life," in *Neighborhood, City, and Metropolis: An Integrated Reader in Urban Sociology,*

edited by Robert Gutman and David Popenoe, pp. 54–69 (New York, 1970).

92. For a refutation of Wirth, see Claude S. Fischer, *The Urban Experience* (New York, 1976). For the persistence of community in urban life, see Claude S. Fischer et al., *Networks and Places: Social Relations in the Urban Setting* (New York, 1977). Thomas Bender has offered an interesting account of American historians' approach to the problem of community. He challenges the Wirthian approach, as well as the approach that uses Ferdinand Tonnies's *Gemeinschaft/Gessellschaft* polarity to demonstrate collapse of community. Bender insists that community need not be tied to place. Bender would probably not agree, however, that Masonry created a community, as his definition of community insists upon more intimate ties than Masonry actually provided (Thomas Bender, *Community and Social Change in America* [New Brunswick, N.J., 1978], pp. 7–8).

CHAPTER 4

1. *Tyler-Keystone* 32 (August 1919): 146, reprinted from *Illinois Freemason*.

2. In the Progressive period, one Masonic editor, Joseph Morecombe of the *American Freemason*, stands out as one of the few authors interested in having Masonry become involved in social problems. He was self-consciously radical on the issue and frequently railed at the conservatism of the rest of the Craft.

3. An example of war relief work was the Masonic War Relief Association formed by the Grand Masters of twenty-eight states. Its purpose was to give relief to the hungry and needy of all the countries touched by the war (*Masonic Home Journal* 33 [15 December 1914]: 1). For Masonic responses to the war, see ibid., 32 (15 September 1914): 3–5; *Builder* 1 (October 1915): 242; *Trestleboard* 29 (February 1916): 227–228; ibid., 29 (November 1915): 125.

4. California's Germania Lodge, for instance, changed its name to Acacia Lodge and voted to stop speaking German (*Calif. Proc.*, 1919, pp. 50, 567–577). See also *Tyler-Keystone* 32 (August 1918): 149.

5. *Tyler-Keystone* 31 (July 1917): 127–128.

6. [Oakland Lodge No. 188], *Fiftieth Anniversary, Oakland Lodge*

No. 188, Free and Accepted Masons, Oakland, California, 1868–1918 ([Oakland, Calif.] 1918), p. 11.

7. *Tyler-Keystone* 32 (January 1918): 15–16.

8. Ibid., 32 (April 1918): 69.

9. *Builder* 9 (January 1923): 15–18.

10. Ibid., 15 (February 1929): 42.

11. *Tyler-Keystone* 33 (January 1919): 10. See also ibid., 31 (July 1917): 123–126; *Illinois Freemason* 32 (20 July 1917): 2.

12. For general accounts of the Red Scare, see Stanley Coben, "A Study in Nativism: The American Red Scare of 1919–1920," *Political Science Quarterly* 79 (March 1964): 52–75; John Higham, *Strangers in the Land: Patterns of American Nativism, 1860–1925* (New York, 1969), pp. 222–263; Robert K. Murray, *Red Scare: A Study in National Hysteria, 1919–1920* (New York, 1955).

13. *Trestleboard* 34 (December 1921): 13.

14. *N.Y. Proc.*, 1920, p. 36.

15. *Calif. Proc.*, 1921, pp. 416–417. Copies of the resolution, as well as the American's Creed, were sent to 68,000 Masons in California.

16. *Southern Masonic Journal* 1 (November 1919): 282.

17. Higham, *Strangers in the Land*, pp. 206–207, discusses the importance of exhortation.

18. *Builder* 10 (September 1924): 287–288; *Tyler-Keystone* 34 (October 1920): 155. Norman Frederick de Clifford, *The Jew and Masonry*, Lion's Paw Series, vol. 2 (Brooklyn, N.Y. [1918]), p. x.

19. Patricia Bryant, "The Ku Klux Klan and the Oregon School Bill" (Master's thesis, Reed College, 1970), p. 58.

20. For Masonic disapproval of the Klan, see *Tyler-Keystone* 38 (May 1923): 93; *Calif. Proc.*, 1925, correspondence, pp. 30–31, 39; *Texas Freemason* 32 (January 1926): 3; *Masonic Review* 2 (October 1921): 53; Donavan Duncan Tidwell, "The Ku Klux Klan and Texas Masonry," *Transactions, Texas Lodge of Research* 14 (1978/1979): 160–176. For Masonry's connection with the Ku Klux Klan, see Kenneth T. Jackson, *The Ku Klux Klan and the City, 1915–1930* (New York, 1967), pp. 29, 95, 134, 143, 161, 162, 191, 203, 204, 290, 219, 259, 277–278, as well as the fourth section of this chapter.

The link between Klansmen and Masons is pronounced in the *Fellowship Forum*. It was established in 1921 by a prominent

Scottish Rite Mason with the heading "Freemasonry's Representative at the Capitol." Dedicated to the purposes of militant Americanism, it included news of Masonry and other fraternal organizations. Within a very short time, although it continued its fraternal news, it became one of the most scurrilous KKK organs. It continually stressed the relationship between the Klan and Masonry, a policy that brought criticism from Masonic officials and authors.

21. *Brotherhood* 9 (December 1920): 3; *Master Mason* 1 (March 1924): 148–150; *Tyler-Keystone* 38 (March 1923): 93; *Square and Compass* 1 (September 1923): 6, 16.

22. *Masonic World* 6 (November 1924): 5–6. See also *Murad's Mirror* 1 (September 1922): 10.

23. *High-Nooner* 1 (November 1925): 18.

24. See, for example, *Masonic Review* 2 (August 1921): 4–5; *Builder* 13 (May 1927): 146–148; *Calif. Proc.*, 1919, correspondence, pp. 13–15. For anti-Catholicism in prewar America, see Higham, *Strangers in the Land*, pp. 175–177.

25. Higham, *Strangers in the Land*, pp. 266, 291–293. For urbanness of Masonry, see my dissertation, appendixes A-2, A-3. On the urban quality of intolerance in the 1920s, see Jackson, *The KKK and the City*, passim.

26. *Masonic Review* 4 (May 1922): 3.

27. *Trestleboard* 34 (April 1921): 15, 16. See also *American Freemason* 10 (January 1919): 118–125; *Shawnee Light* 6 (November 1927): 11.

28. For an excellent discussion of private power and Progressive thought, see Grant McConnell, *Private Power and American Democracy* (New York, 1966), pp. 30–48.

29. On association of lobbying with corruption, see ibid., pp. 11–29.

30. *Masonic Digest* 1 (November 1921): 15.

31. *Southern Masonic Journal* 3 (November/December 1921): 251.

32. For a discussion of the attempts to promote a bill for a federal department of education, see the fourth section of this chapter.

33. For activities of the Scottish Rite in lobbying for educational legislation, see the fourth section of this chapter.

34. *N.C. Proc.*, 1924, correspondence, p. 111; *Kraftsman* 6 (May 1926): 2; *Masonic Outlook* 2 (July 1926): 232; *Calif. Proc.*, 1928, p. 49; ibid., 1920, pp. 45–46; ibid., 1926, pp. 10–12.

35. *Tex. Proc.*, 1925, p. 21; *Texas Freemason* 32 (January 1926): 3–4. The Grand Master of Texas began complaining about KKK infiltration as early as 1921 (*Tex. Proc.*, 1921, pp. 39–48).
36. *Calif. Proc.*, 1925, pp. 399–402. In 1925, the Grand Master included in his questionnaire sent out to Masters a request for information about KKK activities in lodges (ibid., pp. 439–441).
37. See the fourth section of this chapter.
38. *Trestleboard* 38 (October 1924): 9.
39. *Masonic World* 6 (September 1924): 3.
40. Quoted in *Calif. Proc.*, 1922, correspondence, p. 2.
41. *Builder* 6 (April 1920): 100; *Calif. Proc.*, 1920, p. 2; *Trestleboard* 35 (November 1923): 14; *Tyler-Keystone* 38 (June 1923): 111, 125.
42. *Ivanhoe Masonic News* 2 (1 September 1921): 4, reprinted from *Masonic Voice Review*.
43. *Calif. Proc.*, 1919, p. 548; *N.Y. Proc.*, 1923, p. 196. Some speech titles are "Syndicalism and What It Means," "Bolshevism," "The Doom of Democracy," "Mexico, Our Neighbor," "Crime in California," and "Is There a Social Revolution Underway?" (*Live Oak Bulletin*, 1923, p. 196; *Junior Warden* 6 [20 February 1925]: 3; *Masonic Bulletin* [Long Beach, Calif.] 2 [September 1925]: 2; *Trestleboard* 40 [April 1927]: 20–25; ibid., 42 [June 1928]: 26; ibid., 41 [December 1927]: 18).
44. For disapproving Grand Lodges, see, for example, *Calif. Proc.*, 1920, correspondence, pp. 2–3; ibid., 1921, correspondence, p. 92; ibid., 1922, correspondence, p. 390; *Builder* 6 (April 1920): 100.
45. *Builder* 14 (October 1928): 312–313.
46. Allen E. Roberts, *Freemasonry's Servant: The Masonic Service Association of the United States—The First Fifty Years* (New York, 1969), p. 8.
47. An Oklahoma Mason, reflecting on the history of the MSA, claimed that the major motive of the MSA founders was their hostility to Catholics because of the war service issue and that the purpose of the organization was to array Masonic strength against Catholicism (*Calif. Proc.*, 1921, correspondence, p. 73).
48. *Tyler-Keystone* 32 (August 1919): 146, reprinted from *Illinois Freemason; Builder* 6 (January 1920): 8.
49. For a discussion of state MSA activity, see *Calif. Proc.*, 1922,

correspondence, pp. 362, 373; ibid., 1920, correspondence, p. 118; *Southern Masonic Journal* 3 (April 1921): 76–80.

50. Raymond McLaughlin noted the impact of the war on the sense of an educational crisis: "War had revealed definite weaknesses in the educational system, which were highly propagandized. Thousands of men had been found at military camps with little or no education and thousands of others with physical defects which could have been averted by means of better care and training in earlier life. Out of these conditions came cries for 'better schools of all kinds'; for 'physical education'; for 'Americanization' and other means of improvement in the schools" (McLaughlin, *A History of State Legislation Affecting Private Elementary and Secondary Schools in the United States, 1870–1945* [Washington, D.C., 1946], p. 84).

   For the federal survey, see U. S. Bureau of Education, *Biennial Survey of Education, 1916–1918*. For a more detailed discussion of the popularization of the educational crisis, see my dissertation, pp. 226–235.

51. For a detailed account of legislation affecting private schools, see McLaughlin, *A History of State Legislation*, pp. 84–116. McLaughlin reports that 16,000 education laws were enacted in the states between 1919–1920. For the American Legion's involvement in public education, see Marcus Duffield, *King Legion* (New York, 1931), p. 281.

52. *Calif. Proc.*, 1925, pp. 575–588.

53. *Southern Masonic Journal* 1 (November 1919): 298.

54. *Junior Warden* 1 (September 1921): 1–2.

55. *Congressional Record*, 66th Cong., 1st sess., 1919, vol. 58, pt. 4, pp. 3239–3240.

56. Some of the groups were: National Education Association; American Federation of Teachers; American Federation of Labor; National Council of Women; National Congress of Parents and Teachers; Federation of Women's Clubs; National League of Women Voters; Supreme Council, Scottish Rite of Freemasonry, Southern Jurisdiction of the United States; National Woman's Christian Temperance Union; American Association of University Women, National Society; and Daughters of the American Revolution.

   National Education Association, *Proceedings of the 62nd Annual Meeting* 1924, p. 255. Hiram Evans, Imperial Wizard of the Klan, explained his organization's support of the educational bill: "A growing Catholic population in certain sections of the United States threatened to place the control of the public schools of these areas in Catholic hands. The country as a whole, however, was still Protestant and Protestants could still control federal policies. The time had come, therefore, to give the federal government more power over education" (cited in Emerson Hunsberger Loucks, *The Ku Klux Klan in Pennsylvania: A Study in Nativism* [New York, 1936], p. 138).

57. *Builder* 9 (November 1923): 327–338.

58. *Trestleboard* 33 (April 1930): 73; see also ibid., 35 (May 1922): 57; *Southern Masonic Journal* 3 (August 1921): 194; *Duluth Masonic Calendar* 13 (June 1922): 10–12.

59. *Fellowship Forum* 1 (10 February 1922): 6; *Sciots Journal* 4 (December 1922): 4; *Duluth Masonic Calendar* 13 (July 1922): 10–12.

60. For Grand Lodges' responses to the Smith-Towner Bill, see *Builder* 9 (May 1923): 143–144, 155; ibid., 8 (August 1922): 233–243. Scottish Rite publications included the Rite's magazine, *New Age*, local publications, and a newspaper clipping service sent to newspapers throughout the country. See, for example, *Scottish Rite Clip Service*, July, August 1923. For a discussion of Scottish Rite lobbying activities, see my dissertation, pp. 250–255.

61. *Builder* 8 (August 1922): 255.

62. For a more detailed discussion of the Oregon School Bill, see my dissertation, pp. 256–263; M. Paul Holsinger, "The Oregon School Bill Controversy, 1922–1925," *Pacific Historical Review* 37 (August 1968): 327–341; Patricia Bryant, "The Ku Klux Klan"; Lloyd P. Jorgenson, "The Oregon School Law of 1922: Passage and Sequel," *Catholic Historical Review* 54 (1968): 455–466; Stephen Louis Recken, "A Reinterpretation of the Oregon School Bill of 1922: The Concept of the Common School in Progressive America" (Master's thesis, Portland State University, 1973); David Tyack, "The Perils of Pluralism: The Background of the Pierce Case," *American Historical Review* 74 (October 1968): 74–98.

63. Tyack, "The Perils of Pluralism," p. 330; Holsinger, "The Oregon School Bill," p. 328; Bryant, "The Ku Klux Klan," pp. 24–25.

64. Bryant, "The Ku Klux Klan," pp. 79–82.
65. *Builder* 8 (August 1922): 239.
66. Paul L. Murphy, in "Sources and Nature of Intolerance in the 1920s," makes a similar argument about the impact on the native middle class of the increased heterogeneity of American society. Murphy draws upon Ferdinand Tonnies's concept of *Gemeinschaft* and *Gesellschaft* (*Journal of American History* 51 [June 1964]: 60–76).

CHAPTER 5

1. *Saturday Evening Post*, 5 April 1924, p. 174.
2. *Trestleboard* 36 (February 1923): 15.
3. *Masonic World* 8 (May 1927): 5.
4. *Illinois Freemason* 40 (20 September 1924): 9.
5. *N.Y. Proc.*, 1924, correspondence, p. 170.
6. *Proceedings of the First Annual Meeting of the Masonic Service Association* (1919), p. 167; see also *Masonic World* 12 (October 1930): 24.
7. The occupational distribution of new members (those joining between 1918 and 1930) also reveals a shift toward lower-status occupations. In 1920, 20 percent of Live Oak Lodge was high-level white collar, but only 10 percent of the men who joined between 1918 and 1930 were in that category. Conversely, in 1920, 1.5 percent of Live Oak had been semiskilled workers, but for all new members, the figure was 5 percent. A survey of other Oakland lodges' new members reveals a similar pattern. For more details, see my dissertation, appendixes C-7 and C-8.
8. Some of the magazines that encouraged patronage were *Masonic Digest*, *Trestleboard*, and *Masonic World*. As the editor of the *Trestleboard* put it, "Co-operate in business, co-operate in politics, co-operate socially" (*Trestleboard* 35 [October 1921]: 25).
9. See, for example, *Masonic Review, Masonic Digest*, and *Trestleboard*.
10. See, for example, *Calif. Proc.*, 1926, correspondence, p. 4; *Masonic World* 8 (December 1926): 24; *N.C. Proc.*, 1928, p. 28.
11. *Masonic World* 9 (June 1928): 24.
12. *Builder* 15 (September 1929): 261; *Masonic World* 9 (June 1928): 23; ibid., 12 (October 1930): 23; *Illinois Freemason* 4 (20 June 1919): 1.

13. *Trestleboard* 33 (December 1919): 15.
14. *Masonic World* 12 (October 1930): 23. In discussing the rivalry between lodges, one observer noted that "rivalry springs up, at first almost unconsciously, but growing more acute as time goes on. This rivalry usually takes the form of a campaign for members. Of course, solicitation is un-Masonic, and is positively prohibited by Masonic law and usage. But, in their eagerness to increase the rolls of members, Masters and other enthusiastic workers will transgress this rule, sometimes not directly, but by indirect means that are just as reprehensible" (*Trestleboard* 29 [January 1916]: 189).
15. Ibid., 40 (March 1927): 18.
16. *Trestleboard* 33 (February 1920): 5. New members were noticeably younger than the lodge as a whole. For example, 42 percent of new Live Oak members were under thirty, while for the lodge as a whole in 1920, only 17 percent were under thirty. See my dissertation, appendix D-2.
17. *Ivanhoe Masonic News* 2 (May 1921): 28.
18. *Trestleboard* 38 (June 1925): 38.
19. *Masonic Outlook* 1 (May 1925): 205.
20. On the churches' response to social problems, see Henry F. May, *Protestant Churches and Industrial America* (New York, 1967). On religion in the 1920s, see Robert S. Lynd and Helen Merrell Lynd, *Middletown: A Study in Modern American Culture* (New York, 1929), pp. 315–409, passim; Report of the President's Research Committee on Social Trends, *Recent Social Trends* (New York, 1933), 2: 1009–1014; Joseph Wood Krutch, *The Modern Temper: A Study and a Confession* (New York, 1929).
21. Andrew M. Greeley and Robert H. Rossi, *The Denominational Society: A Sociological Approach to Religion in America* (Glenview, Ill., 1972), pp. 128–132.
22. *Secularism* is a problematic term; it is imprecise and can be value laden. Used here it means the declining importance of traditional religion in organizing the lives of individuals. Paul A. Carter offers a helpful suggestion about the use of *secularism* in analyzing the 1920s. *Secularism* "is a useful word, from the very fact that it embraces such a wide spectrum of opinion, all the way from the member of the American Association for the Advancement of Atheism to the man who merely prefers to go fishing on Sunday morning. If the word is not used, then the

side of the 1920s which it connotes would have to be described by some such academic barbarity as 'nonreligiousness.' So I use the word 'secularism' without further apology" (Paul A. Carter, *The Decline and Revival of the Social Gospel: Social and Political Liberalism in American Protestant Churches, 1920–1940* [Ithaca, N.Y., 1954], pp. 85–86).

23. Walter Lippmann, *A Preface to Morals* (New York, 1929), p. 48.

24. It should be noted that the churches' fortunes were not declining in a literal sense; in terms of church property, they were experiencing a healthy expansion. For example, the value of church edifices more than doubled between 1906 and 1926, increasing in value from $1,258,000,000 to $3,840,000,000 (*Recent Social Trends*, 2: 1026–1027).

25. Ibid., p. 1031.

26. Carter, *Decline and Revival of the Social Gospel*, p. 71.

27. Ibid., pp. 70–95; Lynd and Lynd, *Middletown*, pp. 345–349.

28. Lynd and Lynd, *Middletown*, pp. 358–370; *Recent Social Trends*, 2: 1012–1013.

29. Carter, *Decline and Revival of the Social Gospel*, p. 83; Robert Moats Miller, *American Protestantism and Social Issues, 1919–1939* (Chapel Hill, N.C., 1958), pp. 22–25.

30. Bruce Barton, *The Man Nobody Knows: A Discovery of the Real Jesus* (Indianapolis, Ind., 1924), pp. [ii, iv], 9.

31. Richard Weiss, *The American Myth of Success: From Horatio Alger to Norman Vincent Peale* (New York, 1969), pp. 220, 219–222.

32. There were, of course, several magazines that continued to stress religion and ritualism. The *Tyler-Keystone*, for example, was a very traditional magazine. The *Kentucky Home Journal*, the official organ of the Grand Lodge of Kentucky, also tended to have a religious tone. Magazines that had very little on symbolism or ritual included *New England Craftsman, Masonic Outlook, Illinois Freemason, Masonic Review, Southern Masonic Journal, Masonic Analyst*, and such local bulletins as *Palestine Bulletin, Ivanhoe Masonic News*, and *Masonic Bulletin* (Long Beach, Calif.). In 1916, the *Trestleboard* was filled with references to symbolism, religion, and morality, but by 1920, under new management, it had switched to practicality, service, citizenship, Americanism, and calls for the modernization of Masonry. The *Builder*, founded in 1915, was dedicated to Masonic research, and thus included in-

formation on symbolism and history; however, even here the theme of modernizing Masonry was apparent.

33. *Masonic Outlook* 4 (June 1928): 303.
34. *Ivanhoe Masonic News* 2 (1 May 1921): 25.
35. *Trestleboard* 38 (July 1924): 10–11.
36. Ibid., 29 (May 1916): 306–307.
37. For a discussion of the alienation modernists thought fundamentalism produced in thoughtful, intelligent people, see Harry Emerson Fosdick, *The Meaning of Service* (New York, 1920), p. 13; idem, "What Christian Liberals Are Driving At," in *Adventurous Religion and Other Essays* (New York, 1926), pp. 232–257.
38. For Masons' discussions of the religious controversy, see, for example, *N.C. Proc.*, 1930, correspondence, pp. 265–266; *Trestleboard*, 1921 yearbook, pp. 63; ibid., 36 (June 1923): 46–47; *Masonic World* 9 (April 1928): 6.
39. *Masonic Digest* 5 (August 1925): 9; see also *Masonic Analyst* 3 (June 1925): 21; *Capital News Service*, 22 June 1922.
40. *Builder* 14 (October 1928): 313; see also *Masonic World* 8 (September 1926): 6.
41. *Trestleboard* 34 (March 1921): 21.
42. *Masonic World* 9 (July 1927): 12.
43. *Calif. Proc.*, 1925, correspondence, p. 67.
44. Joseph R. Gusfield, *Symbolic Crusade: Status Politics and the American Temperance Movement* (Urbana, Ill., 1963), pp. 139–147. Drawing upon the works of David Riesman, Leo Lowenthal, and others, Gusfield discusses the shift in the acceptability of drinking. "As the new middle class has developed cultural patterns distinctive to it and opposed to nineteenth-century values, the place of impulse gratification in work and leisure has been redefined. Self-control, reserve, industriousness, and abstemiousness are replaced as virtues by demands for relaxation, tolerance, and moderate indulgence. Not one's ability to produce but one's ability to function as an appropriate consumer is the mark of prestige" (p. 146).
45. *Illinois Freemason* 33 (2 March 1918): 1.
46. *Junior Warden* 9 (9 November 1923): 1.
47. For employment bureaus, see *Trestleboard* 37 (July 1923): 14–15; *Builder* 7 (November 1921): 331. For investments, see *Tres-*

tleboard 44 (February 1930): 9; *Masonic Outlook* (New York) 4 (November 1927): 93.

48. Herbert Hoover, *American Individualism* (New York, 1922), pp. 29–30.

49. Ibid., pp. 26–31.

50. An example of the religious uses of Service may be found in Fosdick, *The Meaning of Service*, a book that Fosdick later described as an attempt to explore "the ethical application of the Christian faith and spirit to personal and social problems" (Harry Emerson Fosdick, *The Living of These Days* [New York, 1956], p. 134). The book revealed Fosdick's desire to provide a practical Christianity, unencumbered by denominational and doctrinal squabbles. For the war and Service, see Morrell Heald, "Business Thought in the Twenties: Social Responsibility," *American Quarterly* 13, no. 2 (Summer 1961): 126–139.

51. *Saturday Evening Post* 29 March 1924, p. 76. Barton noted Service's importance in advertising (see *The Man Nobody Knows*, pp. 165–166).

52. Heald, "Business Thought," pp. 126–139.

53. Harold O. Bahlke, "Rotary and American Culture: A Historical Study of Ideology" (Ph.D. dissertation, University of Minnesota, 1956), p. 6.

54. Ibid., pp. 111–112.

55. Krutch, *The Modern Temper*, p. 102.

56. Sinclair Lewis, *Babbitt* (New York, 1922), p. 258.

57. *Ivanhoe Masonic News* 2 (September 1921): 35, reprinted from *Exchange*.

58. For a discussion of civic clubs and "community," see Charles F. Marden, *Rotary and Its Brothers: An Analysis and Interpretation of the Men's Service Club* (Princeton, N.J., 1935), pp. 124–125.

59. *Trestleboard* 37 (January 1924): 73–74.

60. *Scottish Rite Bulletin* 16 (25 October 1925): 5; *Masonic Review* 14 (September 1927): 20; *Bulletin, San Francisco Bodies No. 1, A&ASR* 4 (February 1921): 3.

61. For a discussion of Grand Lodge homes, see *Calif. Proc.*, 1925, pp. 6–9; for criticism of the limits to Grand Lodge charitable activities, see *Builder* 13 (August 1927): 247.

62. *Builder* 8 (January 1922): 22.

63. Ibid., 8 (May 1922): 132; see also *Masonic World* 8 (December

1926): 24–25; *Trestleboard* 36 (June 1924): 54; *Southwestern Freemason* 29 (April 1925): 8.

64. South Dakota Grand Master, 1927, quoted in *Proceedings of the Grand Commandery of Knights Templar of the State of California,* 1928, pp. 85–86.

65. *Builder* 14 (September 1928): 288.

66. Marden, *Rotary and Its Brothers.* Rotary became a federated club system in 1910, but it was not until 1916 that Kiwanis started. In 1933, there were twenty-five associations (most of which started between 1917 and 1922), with a total of 500,000 members (*Recent Social Trends,* 2: 936).

67. Although they ranged from 15 to 500 members, the average club contained somewhere between 25 and 75 men (Marden, *Rotary and Its Brothers,* p. 104).

68. Ibid., p. 23.

69. *Trestleboard* 44 (April 1930): 100.

70. Marden, *Rotary and Its Brothers,* pp. 31–32.

71. Ibid., pp. 61–69.

72. *Recent Social Trends,* 2: 935–936; Lynd and Lynd, *Middletown,* pp. 306–308. The Lynds report, "The great days of lodges as important leisure-time institutions in Middletown have vanished" (p. 306). In their study of Middletown in the Depression, they saw a slight resurgence of interest in lodge activity for the working classes, but for business classes they described lodges as "doomed" (Robert S. Lynd and Helen Merrell Lynd, *Middletown in Transition: A Study in Cultural Conflicts* [New York, 1937], pp. 285–286). See also Marden, *Rotary and Its Brothers,* pp. 150–152.

73. See, for example, *Builder* 15 (May 1929): 132–135; ibid., 14 (November 1928): 321–324; *Illinois Freemason* 53 (20 September 1927): 7; *Freemasonry and Eastern Star* 31 (September 1929): 9; *Masonic World* 10 (July 1928): passim.

74. David Riesman, with Nathan Glazer and Reuel Denney, *The Lonely Crowd: A Study of the Changing American Character* (New Haven, Conn., 1950); Leo Lowenthal, "The Triumph of Mass Idols," in *Literature, Popular Culture and Society,* pp. 145–165 (Englewood Cliffs, N.J., 1961).

75. Paul Carter discusses the decline of the values of Horatio Alger

in the 1920s in *Another Part of the Twenties* (New York, 1977), pp. 145–165.

76. *Trestleboard* 29 (May 1916): 307.

CHAPTER 6

1. *Masonic World* 7 (January 1926): 5.
2. Ibid., 9 (May 1928): 9.
3. *Shawnee Light Bulletin* 5 (October 1925): 7. See also *Calif. Proc.*, 1925, p. 497; *Masonic Outlook* 5 (March 1930): 201–202; *Trestleboard* 39 (September 1925): 47.
4. In 1919, a California official offered an estimate of 15 percent (*Calif. Proc.*, 1919, p. 449). A year later, the Grand Master suggested that 10 percent was a generous figure (ibid., 1920, p. 68). An author in the *Tyler-Keystone* claimed that most observers guessed 10 percent, but that 5 percent was probably more accurate (*Tyler-Keystone* 1 [July 1925]: 233–235).
5. Records for another Oakland lodge—Sequoia—reveal that in 1921, 14 percent was the average attendance at monthly meetings. In 1916, the average attendance was 10 percent (Live Oak and Sequoia were of similar size). If all meetings were taken into account, the figures were 7 percent and 6 percent, respectively.

   Other available attendance figures for the prewar period suggest a much higher level of participation than Live Oak's 1900 average. Figures for the sixteen largest lodges in the United States (ranging in size from 267 to 1,447 members) in 1909 reveal an average attendance of 18 percent (*American Freemason* 1 [May 1910]: 306–307).
6. For details of Indiana and Minnesota attendance, see my dissertation, appendix C-6.
7. "Degree mills" were noted before the war as well: "The Masonic degree mill, so called, has been pummelled vigorously by press and platform of late. . . . The monotony of continuous ritual dulls the imagination and impairs the enthusiasm of the average Mason who is prevented by circumstances from active participation in the work" (*Illinois Freemason* 27 [20 April 1912]: 6).
8. *Trestleboard* 35 (May 1922): 19, 52; *Tex. Proc.*, 1921, p. 21.
9. *Masonic Herald* 26 (February 1920): 35, reprinted from *Masonic Chronicler*. In 1920, one author explained the problem in detail: "The officers cannot feel any personal interest in the candidates,

the knowledge *they* have of the rush, the constant repetition of these labors, brings it down to a mere routine in course of time, while the knowledge the candidates have of their number, and the impersonal feeling about their reception will inevitably . . . reduce to a minimum, if not entirely smother . . . that impression of brotherly love and friendship, which is the great, the real, the ineffable and incommunicable, secret of Freemasonry" (*Tyler-Keystone* 34 [August 1920]: 115–116).

10. *Illinois Freemason* 36 (20 August 1921): 1–2. See also *Trestleboard* 37 (June 1924): 54.

11. *Trestleboard* 36 (March 1923): 23.

12. *Calif. Proc.*, 1920, p. 79.

13. Ibid., 1919, p. 359.

14. *Square and Compass* 2 (January 1925): 22.

15. *Illinois Freemason* 40 (20 December 1924): 1. See also *Calif. Proc.*, 1920, p. 79; *Masonic Analyst* 7 (September 1929): 6; *Masonic Outlook* 1 (July 1925): 233–235.

16. Not surprisingly, large lodges were an urban phenomenon. In 1920, for example, the average size of lodges in California communities of 2,500 or less was 84; the average increased with community size. Lodges in cities of 10,000 to 25,000 averaged 278 members; for cities of more than 25,000, the average was 393 (figures were compiled from *Calif. Proc.*, 1920, and U.S. census data on California).

17. *American Tyler* 19 (15 June 1905): 7; *Palestine Bulletin* 14 (June 1911): 119.

18. *Calif. Proc.*, 1880, 1900, 1920. For more details, see my dissertation, appendix D-8. For an account of large lodges in Massachusetts, see *Mass. Proc.*, 1920, pp. 197–209. Some jurisdictions had more severe large-lodge difficulties. Massachusetts's average lodge size in 1921 was 260; Rhode Island's, 247; Pennsylvania's, 244; Connecticut's, 236, and New York's, 229. Twenty other states had averages between 100 and 200. Twenty-two had averages of less than 100 (*Trestleboard* 34 [January 1921]: 29).

19. [California Grand Lodge of Free and Accepted Masons], *Diamond Jubilee Communication* (San Francisco, 1925), p. 57.

20. *Calif. Proc.*, 1920, correspondence, p. 76; ibid., 1925, p. 361.

21. *Masonic Herald* 31 (August 1924): 156. *Masonic Outlook* 1 (July 1925): 233–235; *Trestleboard* 33 (September 1919): 23.

22. *Trestleboard* 41 (December 1927): back page. The book was serialized in the *Masonic Outlook* in 1926.
23. *Trestleboard* 33 (August 1919): 7; ibid., 34 (August 1920): 22; ibid., 35 (September 1921): 60–63; *Builder* 5 (January 1920): 28.
24. *Trestleboard* 38 (November 1924): 201.
25. *Ill. Proc.*, 1920, correspondence, p. vi.
26. *Calif. Proc.*, 1922, correspondence, pp. 350–351.
27. *Southwestern Freemason* 26 (May 1922): 6.
28. The California Grand Lodge passed legislation to make the forming of new lodges easier in the hopes of relieving the congestion of large lodges; and in fact, between 1920 and 1925, 151 new lodges were constituted. However, lodges with over 300 men still formed 21 percent of all lodges, and 55 percent of all Masons were in these large lodges (*Calif. Proc.*, 1922, pp. 62, 261; ibid., 1925, pp. 727–744). For hostility on the part of existing lodges to the creation of competing new lodges, see *Mass. Proc.*, 1920, pp. 192–209, passim.
29. *Calif. Proc.*, 1919, p. 617.
30. Fisher's explanation for his program stressed attendance. "The time has come to bring into our lodges some up-to-date information concerning arts and sciences of modern civilization, and to interpret for the benefit of Masons the bearing of these arts and sciences upon the affairs of modern life. Degree work alone, although of extreme importance, will not hold attendance up to the desired level. Masters universally desire a good attendance record. Careful execution of this program is the one certain way to secure an increasing attendance on the part of members" (*Masonic World* 9 [February 1928]: 21). See also *Trestleboard* 42 (August 1928): 13.
31. *Masonic World* 10 (May 1928): 10. See also ibid., 8 (September 1926): 6. A telling comment about Masonic education also appeared in a list of questions a proponent of Masonic education, Herbert Hungerford, reported he was most frequently asked. One was, If Masonic education is such a good thing, why is there so much difficulty in putting it across? Hungerford's reply was that "anything worthwhile took pains to establish" (*Builder* 14 [November 1928]: 346).
32. For example, in 1920, the Grand Lodge of California reported that where lodges "had introduced the discussion of public

questions as a part of its regular program the attendance had been more than doubled" (*Calif. Proc.*, 1920, p. 77; see also *Junior Warden* 14 [14 September 1928]: 3).

33. *Masonic Bulletin* (Canton, Ohio) 9 (May 1927): 12. See also *Trestleboard* 37 (June 1924): 54; *Masonic World* 9 (May 1928): 9; *Illinois Freemason* 40 (20 February 1924): 1.

34. *Scottish Rite Bulletin* (Duluth, Minn.) 14 (October 1923): 1.

35. *Masonic World* 7 (January 1926): 5. See also *Masonic Outlook* 5 (March 1929): 201–202; ibid., 1 (May 1925): 185; *Trestleboard* 38 (October 1924): 15–16. Robert C. Hollow, in a recent interview, explained that the duties of the Master of the lodge he was raised in, Detroit's Palestine Lodge (1930), were so consuming that the Master almost had to be affluent enough to leave his job for his year as Master so that his full attention could be given to his Masonic responsibilities.

36. For example, *High-Nooner* (Chicago); *Ivanhoe Masonic News* (Kansas City, Mo.); *Junior Warden* (San Francisco); *Masonic Bulletin* (Long Beach, Calif.); *Palestine Bulletin* (Detroit, Mich.); *Shawnee Light* (Louisville, Ky.); *Temple Topics* (Mount Morris, Ill.); *Masonic Bulletin* (Canton, Ohio); *Acorn News* and *Live Oak Bulletin* (both of Oakland, Calif.).

37. *Live Oak Bulletin*, August 1928; ibid., May 1921; ibid., June 1928.

38. *Masonic World* 9 (June 1927): 28; ibid., 9 (February 1928): 47.

39. Ibid., 9 (June 1928): 94.

40. *Trestleboard* 37 (December 1928): 22.

41. *Pacific Craftsman*, 1927, passim; *Pacific Lodge Bulletin*, 1928–1930, passim.

42. A number of lodges resorted to both professional and amateur talent. The *New England Craftsman* ran ads for amusement agencies that promised "high grade entertainment" for Masonic functions (*New England Craftsman* 17 [January 1922]: 111).

43. *Palestiner* 1 (November 1921): inset.

44. *Square and Compass* 2 (January 1925): 7, 8. See also *Masonic World* 7 (January 1926): 5.

45. Report of the President's Research Committee on Social Trends, *Recent Social Trends* (New York, 1933), 2: 954.

46. As one writer expressed the new trend, "Masons have grown extravagant in the matter of their dining room service just as they have in all other things. Now-a-days they must have chicken,

turkey, tenderloin steak, and all the delicacies of the season. Brethren used to be satisfied with a good old oyster supper with a cup of coffee to accompany it. But now-a-days the oyster supper is merely the first course" (*Illinois Freemason*, 41 [20 December 1925]: 4).

A sense of how complicated Masonic functions had become is evident in a series of articles in the New York *Masonic Outlook* on planning Masonic parties and entertainment (*Masonic Outlook* 6 [December 1929]: 109, 124).

47. *Trestleboard* 33 (June 1920): 17–18, 51–52.

48. This does not mean that Palestine neglected the ritual altogether, however, for apparently the lodge drew upon the entertainment value of the ritual. Robert C. Hollow, who was initiated at Palestine Lodge in 1930, recalls his third degree quite well. Mr. Hollow describes the ceremony as "spectacular." It involved many dramatic sound and lighting effects and "played" to a large audience. Particularly interesting were the devices used to disorient and surprise the candidate. Mr. Hollow explained that he had seen many other lodges' third-degree ceremonies, and that Palestine's was quite unusual (private communication, 1980).

49. *Builder* 1 (October 1915): 239–240. In 1925, the California Grand Lodge reported that lodges throughout the state were "universally either building new Temples or remodelling their old halls, and furnishing club rooms and social quarters" (*Calif. Proc.*, 1925, p. 496).

A particularly ambitious temple built after the war was the 1921 project of Buffalo Masons, who were building a $2 million structure for all of Buffalo's Masonic organizations. It would include a 400-room hotel, an auditorium seating 5,000, a dining room for 3,500, and a gymnasium, among other facilities (*Trestleboard* 34 [January 1921]: 55).

Although the phenomenon of clubhouse-type temples was particularly evident in the 1920s, the trend had begun well before the war. For example, Masons in Detroit in 1905 were planning to include "all the conveniences of a first-class club [that] can be provided for with cafe accommodations, billiard room, etc." (*American Tyler* 19 [1 January 1905]: 282).

50. Robert Moats Miller, *American Protestantism and Social Issues, 1919–1939* (Chapel Hill, N.C., 1958), pp. 22–25. In his autobiography, Harry Emerson Fosdick described the planning stages

of his famous nondenominational Riverside Church in New York City. "Many elements in our program we did, of course, foresee and we provided such equipment as bowling alleys, a gymnasium, a playground, theatrical stages" (Harry Emerson Fosdick, *The Living of These Days: An Autobiography* [New York, 1956], p. 204).

51. *Masonic World* 8 (February 1926): 11.

52. *Trestleboard* 37 (February 1924): 60. Another scheme calling for careful organization was a Syracuse, New York lodge's plan to insure "decent" funeral attendance. The lodge of 1,400 members was organized into clubs of 50 members each. Every member of each club was required to attend the funerals of fellow club members. In addition, they were responsible for visiting fellow members who were sick (*Square and Compass* 1 [April 1924]: 7).

53. "They're all the rage," reported one California official (*Calif. Proc.*, 1926, p. 22). See also *Masonic Review* 14 (August 1927): 17; *Masonic Digest* 1 (August 1921): 24.

54. *Masonic Digest* 5 (December 1925): 18.

55. *Shawnee Light* 5 (December 1925): 7.

56. *Tyler Keystone* 23 (20 March 1909): 509. A National League of Masonic Clubs (NLMC) was formed in 1907 to federate these clubs. In 1909, it had thirty-five clubs with 8,000 members. In 1920, it had 250 clubs with one-tenth of all Masons in the United States (ibid., 23 [20 December 1908]: 270–271; *Masonic Review* 1 [November 1920]: 4). The purpose of the federation was in part to give members club privileges while visiting other cities (each member was given a NLMC traveling card). The NLMC was an important organization in the 1920s. Primarily an East Coast movement, it sponsored huge conventions and had its own magazine (*Kraftsman*). For more on the NLMC, see the next section of this chapter.

57. *Builder* 8 (December 1923): 386–387.

58. Ibid., 8 (April 1923): 112–113.

59. *Southern Masonic Journal* 9 (May 1929): 20, reprinted from *New Hampshire Masonic Bulletin*. See also *Builder* 15 (March 1929): 65; *Trestleboard* 43 (August 1920): 53–55.

60. *Builder* 14 (October 1929): 313.

61. In 1900, only 5 percent of all Masons were in Scottish Rite; by 1925, the figure had risen to 17 percent. Similarly, Shrine's pro-

portion of Masons had grown from 6 percent in 1900 to 20 percent in 1925. York Rite's growth was slower. Already popular in 1900 (27 percent), by 1925, it claimed 30 percent of all Masons (*Proceedings of the Grand Commandery, Knights Templar, of the State of New York at Its Annual Conclave*, 1900, correspondence, p. 249; *World Almanac and Book of Facts* [New York, 1900], pp. 177, 320; personal communications from the Supreme Councils, Southern and Northern jurisdictions of the Scottish Rite; *N.C. Proc.*, 1928, inset, table 23, n.p.).

62. *N.C. Proc.*, 1923, correspondence, pp. 113–114. See also *Kraftsman* 6 (January 1924): 3–4; *Builder* 9 (June 1923): 185–186; ibid., 11 (September 1925): 276; *Trestleboard* 37 (January 1924): 6, 14.

63. *Masonic World* 8 (December 1926): 25.

64. *Trestleboard* 41 (September 1927): 5.

65. *Shawnee Light* 7 (August 1928): 10.

66. A striking example—although a rare one—of the connection between the Shrine and patronage appeared in a full-page ad in the *Masonic World* entitled "Shriners You Should Know," which gave photographs and businesses of thirty-two San Francisco Shriners (*Masonic World* 12 [July 1930]: 11).

67. *Trestleboard* 34 (August 1920): 18. The 1915 roster of the San Francisco Pyramid No. 1, containing a classified business directory of its members, reveals a striking percentage of self-employed and professional men. Of the 640 members for whom occupations are known, 20 percent were professional and high-level white collar; 48 percent were proprietors or self-employed artisans; 21 percent were low-level white collar (of these 10 percent were salesmen); 10 percent were skilled workers; and 1 percent were unskilled ([San Francisco Pyramid No. 1] *Directory*, 1915). Information on Pyramids is quite sketchy. No material on occupations, rosters, etc., is available for Oakland.

68. Sciots Pyramid No. 1, *Bulletin*, May 1917; *Sciots Booster* 2 (1 August 1924): [1].

69. *Trestleboard* 44 (October 1930): 51. See also *Sciots Journal* 7 (February 1925): 9.

70. *Calif. Proc.*, 1920, p. 79. These restrictions included the notion of the lodge as an asylum, as well as the ritualistic and somber quality inherent in Blue Lodge activities. In addition, one of the objectionable restrictions of the Blue Lodges may have been lodge

liquor policies. California did not officially ban alcohol from the lodge room until 1911, but there may have been unwritten laws in effect before then. In contrast, until Prohibition was passed, Sciot announcements of events included liberal mention of alcoholic refreshments. Wine and beer were always on the menu.

71. *High-Twelvian* 1 (May 1927): 11; "What Is the High-Twelve International?" pamphlet no. 3, n.d., p. [1].

72. For a description of High Twelvers as businessmen, see *Fellowship Forum* 1 (2 July 1921): 11; *Trestleboard* 35 (October 1921): 27.

73. *Masonic World* 7 (February 1926): 28–29.

74. *High-Twelvian*'s first issue gave a synopsis of a number of clubs in the United States (*High-Twelvian* 1 [May 1927]: passim).

75. Ibid., pp. 6, 8, 13.

76. Ibid., p. 21.

77. Ibid., p. 17.

78. *Southwestern Freemason* 29 (December 1925): 11–16. See also accounts of New York City's Level Club. With over 1,000 members in 1923, it planned a $1 million clubhouse with auditorium, pool, gymnasium, etc. (*New York Times*, 23 June 1923).

79. *Calif. Proc.*, 1925, p. 36.

80. Others were associated with the San Francisco City Hall Employees, Express Company, Spanish-American Veterans, Military Service, Commission Markets, Building of Public Works, San Francisco and Oakland Police, Post Office, Pacific Auto Club, Standard Oil, Howard Automobiles, Anglo-American Trust, Key System Transit, Judson Iron Works, Capwell's Department Store, and Westinghouse.

81. *Trestleboard* 38 (August 1924): 26. See also *Masonic Bulletin* (Long Beach, Calif.) 3 (August 1926): 5; *Trestleboard* 29 (November 1915): 137.

82. Ibid., 38 (August 1924): 26.

83. For example, Railway Express, Sanitary Manufacturing Company of Indiana, Belknap Hardware and Manufacturing Company of Kentucky, and the California Packing Corporation (*Trestleboard* 35 [March 1922]: 21; *Masonic Home Journal* 45 [15 January 1928]: 2; *Masonic Digest* 5 [July 1925]: 4; *Universal Craftsman* 2 [21 May 1923]: 4; *Southwestern Freemason* 5 [June 1921]: 13).

84. *Universal Craftsman* 2 (21 May 1923): 4.

85. *Freemasonry and Eastern Star* 32 (February 1930): 15.
86. *Southwestern Freemason* 5 (June 1921): 13.
87. *Masonic Digest* 5 (July 1925): 41.
88. *Kraftsman* 5 (October 1924): 4.
89. Most accounts of clubs' origins described them as springing from the desire of Masons to promote a greater spirit of fraternal spirit among men working together. See, for example, *Masonic World* 6 (October 1924): 4, 45.
90. *Masonic Review* 4 (July 1922): 24; ibid., 4 (June 1922): 49; *Calif. Proc.*, 1927, correspondence, p. 12.
91. *Masonic Review* 7 (June 1922): 22–25.
92. *American Freemason* 6 (July 1915): 444–445; *Masonic Review* 19 (November 1929): 14. For more on the councils, see my dissertation, pp. 377–382.
93. *American Freemason* 6 (July 1915): 444.
94. *Universal Craftsman* 6 (15 December 1927): [23].
95. *American Freemason* 6 (July 1915): 445.
96. *Builder* 8 (March 1922): 73.
97. One further aspect of occupational identity within Masonry should be noted. In many instances, entire lodges were known for their occupational character. Plymouth Lodge in Oakland, for example, was unofficially known as the "Key Route Lodge." The same lodge was also noted for having a large number of employees of the Pacific Telephone Company. Although no official count was ever made, the lodge's historian claimed that the lodge was one-third Key Route, one-third telephone company, and one-third independents. Similarly, Alcatraz Lodge in Oakland was noted as a railroad lodge. There is some evidence to suggest that a number of lodges in the Oakland area had a very high percentage of men in professional and high-status occupations, while others had a high proportion of skilled laborers (Clyde M. Stine, *Plymouth's Progress—Fifty Golden Years: The Story of Plymouth Lodge No. 560 F.&A.M. of California* [Oakland, Calif., 1974], p. 14). Alcatraz Lodge's railroad connection was recalled by Mr. Raymond Leavitt (personal communication, 1980). Compared to Live Oak Lodge, Durant Lodge in Berkeley had a greater proportion drawn from the highest occupational group.
98. Robert S. Lynd and Helen Merrell Lynd, *Middletown; A Study in Modern American Culture* (New York, 1929), pp. 251–312. *Recent Social Trends*, 2: 933–939.

CONCLUSION

1. Noel Pitts Gist, "Secret Societies: A Cultural Study of Fraternalism in the United States," *University of Missouri Studies* 15 (October 1940), passim.
2. Two major studies of other fraternal orders suggest the ways in which they articulated the values of their members. Christopher Kauffman's *Faith and Fraternalism: The History of the Knights of Columbus, 1882–1982* (New York, 1982) suggests that the Knights of Columbus provided Irish Catholics with a means of expressing pride in their Catholicism, while at the same time indicating their patriotism and adherence to "respectable" values. Kauffman clearly sees the order as an agency of assimilation. As he sums it up, "By proclaiming the nobility of the American-Catholic experience and by conspicuously avoiding any association with the Old World, the Knights of Columbus are a classic instance of a minority drive to assimilate into the larger society" (p. 71). Similarly, in his study of black Masons, *Middle-Class Blacks in a White Society: Prince Hall Freemasonry in America* (Berkeley, Calif., 1975), William Alan Muraskin provides another example of a fraternity attempting to provide a marginal group with a vehicle for assimilation into mainstream society. Muraskin sees the order's stress on morality as indicative of black middle-class men's desire to adopt middle-class white values, but he also notes that Prince Hall Masons expressed a sense of race pride and race solidarity. Brian Greenberg, in an article on the Odd Fellows in Albany, New York, indicates the way in which that fraternity articulated the ideals of Albany workers by expressing a free-labor ideology similar to nineteenth-century Masonic values. Because of its ideology and its inclusion of workers and middle-class men, Greenberg sees the Odd Fellows as contributing to "community" rather than class consciousness (Brian Greenberg, "Worker and Community: Fraternal Orders in Albany, New York, 1845–1885," *Maryland Historian* 8 [Fall 1977]: 38–53).
3. Charles Beard and Mary Beard, *The Rise of American Civilization* (New York, 1927), 2: 763.

Selected Bibliography

UNPUBLISHED MATERIAL

A&ASR Orient of Texas. Library of the Supreme Council Southern Jurisdiction of Scottish Rite Masons. Letters from the Department of Education.

Live Oak Lodge, Oakland, California. Live Oak letters.

GOVERNMENT PUBLICATIONS

Congressional Record. 66th Cong., 1st sess., 1919. Vol. 58, pt. 4.

U.S. Bureau of the Census. *Tenth Census, 1880: Social Statistics of Cities*. Pt. 2.

————. *Eleventh Census, 1890: Population*. Pt. 1.

————. *Twelfth Census, 1900: Population*. Pt. 2.

U.S. Department of Commerce. *Historical Statistics of the United States: Colonial Times to 1970*. 2 parts. Washington, D.C., 1975.

U.S. Department of the Interior. Bureau of Education. *Biennial Survey of Education*. Washington, D.C., 1919, 1926.

MASONIC GRAND LODGE PROCEEDINGS
(titles vary slightly)

Proceedings of the M.W. Grand Lodge of Free and Accepted Masons of Arizona

Proceedings of the M.W. Grand Lodge of F. and A. Masons of the State of Arkansas

Proceedings of the M.W. Grand Lodge of Free and Accepted Masons of the State of California

Proceedings of the Grand Lodge of the Most Ancient and Honorable Free and Accepted Masons of the State of Connecticut

Proceedings of the Annual Communication of the M.W. Grand Lodge, Ancient, Free and Accepted Masons of Dakota

Annual Communication of the M.W. Grand Lodge of Ancient, Free and Accepted Masons of the State of Idaho

SELECTED BIBLIOGRAPHY

Proceedings of the Grand Lodge of the State of Illinois, Free and Accepted Masons

Proceedings of the Annual Meeting of the M.W. Grand Lodge of Free and Accepted Masons of the State of Indiana

Annals of the Grand Lodge of Iowa, A.F.&A.M.

Proceedings of the Grand Lodge of Ancient and Accepted Masons of the State of Maine

Proceedings of the Most Worshipful Grand Lodge of Ancient Free and Accepted Masons of the Commonwealth of Massachusetts

Proceedings of the Grand Lodge of Ancient Free and Accepted Masons of Minnesota

Proceedings of the Grand Lodge, F.&A.M. of the State of Mississippi

Proceedings of the Grand Lodge of the Most Ancient and Honorable Society of Free and Accepted Masons for the State of New Jersey

Proceedings of the Grand Lodge of Free and Accepted Masons of the State of New York

Proceedings of the Grand Lodge of North Carolina

Proceedings of the M.W. Grand Lodge of the Most Ancient and Honorable Fraternity of Free and Accepted Masons of the State of Ohio

Proceedings of the Grand Lodge of Ancient Free and Accepted Masons of Oregon

Proceedings of the Right Worshipful Grand Lodge of the Most Ancient and Honorable Fraternity of Free and Accepted Masons of Pennsylvania

Proceedings of the Grand Lodge of Free and Accepted Masons, Tennessee

Proceedings of the M.W. Grand Lodge of Texas

Proceedings of the M.W. Grand Lodge of the State of Utah

Proceedings of the M.W. Grand Lodge of Free and Accepted Masons of the State of Vermont

Proceedings of the M.W. Grand Lodge of Free and Accepted Masons of Washington

OTHER MASONIC PROCEEDINGS

Proceedings of the . . . Annual Meeting of the Masonic Service Association of the United States

Proceedings of the Grand Commandery of Knights Templar of the State of California

Proceedings of the Grand Commandery of Knights Templar, for the State of Maine

SELECTED BIBLIOGRAPHY

Proceedings of the Grand Commandery, Knights Templar, of the State of New York

Proceedings of the Supreme Pyramid of California A.E.O.S. [Sciots]

Transactions, Supreme Council 33°, A&ASR Southern Jurisdiction of the United States of America

MASONIC MAGAZINES AND LOCAL LODGE BULLETINS

Acorn News (Oakland, Calif.)

American Freemason (Storm Lake, Iowa)

American Mason (Washington, D.C.; also known as the *Kraftsman*)

American Tyler (Detroit and Grand Rapids, Mich.; also known as *Tyler-Keystone*)

Brotherhood (New York)

Builder (Anamosa, Iowa)

Bulletin, San Francisco Bodies No. 1, A&ASR (San Francisco)

Capital News Service (Washington, D.C.)

Duluth Masonic Calendar (Duluth, Minn.)

Fellowship Forum (Washington, D.C.)

Freemason (Los Angeles)

Freemasonry and Eastern Star (Los Angeles; also known as *Southwestern Freemason*)

Freemasons' Repository (Providence, R.I.)

High Nooner (Chicago)

High-Twelvian (Kansas City, Kans.)

Illinois Freemason (Bloomington)

Indiana Freemason (Franklin)

Ivanhoe Masonic News (Kansas City, Mo.)

Junior Warden (San Francisco)

Kansas City Freemason (Kansas City, Kans.)

Kraftsman (see *American Mason*)

Live Oak Bulletin (Oakland, Calif.)

Masonic Advocate (Indianapolis, Ind.)

Masonic Analyst (Portland, Oreg.)

Masonic Bulletin (Canton, Ohio)

Masonic Bulletin (Cleveland, Ohio)

Masonic Bulletin (Long Beach, Calif.)

Masonic Chronicle (Columbus, Ohio)

Masonic Digest (Los Angeles)

Masonic Herald (Rome, Ga.)

Masonic Home Journal (Louisville, Ky.)

283

SELECTED BIBLIOGRAPHY

Masonic Monthly (San Francisco)
Masonic Outlook (New York)
Masonic Record (San Francisco)
Masonic Review (Cincinnati, Ohio)
Masonic Review (New York)
Masonic Standard (New York)
Masonic World (San Francisco)
Master Mason (Washington, D.C.)
Murad's Mirror (Burlington, Iowa)
New Age Magazine (Washington, D.C.)
New England Craftsman (Boston)
Oklahoma Mason (McAlester, Okla.)
Pacific Craftsman (San Francisco; also known as *Pacific Lodge Bulletin*)
Pacific Mason (Seattle, Wash.; also known as *Pacific Freemason*)
Sciot Booster (Sacramento, Calif.)
Sciots Journal (San Francisco)
Scottish Rite Bulletin (Duluth, Minn.)
Scottish Rite Clip Service (Washington, D.C.)
Shawnee Light (Louisville, Ky.)
Short Talk Bulletin of the Masonic Service Association of the United States (Washington, D.C.)
Southern Masonic Journal (Birmingham, Ala.)
Southwestern Freemason (see *Freemasonry and Eastern Star*)
Square and Compass (Utica, N.Y.)
Stockton Trumpeter (Stockton, Calif.)
Temple Topics (Mount Morris, Ill.)
Texas Freemason (San Antonio)
Texas Masonic Journal (Fort Worth)
Trestleboard (San Francisco)
Trestleboard of New York (New York)
Tyler-Keystone (see *American Tyler*)
Universal Craftsman (Cleveland, Ohio)
Universal Engineer (New York)
Voice of Masonry (Chicago)

OTHER PERIODICALS

Chicago Tribune
Collier's Weekly

SELECTED BIBLIOGRAPHY

Fraternal Monitor
Fraternal Record
National Education Association Journal
New York Times
Oakland Tribune
Proceedings of the Annual Meeting of the National Education Association
Saturday Evening Post
School and Society
School Life

BOOKS AND ARTICLES

Abbott, Lyman. *The Evolution of Christianity*. Boston, 1897.

Abell, Aaron Ignatius. *The Urban Impact on American Protestantism, 1865–1900*. Harvard Historical Studies, vol. 54. Cambridge, Mass., 1943.

Ahlstrom, Sydney E. *A Religious History of the American People*. New Haven, Conn., 1972.

Andersen, Arthur R. *How Sturdy an Oak: A Centennial History, Live Oak Lodge No. 61, Free and Accepted Masons in California*. Oakland, Calif., 1954.

Anderson, James Wright. *A Masonic Manual*. San Francisco, 1893.

Bahlke, Harold O. "Rotary and American Culture: A Historical Study of Ideology." Ph.D. dissertation, University of Minnesota, 1956.

Barber, Bernard. "Participation and Mass Apathy in Associations." In *Studies in Leadership: Leadership in Democratic Action*. Edited by Alvin W. Gouldner. New York, 1950.

Barton, Bruce. *The Man Nobody Knows: A Discovery of the Real Jesus*. Indianapolis, Ind., 1924.

Basye, Walter. *History and Operation of Fraternal Insurance*. Rochester, N.Y., 1919.

Beard, Charles, and Beard, Mary. *The Rise of American Civilization*. 2 vols. New York, 1927.

Bender, Thomas. *Community and Social Change in America*. New Brunswick, N.J., 1978.

Berthoff, Roland. *An Unsettled People: Social Order and Disorder in American History*. New York, 1971.

Boyer, Paul. *Urban Masses and Moral Order in America, 1820–1920*. Cambridge, Mass., 1978.

Brownell, John H., ed. *Gems from the Quarry and Sparks from the Gavel*. 2 vols. Detroit, Mich., 1893.

Bryant, Patricia. "The Ku Klux Klan and the Oregon School Bill." Master's thesis, Reed College, 1970.

Buck, J. D. *The Genius of Free-Masonry and the Twentieth-Century Crusade*. Chicago, 1907.

Calhoun, Arthur M. *A Social History of the American Family*. Vol. 3, *From 1865 to 1919*. New York, 1919.

[California Commandery Knights Templar No. 1.] *Itinerary of California Commandery No. 1, K.T., Twenty-eighth Triennial Conclave at Louisville, Kentucky*. San Francisco, 1901.

[California Grand Lodge of Free and Accepted Masons.] *The California Digest of Masonic Law*. San Francisco, 1867.

————. *Diamond Jubilee Communication*. San Francisco, 1925.

————. *A History of the Masonic Widows' and Orphans' Home of California*. San Francisco, 1898.

————. *The Monitorial Work of the Three Degrees of Masonry: Revised and Approved by the Grand Lodge*. [San Francisco], 1879.

Carter, Paul A. *Another Part of the Twenties*. New York, 1977.

————. *The Decline and Revival of the Social Gospel: Social and Political Liberalism in American Protestant Churches, 1920–1940*. Ithaca, N.Y., 1954.

————. *The Spiritual Crisis of the Gilded Age*. De Kalb, Ill., 1971.

Cauthen, Kenneth. *The Impact of American Religious Liberalism*. New York, 1962.

Cawelti, John. *Apostles of the Self-Made Man: Changing Concepts of Success in America*. Chicago, 1965.

Cleveland, William F. *History of the Grand Lodge of Iowa A.F.&A.M.* 2 vols. Cedar Rapids, Iowa? 1913.

Coben, Stanley, "A Study in Nativism: The American Red Scare of 1919–1920." *Political Science Quarterly* 79 (March 1964): 52–75.

Condit, Carl W. *The Chicago School of Architecture: A History of Commercial and Public Building in the Chicago Area, 1875–1925*. Chicago, 1965.

Cronin, Joseph M. *The Control of Urban Schools: Perspectives on the Power of Educational Reformers*. New York, 1973.

Davis, David Brion, ed. *The Fear of Conspiracy: Images of Un-American Subversion from the Revolution to the Present*. Ithaca, N.Y., 1971.

Davis, David Brion. "Some Themes of Counter-Subversion: An Analysis of Anti-Masonic, Anti-Catholic, and Anti-Mormonism Literature." *Mississippi Valley Historical Review* 47, no. 2 (September 1960): 205–224.

de Clifford, Norman Frederick. *The Jew and Masonry.* Lion's Paw Series, vol. 2. Brooklyn, N.Y. [1918].

Degler, Carl N. *At Odds: Women and the Family from the Revolution to the Present.* New York, 1980.

Douglas, Ann. *The Feminization of American Culture.* New York, 1977.

Duffield, Marcus. *King Legion.* New York, 1931.

Dumenil, Lynn. "Brotherhood and Respectability: Freemasonry and American Culture, 1880–1930." Ph.D. dissertation, University of California, Berkeley, 1981.

Eliade, Mircea. *Rites and Symbols of Initiation: The Mysteries of Birth and Rebirth.* New York, 1965.

Elson, Ruth Miller. *Guardians of Tradition: American Schoolbooks of the Nineteenth Century.* Lincoln, Nebr., 1964.

Ferguson, Charles Wright. *Fifty Million Brothers: A Panorama of American Lodges and Clubs.* New York, 1937.

Filene, Peter Gabriel. *Him/Her/Self: Sex Roles in Modern America.* New York, 1974.

Fischer, Claude S. *The Urban Experience.* New York, 1976.

Fischer, Claude S. et al. *Networks and Places: Social Relations in the Urban Setting.* New York, 1977.

Formisano, Ronald. *The Birth of Mass Political Parties: Michigan, 1827–1861.* Princeton, N.J., 1971.

Formisano, Ronald, and Kutolowski, Kathleen Smith. "Antimasonry and Masonry: The Genesis of Protest, 1826–1827," *American Quarterly* 29, no. 2 (Summer 1977): 139–165.

Fosdick, Harry Emerson. *The Meaning of Service.* New York, 1920.

———. "What Christian Liberals Are Driving At." In *Adventurous Religion and Other Essays*, pp. 232–257. New York, 1926.

———. *The Living of These Days: An Autobiography.* New York, 1956.

Friedlander, Peter. *The Emergence of a UAW Local, 1936–1939: A Study in Class and Culture.* Pittsburgh, Pa., 1975.

Gellermann, William. *The American Legion as Educator.* Teachers College, Columbia University, Contributions to Education, no. 743. New York, 1938.

Gist, Noel Pitts. "Secret Societies: A Cultural Study of Fraternalism in the United States." *University of Missouri Studies* 15 (October 1940).

Gompers, Samuel. *Seventy Years of Life and Labor.* 2 vols. New York, 1925.

Goodwyn, Lawrence. *The Populist Moment.* New York, 1978.

Greeley, Andrew M., and Rossi, Robert H. *The Denominational Society: A Sociological Approach to Religion in America.* Glenview, Ill., 1972.

Greenberg, Brian. "Worker and Community: Fraternal Orders in Albany, New York, 1845–1885," *Maryland Historian* 8 (Fall 1977): 38–53.

————. "Worker and Community: The Social Structure of a Nineteenth-Century American City, Albany, New York, 1850–1884." Ph.D. dissertation, Princeton University, 1981.

Griffin, Clifford S. "Religious Benevolence as Social Control, 1815–1860." In *Ante-Bellum Reform,* edited by David Brion Davis, pp. 81–107. New York, 1967.

Gusfield, Joseph R. *Symbolic Crusade: Status Politics and the American Temperance Movement.* Urbana, Ill., 1963.

Handy, Robert T. *A Christian America: Protestant Hopes and Historical Realities.* New York, 1971.

Harrell, David Edwin, Jr. *The Social Sources of Division in the Disciples of Christ, 1865–1900.* 2 vols. Atlanta, Ga., 1973.

Heald, Morrell. "Business Thought in the Twenties: Social Responsibility." *American Quarterly* 13, no. 2 (Summer 1961): 126–139.

Herberg, Will. "Religion and Education in America." In *Religious Perspectives in American Culture,* edited by James Ward Smith and A. Leland Jamison, 2: 11–52. Princeton, N.J., 1961.

Higham, John. *Strangers in the Land: Patterns of American Nativism, 1860–1925.* New York, 1969.

Hill, Walter B. "The Great American Safety-Valve." *Century* 44 (July 1892): 383–384.

Holsinger, M. Paul. "The Oregon School Bill Controversy, 1922–1925." *Pacific Historical Review* 37 (August 1968): 327–341.

Hoover, Herbert. *American Individualism.* New York, 1922.

Hudson, Winthrop S. *The Great Tradition of the American Churches.* New York, 1953.

————. *Religion in America.* New York, 1965.

Hutchison, William R. *The Modernist Impulse in American Protestantism.* Cambridge, Mass., 1976.

Jackson, Kenneth T. *The Ku Klux Klan and the City, 1915–1930.* New York, 1967.

Jorgenson, Lloyd P. "The Oregon School Law of 1922: Passage and Sequel." *Catholic Historical Review* 54 (1968): 455–466.

Katz, Jacob. *Jews and Freemasons in Europe, 1723–1939.* Translated by Leonard Oschry. Cambridge, Mass., 1970.

Kauffman, Christopher. *Faith and Fraternalism: The History of the Knights of Columbus, 1882–1982.* New York, 1982.

Kilby, Clyde S. *Minority of One: The Biography of Johnathan Blanchard.* Grand Rapids, Mich., 1959.

Kleppner, Paul. *The Cross of Culture: A Social Analysis of Midwestern Politics, 1850–1900.* New York, 1970.

Köcka, Jurgen. *White Collar Workers in America, 1890–1940: A Social-Political History in International Perspective.* London, 1980.

Krutch, Joseph Wood. *The Modern Temper: A Study and a Confession.* New York, 1929.

Landis, Abb. "Life Insurance by Fraternal Orders." *American Academy of Political and Social Science Annals* 24 (1904): 474–488.

Lanier, John L. *Masonry and Protestantism.* New York, 1923.

Larrabee, Eric, and Meyersohn, Rolf, eds. *Mass Leisure.* Glencoe, Ill., 1958.

Lewis, Sinclair. *Babbitt.* New York, 1922.

Lippmann, Walter. *A Preface to Morals.* New York, 1929.

Lipson, Dorothy Ann. *Freemasonry in Federalist Connecticut, 1789–1835.* Princeton, N.J., 1977.

Lischka, Charles N. *Private Schools and State Laws.* Washington, D.C., 1924.

[Live Oak Lodge.] *Souvenir: Fortieth Anniversary Celebration of Live Oak Lodge.* Oakland, Calif., 1896.

Loucks, Emerson Hunsberger. *The Ku Klux Klan in Pennsylvania: A Study in Nativism.* New York, 1936.

Lowenthal, Leo. "The Triumph of Mass Idols." In *Literature, Popular Culture and Society,* pp. 145–165. Englewood Cliffs, N.J., 1961.

Lundberg, George A.; Komarovsky, Mirra; and McInerny, Mary Alice. *Leisure: A Suburban Study.* New York, 1969.

Lynd, Robert S., and Lynd, Helen Merrell. *Middletown: A Study in Modern American Culture.* New York, 1929.

Lynd, Robert S., and Lynd, Helen Merrell. *Middletown in Transition: A Study in Cultural Conflicts.* New York, 1937.

McConnell, Grant. *Private Power and American Democracy.* New York, 1966.

MacDonald, Fergus. *The Catholic Church and the Secret Societies in the United States.* United States Catholic Historical Series Monograph 22. New York, 1946.

Mackey, Albert G. *A Manual of the Lodge; or, Monitorial Instructions in the Degrees of Entered Apprentice, Fellow Craft, and Master Mason.* New York, 1871.

———. *The Symbolism of Freemasonry.* New York, 1869.

McLaughlin, Raymond. *A History of State Legislation Affecting Private Elementary and Secondary Schools in the United States, 1870–1945.* Washington, D.C., 1946.

Macoy, Robert. *The True Masonic Guide.* New York, 1870.

———. *Worshipful Master's Assistant: The Encyclopedia of Useful Knowledge.* New York, 1885.

Malinowski, Bronislaw. "Magic, Science and Religion." In *Magic, Science and Religion and Other Essays.* Glencoe, Ill., 1948.

Marden, Charles F. *Rotary and Its Brothers: An Analysis and Interpretation of the Men's Service Club.* Princeton, N.J., 1935.

Marty, Martin E. *The Infidel: Freethought and American Religion.* Cleveland, Ohio, 1961.

May, Henry F. *Protestant Churches and Industrial America.* New York, 1967.

Mead, Sidney E. *The Lively Experiment: The Shaping of Christianity in America.* New York, 1963.

Melendy, Royal B. "The Saloon in Chicago." *American Journal of Sociology* 6 (January 1901): 433–440.

Melish, William B., et al. *The History of the Imperial Council Ancient Arabic Order Nobles of the Mystic Shrine for North America, 1872–1921.* Cincinnati, Ohio, 1921.

Merton, Robert K. *Social Theory and Social Structure.* Glencoe, Ill., 1949.

Meyer, B. H. "Fraternal Beneficiary Societies in the United States." *American Journal of Sociology* 6 (March 1901): 646–661.

Meyers, Marvin. *The Jacksonian Persuasion: Politics and Belief.* Stanford, Calif., 1957.

Michels, Robert. *Political Parties.* Glencoe, Ill., 1949.

Miller, Robert Moats. *American Protestantism and Social Issues, 1919–1939*. Chapel Hill, N.C., 1958.

Miller, William Lee. "American Religion and American Political Attitudes." In *Religious Perspectives in American Culture*, edited by James Ward Smith and A. Leland Jamison, 2: 81–118. Princeton, N.J., 1961.

Mills, C. Wright. *White Collar: The American Middle Classes*. New York, 1951.

Muraskin, William Alan. *Middle-Class Blacks in a White Society: Prince Hall Freemasonry in America*. Berkeley, Calif., 1975.

Murphy, Paul L. "Sources and Nature of Intolerance in the 1920s." *Journal of American History* 51 (June 1964): 60–76.

Murray, Robert K. *Red Scare: A Study in National Hysteria, 1919–1920*. New York, 1955.

Oakland (California) Board of Trade. *Oakland, California*. [Oakland, Calif.], 1886.

[Oakland Lodge No. 188.] *Fiftieth Anniversary, Oakland Lodge No. 188, Free and Accepted Masons, Oakland, California, 1868–1918*. [Oakland, Calif.], 1918.

Odegard, Peter H. *Pressure Politics: The Story of the Anti-Saloon League*. New York, 1928.

Pettibone, James, ed. *The Lodge Goat, Goat Rides, Butts, and Goat Hairs: Gathered from the Lodge Rooms of Every Fraternal Order*. Cincinnati, Ohio, 1902.

Pierce, Bessie Louise. *Citizens' Organizations and the Civic Training of Youth*. Report of the Commission on the Social Studies, pt. 3. New York, 1933.

———. *Civic Attitudes in America School Textbooks*. Chicago, 1930.

Pollard, Ralph J. *Freemasonry in Maine, 1726–1945*. Portland, Maine, n.d.

Powderly, Terrence V. *The Path I Trod: The Autobiography of Terrence V. Powderly*. Edited by Harry J. Carman, Henry David, and Paul N. Guthrie. New York, 1968.

Ratner, Lorman. *Antimasonry: The Crusade and the Party*. Englewood Cliffs, N.J., 1969.

Ravitch, Diane. *The Great School Wars: New York City, 1805–1973*. New York, 1974.

Recken, Stephen Louis. "A Reinterpretation of the Oregon School Bill of 1922: The Concept of the Common School in Progressive America." Master's thesis, Portland State University, 1973.

Report of the President's Research Committee on Social Trends. *Recent Social Trends*. 2 vols. New York, 1933.

Revised Constitution, General Regulations and Grand Lodge Standing Resolutions with Annotated Decisions of the Grand Lodge of Free and Accepted Masons of Minnesota. [Saint Paul, Minn.], 1915.

Riesman, David, with Glazer, Nathan, and Denney, Reuel. *The Lonely Crowd: A Study of the Changing American Character*. New Haven, Conn., 1950.

Rodgers, Daniel T. *The Work Ethic in Industrial America, 1850–1920*. Chicago, 1978.

Rosenzweig, Roy. "Boston Masons, 1900–1935: The Lower Middle-Class in a Divided Society." *Journal of Voluntary Action Research* 6 (July 1977): 119–124.

Ross, John Stewart, ed. *Digest and Compilation of Approved Decisions and Regulations by the Grand Lodge of Free and Accepted Masons of California, 1850 to and including the Annual Communication, October 1931*. San Francisco, 1932.

Rothman, David J. *The Discovery of the Asylum: Social Order and Disorder in the New Republic*. Boston, 1971.

Roy, Thomas Sherrard. *Stalwart Builders: A History of the Grand Lodge of Masons in Massachusetts, 1733–1970*. Boston, 1971.

[San Francisco Sciots Pyramid No. 1.] *Directory*. San Francisco, 1915.

Saunders, George M. *A Short History of the Shrine*. Chicago, n.d.

Schlesinger, Arthur M. "Biography of a Nation of Joiners." In *Paths to the Present*, pp. 24–50. Boston, 1949.

————. *The Rise of the City, 1878–1898*. Vol. 12 of *A History of American Life*, edited by Arthur M. Schlesinger and Dixon Ryan Fox. New York, 1933.

Schmidt, Alvin J. *Oligarchy in Fraternal Organizations: A Study in Organizational Leadership*. Detroit, Mich., 1973.

Schneider, Herbert W. *Religion in Twentieth Century America*. Cambridge, Mass., 1952.

Sheldon, Charles M. *In His Steps*. Chicago, 1897.

Sherman, Edwin A. *Fifty Years of Masonry in California*. 2 vols. San Francisco, 1898.

Sills, David. "Voluntary Associations: Sociological Aspects." In *International Encyclopedia of the Social Sciences* (New York, 1968), 16: 362–379.

————. *The Volunteers: Means and Ends in a National Organization*.

A Report of the Bureau of Applied Social Research. New York, 1957.

Simmel, Georg. *The Sociology of Georg Simmel*. Translated by Kurt H. Wolff. Glencoe, Ill., 1950.

Sinclair, Andrew. *Era of Excess: A Social History of the Prohibition Movement*. New York, 1962.

Smith, Constance, and Freedman, Ann, eds. *Voluntary Associations: Perspectives in the Literature*. Cambridge, Mass., 1972.

Stevens, Albert C. *The Cyclopaedia of Fraternities*. New York, 1907.

Stine, Clyde M. *Plymouth's Progress—Fifty Golden Years: The Story of Plymouth Lodge No. 560, F.&A.M. of California*. Oakland, Calif., 1974.

Sullivan, Mark. *Our Times: The United States, 1900–1925*. 6 vols. New York, 1926.

Thernstrom, Stephan. *The Other Bostonians: Poverty and Progress in the American Metropolis, 1880–1970*. Cambridge, Mass., 1973.

Thorp, Winthrop. "The Religious Novel as Best Seller in America." In *Religious Perspectives in American Culture*, edited by James Ward Smith and A. Leland Jamison, 2: 195–242. Princeton, N.J., 1961.

Tidwell, Donavan Duncan. "The Ku Klux Klan and Texas Masonry." *Transactions, Texas Lodge of Research* 14 (1978/1979): 160–176.

Tiger, Lionel. *Men in Groups*. New York, 1969.

Tyack, David. *The One Best System: A History of American Urban Education*. Cambridge, Mass., 1976.

———. "The Perils of Pluralism: The Background of the Pierce Case." *American Historical Review* 74 (October 1968): 74–98.

Warner, W. Lloyd. *Democracy in Jonesville*. New York, 1949.

Warren, Sidney. *American Freethought, 1860–1914*. Columbia University Studies in History, Economics and Public Law, no. 504. New York, 1966.

Weiss, Richard. *The American Myth of Success: From Horatio Alger to Norman Vincent Peale*. New York, 1969.

Wesley, Edgar B. *NEA—The First Hundred Years: The Building of the Teaching Profession*. New York, 1957.

Wiebe, Robert H. *The Search for Order, 1877–1920*. New York, 1967.

Williams, Loretta J. *Black Freemasonry and Middle-Class Realities*. Columbia, Mo., 1980.

Williams, Michael. *The Shadow of the Pope*. New York, 1932.

Wirth, Louis. "Urbanism as a Way of Life." In *Neighborhood, City, and Metropolis: An Integrated Reader in Urban Sociology*, edited by Robert Gutman and David Popenoe, pp. 54–69. New York, 1970.

World Almanac and Book of Facts. New York, 1900.

Index

Acacia Club of Shawnee Light Lodge, Louisville, Ky., 200
Acacia Lodge, Ca., 258n4
Admission to Masonry: saloon-keepers, 77; standards for, 9-13, 80-82, 153-54, 187. *See also* Recruitment of Masons
Age of Masons, 265n16
Agnosticism, 68
Alabama Masons, 53; and public school funding, 139
Alcatraz Lodge, Oakland, Ca., 229, 236n9, 239n18, 278n97
Allen, C. H., 87-88
Allen, William Paggett, 72
American Association of University Women, National Society, 262n56
American Federation of Labor, 262n56
American Federation of Teachers, 262n56
Americanism, 100 percent, 120-22, 145-47; and education, 140, 142; glorification of, 130; identified with Protestantism, 125-26; and Masonic education, 192; Masonic promotion of, 126, 130-31, 135-37, 153, 259n15; and modernization, 155-56; and service, 175; within Masonry, 117
American Legion, 137, 219
American Party, 249n61
American Protective Association, 143
Amex Masonic Club, Camp de Souge, France, 118
Ancient and Accepted Order of Freemasons. *See* Masonry
Ancient Arabic Order of the Nobles

of the Mystic Shrine. *See* Shrine and Shriners
Ancient Egyptian Order of Sciots. *See* Sciots, Ancient Egyptian Order of
Ancient Order of United Workmen, 220, 238n16
Anti-Catholicism, 6; of Masonic Service Association, 135, 261n47; of Masons, 11-12, 124-26, 237n12; of public education campaigns, 137-38, 139, 140, 143, 144-45. *See also* Catholic opposition to Masonry
Anti-Masonic sentiment, 3, 5-7, 25, 249n61; abatement of, 8-9, 52-53
Anti-materialism and anti-commercialism, 93, 94-96, 171-72, 176, 182, 208; declining emphasis on, 151-52, 166, 206-207. *See also* Success as defined by Masons
Anti-Mormonism, 6
Anti-saloonkeeper laws, 11, 75-78, 137, 251n15. *See also* Saloons near lodges
Anti-Saloon League, 76
Anti-Semitism, 122, 123. *See also* Jewish Masons
Apathy. *See* Attendance at lodges; Inactive members
Aquart, A. V., 150
Arthur, John, 16-17
Asylum motif. *See* Exclusion of profane
Atheism, agnosticism, and Deism, 3, 36, 48, 50, 54, 59-61, 68. *See also* Enlightenment influence on Masonry; Freethinking Attendance at church, 159

295

Immigrant Masons, 10-11, 236*n*9, 240*n*33. *See also* German-American Masons; Jewish Masons
Immigrants and immigration, 43, 47, 90, 120-24; and education, 140; Masonic activism against, 129
Inactive members, 29, 40, 244*n*57. *See also* Attendance at lodges
Indiana Masons' attendance, 187, 189
Individual morality as solution to social problems, 91, 92-95, 131
Individual motivation as solution to Masonic apathy, 155
Ingersoll, H. H., 63
Ingersoll, Robert B., 45, 46
Innes, William P., 100
Instrumental organizations, xii. *See also* Practical benefits of Masonry
Iowa Masons; buildings of, 235*n*6; Leighton Lodge No. 387, 241*n*34; temperance of, 86
Island communities in nineteenth-century America, 89, 109, 146
Italiana Speranza Lodge, San Francisco, Ca., 10
Italy, Masonry in, 129

Jackson, Kenneth, 146
Jamestown, N.Y., Fellow Craft Club, 201-202
Jewels, 15
Jewish Masons, 11, 55-56, 69-70, 122, 237*nn*10, 11, 246*n*17. *See also* Anti-Semitism
John the Baptist, 37, 246*n*17
John the Evangelist, 37, 246*n*17
Jones, John Paul, 87
Jones, Richard Saxe, 67-68
Joseph Webb Lodge, Boston, Mass., 236*n*9

Kadosh, Council of, 15
Kauffman, Christopher, 279*n*2
Kent, Frederic H., 21
Kenwood Lodge, Wisc., 199
Key Route Masons, 277*n*80, 278*n*97
Kiwanis, 172, 178-79, 269*n*66

Knights of Columbus, 119, 125, 134, 172, 220; Kauffman on, 279*n*2
Knights of Labor, 75
Knights of Pythias, 220, 234*n*3
Knights Templar, 11, 15, 54, 240*n*28; charity of, 105; regalia of, 16, 240*n*27
Know-Nothings, 143
Krutch, Joseph Wood, 173, 184
Ku Klux Klan, 146-47; and education bills, 141, 143-44, 262*n*56; and Masonry, 122-23, 129-30, 137, 259*n*20, 261*n*35
Kutolowski, Kathleen Smith, 6

Lafayette, Marquis de, 49
Larger, T. J., 58
Laughlin, L. C., 83
League of Women Voters, National, 262*n*56
Lee, W. W., 65
Legalism, 10, 28-29. *See also* Trials under Masonic law
Leighton Lodge No. 387, Iowa, 241*n*34
Leisure: in late nineteenth century, 25, 30; in 1920s, 181, 193, 216. *See also* Production vs. consumption society
Leo XIII, Pope, 12
Level Club, New York City, 277*n*78
Lewis, Sinclair, 173
Liberal Masons. *See* Modernization of Masonry
Lindbergh, Charles, 149
Lions, 178-79
Lippitt, Costello, 88
Lippmann, Walter, 158, 184
Lipson, Dorothy, 4-5, 7, 25
Live Oak Lodge No. 61, Oakland, Ca., xv, 84; age of members of, 265*n*16; attendance at, 186-87, 202, 230-31, 243*n*52; immigrants in, 236*n*9; occupations of members of, 12-13, 21-22, 151, 227-28, 238*n*15, 264*n*7; programs at, 194-95
Lobaugh, A. G., 59-60

Library of Congress Cataloging in Publication Data

Dumenil, Lynn, 1950-
    Freemasonry and American culture, 1880-1930.

    Bibliography: p.
    Includes index.
    1. Freemasonry—United States—History—19th century. 2. Freema-
sonry—United States—History—20th century. 3. United States—Social conditions—1865-1918. 4. United States—Social conditions—1918-1932. 5.
WASPs (Persons)
    I. Title.
HS529.D86   1984   366'.1'0973   84-42594
    ISBN 0-691-04716-2 (alk. paper)